FINDING HOPE

FINDING HOPE

AURA POLANCO

To order additional copies of this book, contact:
Xlibris
1-888-795-4274
www.Xlibris.com
Orders@Xlibris.com
755024

CONTENTS

Prologue ix

Chapter 1: Until We Meet Again 1

Chapter 2: The Goto Flower Hotel 7

Chapter 3: James..17

Chapter 4: Rey..23

Chapter 5: Japan..33

Chapter 6: New York 51

Chapter 7: Farewells 77

Chapter 8: Breathe..81

Chapter 9: First Time Ever I Saw Your Face.............................93

Chapter 10: Trevor Miles...113

Chapter 11: White Rose Cottage 127

Chapter 12: Declaration 153

Chapter 13: Touchy and Bold 167

Chapter 14: New York City Christmas 179

Chapter 15: New Year's Eve 197

Chapter 16: Tiffany's and a Pied-à-Terre 205

Chapter 17: Enter Mr. Wolf..217

Chapter 18: Guilt 227

Chapter 19: Starting Over 235

Chapter 20: Farewell, Angie...239

Chapter 21: Aiko and Samu 245

Chapter 22: Lonely Planet 249

Chapter 23: Bougainvillea Heaven..261

Chapter 24: Hope...279

Epilogue..291

For R.I.

For all who believe that everyone deserves a second or third chance,

For all who understand that love comes in the
most unexpected ways into our lives,

For all who believe that where there is
love, there will always be hope,

For Maria, my greatest example of hope and love.

In my office, tucked away in a decorative box, are several dusty little books filled with ideas, plots, and characters. The pages in these books have yellowed over the years but the contents remain as rich to me as when I jotted down these ideas.

After publishing my first book, *The Acquisition*, it was very obvious to me that there was no possibility of squelching my love of writing. Creating stories and using my imagination to build characters, themes, and plots is a task I enjoy, and that feeds my need for creativity.

With the completion of my second novel, *Finding Hope*, I can no longer imagine life without writing. My writing is centered on taking my readers' to sunnier shores and into the lives of characters they can love or dislike. In *Finding Hope*, my goal was to have the reader wonder and question his or her own capacity for forgiveness and love.

Thank you to the lovely people at Xlibris for your professional guidance and patience, and to my family, friends, and readers for your continued support and encouragement.

PROLOGUE

It was Labor Day weekend with just a few days before the new school term began. Kate Connor and her son Oliver walked along West End Avenue, testing the new bicycle he received from his parents on his tenth birthday. Oliver had requested two things, a Trek mountain bike and a family dinner. The plan was to spend a few hours at Riverside Park and go shopping for groceries at Fairway, as Oliver wanted his mother to make his favorite meal of spaghetti and meatballs that evening. He was happy because his parents were going to share their first meal together as a family since the divorce five years before.

The day was hot, humid, and eerily quiet. Small waves of traffic came and went on the usually busy two-way avenue, and few people walked along the streets. The only noise came from the incessant buzzing of overworked and sweating air conditioners that protruded from apartment windows overhead. It was around noon when they went to make a turn on Ninety-Second Street and Riverside Drive to walk across the street and enter the park. They never made it beyond that point because a black SUV swerved out of control as it took the corner at a high speed, jumped the curb, and smashed into their lives.

The next day, Kate awoke in the hospital in tremendous pain and confusion. A hospital chaplain and a doctor explained what had happened as her former husband and Oliver's father cried into his hands. She heard James calling her name and saying encouraging things to her. James was always strong and dependable. His voice soothed her as she drifted in and out of consciousness. The heavy narcotics kept Kate numb and in a haze, yet inside her body, she was screaming and in a complete state of total despair. Despite the haze that was her mind, with crystal clarity, she realized that going forward with her life—as she knew it to be—was over because her son was gone forever.

The decision to leave it all behind came while she recovered in the rehabilitation facility. Doctors and therapists were encouraging and taught her to walk again after her left leg was crushed under the weight of the car. Although Kate's body healed slowly, the best psychiatric efforts could not get her to relive the tragedy and help her out of what they called a self-imposed denial. What they did not know was that Kate had chosen to secretly go mute and disconnect to avoid the prying doctors and people who never left her alone. Kate, pretended to be in a trance to get through the grueling physical therapy and recover enough to leave what had become a prison. She learned to say all the right things to keep the resident psychiatrist at bay and avoid mind-altering medication. Remaining lucid was important, as she did not want to be under anyone else's control.

Greater than the physical anguish was the emotional pain. This was beyond anything Kate could have imagined. Oliver had been her center and focus for ten years, and now what Kate loved above all else was no longer. Becoming physically strong and able to walk again was all she wanted because she knew her son would have wanted this as well. Only in the deep darkness of night while the rehabilitation center heaved in slumber did Kate wail into her pillow. It was only during this very personal and quiet time that the pain surfaced and became one with the loss of her son. Recalling every minute detail of his face and body and the little conversations they shared was the daily nourishment she required to stay alive. The image of Oliver's dimpled smile and sandy hair from his last school picture and a small collection of photographs chronicling his young life were the only luxuries she kept. The last memory she had of her son was the joy in his face as he chatted about how he wanted to go to Bear Mountain the following weekend to properly test his new bike.

CHAPTER 1

Until We Meet Again

James was worried with the sudden decisions Kate had recently made. She decided to sell the home she had shared with her son and go to an isolated location. He feared her emotions were too fragile for such change, but he also knew her to be a decisive and determined woman. At her request, he reluctantly booked a one-way ticket to Okinawa, Japan, and drove her to the airport.

James and Kate grew up in the same foster home. They were in the same school since kindergarten and were fortunate to have the same foster parents throughout their lives. They were young adults when their foster parents passed away, and from that moment on, they knew they only had each other and the fond memories of their devoted parents.

Trying not to spill tears and cause an already difficult farewell to be impossible, James focused on a memory from grade school. He smiled as he recalled when Kate walked up to a boy who had been bullying him relentlessly and forcing him to give up his change, lunch, or pencils. Compared to the bully, Kate was small, but she summoned the courage to ask him to stop hurting her brother. The pathetic angry boy laughed at her reference to James as her brother because he was black and she white. The foolish bully never expected the little girl to kick him in the groin. Her actions were enough to keep the bully from bothering James again, and he also stayed clear of the little girl with the long chestnut ponytail who had brought him to his knees. Throughout the years, that same bond grew in strength into one of mutual respect and love.

Kate gave her foster brother, James Adderley, the keys to her condominium on West Eighty-Eighth and Columbus Avenue, with instructions to sell the property at market value, donate all the furniture and clothing, and deposit the check into her account. Further instructions were left to pay off all remaining bills and cancel utilities. She also resigned from her job as a studio arts professor at the prestigious Barton College after fifteen years of service and contacted the few friends and family close enough to care that she was disconnecting her mobile. Some expressed concern, while others shared empathy, but none were alarmed, as they expected this moment to happen for some time. Kate had nothing left that mattered to her in New York; in fact, nothing else was important to her anywhere in the world. She was desperate to get off the grid, out of the fray of daily existence with intrusive technology and oppressive schedules that robbed one of time. The emptiness and despair from losing her son had taken its toll on her emotions. Her battered body, while healing, showed the aftermath of the accident, as she had an obvious limp. But despite the ever-present pain, what Kate desired most was to inhale and exhale deep breaths. Her breathing was often shallow, and in her chest was nestled a permanent lump of sorrow that stole away every full breath of air.

James pulled his convertible Mini Coop in front of the Japan Airlines terminal at John F. Kennedy Airport. He looked over at

Kate sitting in the passenger seat and realized that saying good-bye to his best friend and sister was starting to be difficult as he could barely speak without getting all choked up. Kate sat quietly holding the Lancôme duffel bag she was gifted for buying cosmetics at Bloomingdale's some years ago. She traced over the puffy designer letters, briefly remembering a time when her cares were few. In the bag, she had carelessly placed some underwear, a sweater, one pair of flip-flops, one blouse, T-shirts, one skirt and a pair of capris that would hide the numerous red scars that traveled down her left leg like a wayward tattoo, and a photo album filled with photographs of her Oliver.

James took her left hand and held it between his two large brown ones and said quietly, "You know, you don't have to go so far away."

His eyes were brimming with tears when she cleared her throat to say in a barely audible voice, "James, you know how important it is for me to disappear. Actually, what I would prefer is to die, but I'm too chicken to kill myself. And besides, I think Oliver would be disappointed if I did anything stupid like that. I love you, Jamesy. You are my best friend and brother. I just need you to take care of the business that was my life."

James sighed and shuddered as Kate reached over and hugged him tightly. He whispered, "Remember what Mom always said about keeping hate in your heart. It is like a cancer that grows and consumes you."

Kate stared ahead and responded quietly to his comment. "Tell that to my heart because it is broken forever."

James opened his window and inhaled to avoid exploding into tears. "Yes, I know your heart is broken. I have to know you arrive safely. I hate that you refuse to have a phone. That is so last century. So promise me that you won't move from this hotel without letting me know."

Kate looked up into his handsome chiseled face. Giving him a loving kiss on the cheek, she promised, "I will call from time to time. Don't bug me with stupid business stuff but definitely call or leave me a message about what's going on with you. I just feel like an empty vessel, and I don't know if I will ever feel whole again. I miss my baby every second of the day. Every time I take a breath, it hurts, so I really need for you to have my back, okay?"

James hugged Kate tightly and kissed the top of her head. He ran his left hand down her shoulder-length hair. Hugging her, he whispered, "I have your back, Katie, always will, but I'm going to miss you so much. Please come back to me so we can grow old together. I want you to be my dance partner when I'm eighty-seven years old and looking like a tired old fag in Boca." Neither of them laughed.

His tears threatened to fall, but she gave him a cross-eyed look that always cracked him into a laugh. Despite her silliness, it was not lost on James that the goofy expression was not followed by her beautiful smile and the deep dimples that formed like two teacups on her cheeks. Breaking away from his embrace, she moved quickly out of the car. Quietly in his heart, he said a prayer to God asking him to help Kate find her smile again and heal her mind and soul as he watched her limp away into the terminal.

Kate left New York to heal in her own way. Having missed the wake and funeral for her son because she was in the hospital had kept many people from looking upon her with pity for a time after Oliver's passing. Just the same, people felt the need to make well-meaning but silly and often rude comments such as "He's an angel now" or "You have to sue the other insurance" or the dreaded "Luckily, you are young enough to have more children." People may have meant well, but the comments and sorrowful grins made Kate feel like screaming and hitting something. The last thing she ever wanted was to be pitied or reminded of what Oliver would never become. While she was a resident at Burke Rehabilitation in White Plains, several of Oliver's closest friends came over to see her to pay their respects. Those were the most agonizing moments since the accident when Kate had to look upon those young boys' faces full of energy and life and imagine her own son cold and dead.

CHAPTER 2

The Goto Flower Hotel

The Goto Flower Hotel offered no amenities that were often expected by tourists, but it was clean and private, and the food was organic. This suited Kate, as she tended to dislike the predictable when traveling. The hotel was nestled just off the beach behind a group of Yonehara palm trees that led down a neat stone path into tiny gardens that invited meditation and repose. The polished wood doors led guests into an airy reception area with varied orchid plants and a sizable saltwater tank with colorful clown fish. A sense of calm and quiet permeated the space as did the scent of flowers and nature.

The proprietors, Mrs. Goto and her daughter Aiko, were accommodating and respectful and very protective of their guests. They sensed from the moment Kate arrived that she was a woman in great pain and in search of hope. They took notice that, during her first days at the hotel, Kate never left her room. The maid reported to Mrs. Goto and Aiko that she had heard and seen Kate crying and staring at photographs in a book. Upon learning this, Mrs. Goto presented Kate every evening in the privacy of her room a cup of warm *matcha* tea. Initially, Kate was embarrassed and tried to reject the older woman's attempt for going to such trouble. Mrs. Goto's limited command of English and Kate's few words in Japanese eventually helped both women relax and accept each other as the tea continued to arrive nightly with a smile and a bow.

Soon thereafter, a small yellow or pink orchid flower and note written in perfect calligraphy appeared with the tea. The messages were about love, strength, and peace. This was followed by more orchids and messages accompanied with every breakfast. At first, Kate thought it strange that the flowers and notes came her way and wondered if other guests received these warm gestures.

The hotel had six suites and a small cottage to the side, where Mrs. Goto and her daughter lived. Behind their cottage and hidden away by more palm trees stood a wrought iron gate that led down a short path into a lush green space. Off to the side, there was a clearing where Mrs. Goto tended to her vegetable garden; but to the right, a graceful glass-enclosed greenhouse stood holding nature's treasures. Mrs. Goto grew orchids of several varieties, but her specialty was the tiny pink and yellow ones that floated in elegant round bowls on every dining table as centerpieces and graced the coffee tables in guests' suites.

Mrs. Goto and Aiko were well respected and liked for leaving guests to their privacy. They were popular with international people visiting and native travelers from busy cities like Tokyo. The latter came yearly to rest and recover before returning to insanely overscheduled city lives.

Okinawa, Japan, pulled at Kate's emotions with its pristine, untouched beaches and natural wildlife. These remote islands had few tourists and busy resorts. It was the place of peace and healing that Kate yearned for. This had also been the last overseas trip she took with Oliver when he was eight years old. For Oliver, experiencing Okinawa was the highlight of that year. He had returned to school enthusiastically and shared his experiences in a collage of his trip. For Kate, the three weeks she spent there with Oliver flew by sailing with local fishermen, scuba diving, and exploring the water caves. Oliver loved the water and the beach, where he played for hours with just his imagination and the silvery fish that tickled his toes. Kate recalled how Oliver went to bed crying one night because she forbade him from asking the concierge of the hotel to teach him to dive like the champion divers who frequented the island. Oliver's little crooked smile was plastered in Kate's mind, and this was the only medication she needed to find peace and forgiveness.

She had this immense need to breathe. For months following the tragedy, Kate was unable to take a deep breath. Even the years of yoga breathing could not help her take that deep belly breath that filled the lungs and cleansed from within. At first, Kate figured this was a medical problem due to the broken ribs from the accident. When the problem persisted after her body had healed, she realized that she was in need of a different release, something more akin to leaving her life in New York. Kate knew somewhere deep in the recesses of her mind that on the islands of Okinawa with the Kerama blue waters and its large population of wise and friendly people was where she might learn to live and breathe again.

Kate welcomed the soft and velvety sensation of the downy white sand beneath her feet as she walked along the glistening waters on the deserted beach. The sun was high and not yet its hottest in the early morning hours in Yonehara Beach on the island of Ishigaki. The sun's rays encircled her battered body in warmth as the gentle sound of waves whispered a longing in her ear that left a lump in her throat. Microscopic beads of sweat burst upon the bridge of her nose and collarbone, teasing her to enter the tepid aquamarine water, but all she wanted to do was walk quietly along the edge where sand and water kissed. Silvery fish darted alongside her every step as water slapped the hem of her long and gauzy white dress. Kate did not recall the last time she had felt so alive and at peace. The only other sensation that compared and rivaled this one was when she gave birth to Oliver and looked upon his round pudgy face and bright green eyes. At that moment, she felt her heart swell with a capacity for love unlike anything she had ever experienced.

The foamy water hit her ankles, and when it receded, Kate saw the tiny sea horse lying motionless on the sand. Picking it up, she gently held it in her palm and studied the perfect beauty of such a tiny organism. She remained transfixed, observing this little lifeless creature. Looking up into the bright blue sky, she held the sea horse to her breast and allowed the wave of emotion to hit her. The pain built like a crescendo and settled in her throat until it exploded into a flood of tears. Collapsing onto the sand, she cried and rocked her body until all her tears were spent and her head ached from the heavy anguish.

The bright yellow sky turned to a murky gray with huge clouds forcing their way across. It was the season for this type of sudden change in the weather, and avoiding it was important because of high winds and floods. Kate's forehead wrinkled upward, as she noticed the change in the sky. Quickly, she gently placed the tiny sea horse into the water and walked off the beach and toward the greenhouse as quickly as her legs would go, but the rain came down in torrents and soaked her in an unwanted cold bath. The greenhouse door was opened, and Kate moved in right away, shaking out her dress and smoothing down her hair. There wasn't anyone around giving her a chance to warm up and explore. The violent rain hit the glass ceiling hard, startling Kate on several occasions.

Moving along, she admired the beautiful orchids and plants. The potted orchids were placed alongside lilies and roses and were organized based on varieties and sizes on several narrow and long wooden tables. Quite a few of the orchids were as tall as two feet, while others—like the ones used throughout the hotel—were dainty and small and floated in large shallow bowls. The perimeter of the greenhouse was decorated with several love seats both upholstered and in intricately carved wood.

The air was moist and very warm in the greenhouse. Not liking hot and clammy weather, Kate looked for an air conditioner and thought how silly she was, as these flowers would not thrive in cold temperatures. Settling on a plush loveseat and curling her right leg under her, Kate closed her eyes and practiced some breathing techniques she knew from yoga that would cool her down. Within minutes, her heart was calmer, and the moistness in the greenhouse did not bother her at all. A while later, as she sat there taking in the lushness of the foliage, the rain stopped, and the sun slowly peeked its way out from behind the gloomy clouds and brightened up the wet morning in a buttercup yellow glow.

Returning to the hotel, Kate changed out of her damp clothing and decided to contact James. He had left a message with reception a week ago to call him regarding the sale of the condominium. She suspected James might be upset with her for not responding in a timely manner and determined to call him instead from her room for privacy. Dialing his mobile number from the phone at her bedside, she waited for just one ring to end before his animated voice shouted through. "She lives!" Sarcastically, he continued. "I could be dead in a ditch, but *no*, my sister would not care a bit. What the heck took you so long to return my call?"

Kate was earnest when she said, "I'm sorry, James. You are right. I am an awful person for just making you wait like that. I don't have an excuse, but disconnecting from everything has been very helpful."

"Okay, that sounds wonderful, Katie. Tell me how you are wherever the heck it is you are right now." He chuckled into the phone. Kate took a deep breath, but before she could say anything, James jumped in again. "Oh my god, was that a deep breath I heard? Hooray! You are breathing again. I haven't heard from you in so long. Okay, tell me everything about this magical place."

Kate smiled despite herself and extended on the bed to talk leisurely with James. "Well, this is a very beautiful and calming environment. This beach town is so quiet and quaint that I feel I could heal a little more here. Every day, I make a pilgrimage to the beach, where I walk and relax. Walking on the sand has helped strengthen my back, and that feels much better. Today I found a tiny sea horse, and although it wasn't alive, I was in awe of its beauty. The water is spectacularly bright, like a blue green gemstone. Oh, James, I wish you were here with me and not in cold and dreary New York."

It was early March in New York, and the weather was unpredictable and just generally nasty. Kate continued. "The pain in my leg has lessened, and I have to thank the ocean for that. When I'm in the water, it is very therapeutic. So let's see, it looks and feels like I lost some weight, which is always a plus, and my hair is now past my shoulder blades, but I know I need a trim badly. Hmm, that's really it. Anyway, so tell me about the condo. Is it finally sold?"

James was eating with gusto a snack of Swedish fish, prosciutto, and cheese. He gulped down some Riesling to respond to Kate. "Well, all that news makes me happy. So here's your good news. The condo is sold, and the check was deposited and should have cleared by now, and we got it at full price. So once you give me the authority, I will set up two other accounts to split the money and guarantee protection until you decide how you want to invest it. You are now considered either very, very comfortable or just plain old rich."

James popped more Swedish fish into his mouth as Kate responded, "Good, now I will leave this all behind for good."

Upon hearing this, James stopped chewing immediately and sat up and in an alarmed tone asked, "Kate, what are you saying? You are leaving what behind? This was supposed to be for a while, not forever. I miss you and want you to come back home. We are the only family we have."

The desperation in his voice rang clearly to Kate, but she had already determined never to return to New York City or even perhaps the United States. "James, I cannot face New York ever again. Everything about it reminds me of Oliver and the ten wonderful years that I was blessed with my son. It isn't ever happening again. Sorry, James."

The silence on the other end was hollow and empty. James could not believe Kate never planned to return to the only home she ever knew. Taking a different approach to not alienate her, he added, "I understand. I do not like it, but I cannot imagine what it is to lose a child. It must be like losing a giant part of one's heart."

Kate's heart swelled with emotion upon hearing the understanding in his voice. He changed the subject because discussing this over the phone was not a good idea. James added, "I met someone. His name is Sebastian, and we are getting on so well, Katie. I know I've had plenty of boyfriends, but this one is so different. I need for you to meet him. We were thinking of a trip soon, so if you don't mind and he's agreeable, can we come to the ends of the earth so you can meet him?"

Kate sat up in her bed and enthusiastically exclaimed, "I would love to see you and check out lover boy. Oh, James, I'm sorry that I haven't been there for you. Hey, I haven't paid you yet, so take out of my account the fare for both flights to Japan."

Laughing richly, James joked back, "Oh, so you rolling like that these days, huh? No problem, baby girl, I will be there inside of a month, so don't go anywhere else. I have the hotel info, so I'll book it myself. I can't wait to see you. Oh, I almost forgot, a letter addressed to the firm arrived, but inside is a sealed one for you with bold letters on the outside stating, 'Confidential: For Katherine Connor.' I'm bringing it with me because, whatever it is, it seems important."

Kate moved off the bed and walked over to the picture window overlooking the ocean. She wondered what the mysterious correspondence was all about and inquired further with James. "Oh really? Perhaps it's from Barton." Kate suppressed a yawn.

James thought before answering, as he was a bit surprised at her lack of concern. "I'm not sure. It seems suspicious at best. Any clue who could be writing you?"

"I haven't the slightest clue, or it's probably one of those dumb chain letters. Just open it, and if it's junk, then throw it away."

James was surprised at Kate's casual regard to a letter addressed to her. He knew her to be careful and attentive to such matters regarding anything with her name and knew she would never be flippant. Not wanting to press, he quickly added, "No worries, I'll open it, and if it is junk, then I'll dump it. Are you sure you are cool with that?"

"James, I no longer care about such things. I have enough in the bank to be okay, and if I ever want to do anything to keep busy, then I'll think about it then. Open and throw away. It's probably just junk mail. I have to go now because I'm starving, and lunch is being served." This time, Kate yawned into the phone.

"See you soon, Katie, and it's really good to hear you smiling over the phone again."

Kate's laugh filled James with a peace that even surprised him. "I love you, Jamesy. Come soon and bring Sebastian. I can't wait to meet him. Be safe."

"Love you more, Katie." James proceeded to call Sebastian and secure a flight for two in business class for later that month to Tokyo.

CHAPTER 3

James

It was well past seven in the evening, and a late winter snow was falling upon New York City. The rush hour traffic and the day's hustle were slowing and welcoming the night. James stared down from his office window onto Park Avenue below. His head kept debating whether to make the call he was dreading all day. Following his conversation with Kate a week ago, he proceeded to plan his trip to Japan with Sebastian; but with the excitement that a vacation brought forth, he had completely forgotten about the mysterious envelope addressed to Kate. That morning, as he walked around the multiple boxes and folders strewn about his office, he saw the yellow manila envelope casually resting on a box filled with tax documentation. Sipping a double espresso laced with sambuca, James opened the envelope marked CONFIDENTIAL: FOR KATHERINE CONNOR. He carefully read a one-page letter in neat cursive handwriting and signed by a Rey Aguilar. The name rang a bell, but James could not place it at the moment.

Dear Ms. Connor,

My name is Rey Aguilar. I know I have no business writing you, but I feel I must. Forgive me for being so bold, but I believe you deserve an explanation of what really happened. But before you read this letter, I want to let you know that I am the man who was driving the car that killed your son and caused you injuries.

If you have not yet destroyed this letter, then thank you because I must share something else with you. It is in shame and humility that I share how sorry I am for what happened. Although I was driving the SUV, I must let you know that I lost control of the car because of a defect with the steering and brakes. I took that corner at 15 mph and signaled, yet the car sped to a much higher speed, the steering locked, and the brakes failed.

Despite my best efforts to move that wheel one way or another, it remained fixed and moving in the direction where you and your son were standing. I am not trying to deflect my part in this tragedy. I just believe that you deserve a clear explanation and know that I am not some random irresponsible drunk or crazy man out to hurt anyone.

About three weeks after the accident, I was informed of the extent of what happened. And since then, I have had a need to contact you and tell you how terribly sorry I am over your immense loss. Sadly, I am aware that nothing I say will bring back your son and that nothing I do will make a difference. The car manufacturer has issued in my name a substantial check for what they call pain and suffering. I will not keep this money but would like to donate it in your son's name. To do this, I need your permission and input.

I just needed you to know how sorry I am and how I dread with all my life what happened. I am so deeply sorry, and if I could change anything, I honestly wish it were me who had lost his life and not your son.

Respectfully,
Rey Aguilar

P.S. When and if you are ready to call, my number is 917-222-6579.

The contents of the letter gave James goose bumps, yet he found himself sympathizing with this man. Rey Aguilar sounded serious, earnest, and full of remorse. Walking away from the window, James picked up his cell phone and dialed the number on the letter. The phone rang several times, and just when James was about to end the call, a deep baritone answered. "Hello?" It was a clear, strong, and manly voice; and to James, it even sounded sexy.

Clearing his throat, James said, "Yes, hello. My name is James Adderley. I represent Kate Connor, the woman you wrote a letter to back in November of last year. I'm calling about that letter."

There was obvious hesitation on the other end before a response came through. "Why are you the one calling? The letter was addressed to Ms. Connor." This statement was made without any animosity, just concern.

James sensed this and wanted to get more information. "Ms. Connor has left me in charge of all her correspondence and affairs. I opened this letter on her instructions and am calling you—" James stopped talking, as he was not certain why he was calling this man. Feeling foolish and desperate to hang up, he added hurriedly, "Uh, I will inform Ms. Connor of the contents of the letter, and she will determine if she wants to contact you going forward."

Rey Aguilar was displeased that a letter that cost him difficulty to write had been read by a person other than the addressed party. Keeping his annoyance in check, he made his point as clearly and as firmly as possible without sounding desperate. "Mr. Adderley, without sounding like a total jerk, I am also a victim in this accident, and I need closure for my own sanity. I would appreciate it very much if you gave Ms. Connor my letter to read. I need to know she doesn't think her boy's life was ended by some monster."

The last line about being a monster had James choking up just thinking about Oliver and how much he had adored Kate's son from the time he was a baby. Rey Aguilar was too real and honest for James to dismiss, and he determined at that moment that he would show Kate the letter. Controlling his emotions, James spoke honestly to Rey. "I will promise you that I will give Kate the letter. Whether she will read it or not is up to her. What happened, you can imagine, has been a nightmare for her. I will see her by the end of this month, and again, I will present her with the letter. Thank you for your honesty, and be well, Mr. Aguilar."

Rey wanted to get off the phone as the jarring yet blurred images of the SUV hitting the boy and his mother were haunting his mind. With great effort, he pushed the dark thoughts aside and rolled over to the window. Watching how the snow settled on the branches outside his window made him grin despite the pain he felt everywhere on his broken body and mind. He whispered, "Thank you," before ending the call.

There was something about Rey Aguilar that intrigued James. He determined that tomorrow he would do some snooping on this mysterious and interesting man before he showed Kate the letter.

CHAPTER 4

Rey

"You are doing so well, Mr. Aguilar," was the sugary cheer from the physical therapist at the rehabilitation center that Rey attended three days per week. The hydrotherapy was easier than most exercises, but even this drove him mad with piercing pain and exhaustion. The support belt around his waist was removed, and with the assistance of an attendant, he was helped out of the pool. Feeling like an enormous weight settled in his lower back, Rey collapsed on the bench with a thud, prompting a petite female therapist to hurry over and inquire with concern. He detested all the attention from strangers and waved her away. Resting his elbows on his knees, he took the towel by his side and hid his face to control the frustration and fury that wanted to explode every time he had therapy.

Several therapists looked over at Rey. He had developed a reputation of being ornery and angry. They were sympathetic, but some of the young female therapists gushed over his powerful masculine physique and features. Too often, they whispered how handsome he was and made references about his sex appeal. Rey could feel all eyes on him and hated every minute of it but guarded his temper because, in the end, he knew this therapy was the way out of the insufferable wheelchair.

After the van hit Oliver and Kate, it careened into the edge of the building. The intensity of the collision was such that it tore through Rey's spine, tearing disks and nerves and sending bone fragments throughout. After four difficult surgeries, the team of doctors at Hospital for Special Surgery was able to restore most of the nerve endings and replaced disks with plastic and metal parts, while a titanium rod supported the thoracic and lumbar spine and held it all in place. Rey was once again able to walk but only for tiny distances much akin to a toddler taking his first steps before collapsing. Doctors and therapists alike wondered how this man could even take one step after such an injury, but it was with Rey's sheer force of will that those steps even happened.

Slowly and with the support of a cane, he made his way into the dressing room, where he changed and anguished while he bent over to put on his boots. Every physical move was painful and accompanied by grunts and swear words. The male attendant discreetly stood nearby to supervise. He pretended to wring out some towels without offering any assistance, as he knew how tough and proud Rey was and how he disliked people hovering over him. He stood up with more difficulty and held himself up to his full height of six feet four inches.

The attendant came toward him with the wheelchair. The sight of it made him want to vomit, but he approached it with a poker face and sat down, allowing an attendant to maneuver him and the chair over to the elevator bank. Thanking the man, he pressed the down button and waited as he lost himself in a daydream of when he played his sax at the Blue Note and other venues with notable musicians. He recalled how he and his sax became one with the music. When Rey was in the zone, he was a force on stage. His imposing height and the way he held the instrument made women in the audience go wild with cheers. Rey played the sax as if he were making love to it, and it reciprocated by filling his heart and soul with joy. The ding of the elevator brought him back to his reality as he maneuvered the powered chair backward into the elevator. Once inside, he pressed L for the lobby and proceeded to a waiting car that took him home.

Getting back home was the goal because, after six difficult, lonely long months, his beloved rottweiler Captain was returning to him. After the accident, Rey was intubated and unable to speak, but he scribbled down that he had a dog at home. The American Society for the Prevention of Cruelty to Animals (ASPCA) picked up the huge dog and held him at their facilities until Rey's closest friend and fellow musician Paco Nieves picked him up. Paco visited Rey in the hospital and assured him Captain would be well loved and cared for at his family's home in Tampa, Florida.

The building superintendent's wife, Olga, did Rey's weekly shopping and cleaned the duplex loft apartment. Since the accident, his neighbors had been kind and very willing to help, but Rey discouraged favors and paid Olga while keeping his distance from everyone else.

The apartment was on a short block with two trees one on either side in the SoHo neighborhood. It was a narrow one-way street with cars tightly parked. The other two buildings on the block had storefronts. Café Memento served fancy coffees and sandwiches during the week, but Thursday through Sunday, it was busy serving a menu of Italian dishes. The locals and tourists flocked to the popular restaurant because the food was exquisitely prepared, and Zagat had rated it 4.5 for food, price, and decor. The other building had a larger storefront where two different businesses shared the space within. On one side was Soaps and Suds Laundromat, and the other half had the trendy Voodoo Vapor Lounge. This shop was always busy with a grungier younger crowd. Despite the million-dollar condominiums going up and old walk-up buildings being turned into cooperative apartments, this part of town had not lost its gritty appeal and early New York charm. Rey liked where he lived and enjoyed opening his windows during summer days and listening to the city sounds. Many of his most popular sax pieces were inspired by the experiences and stories of the people he knew and especially the numerous women who had shared his bed.

During his twenties and thirties, Rey traveled extensively throughout the world on tours and was without much care to establishing any solid relationship. His parents were living in Florida in a retirement community, and he visited them once or twice a year when he was heading to or from that general direction from tours or gigs. Musicians often teased him about being a lone wolf and about being afraid of commitment, but he always told them confidently that he was not the marrying kind and was the "one and done" type of man where women were concerned. His friends had envied his free lifestyle, how he always had a gorgeous lady or two hanging around him at parties, and how he so nonchalantly floated throughout life without a care for anyone else.

They say, your life can change in a second, and in the case of Rey Aguilar, this was true. The doorbell rang, and he moved himself over to open it. Being so tall, he reached up easily and turned the dead bolt. On the other side, he heard Captain's heavy breathing and his rough pawing at the door. Swinging the door open, the massive black dog stared wildly at Rey; he whined like a puppy and then jumped onto his lap and proceeded to lick his face and neck and make more sounds.

Rey hugged Captain back and held in his own pain from the weight of the dog on his lap; he rubbed his head and then encouraged the heavy dog to get off. Captain ran around his familiar surroundings and drank a copious amount of freshwater from his bowl. He found a large bully stick on his freshly laundered bed and settled into this with gusto. Paco Nieves watched the entire exchange of affection between man and dog and followed suit with a huge hug and handshake for his friend.

Paco was a jazz percussionist, a conguero, and a former schoolmate of Rey's at Berklee College of Music in Boston. It was Paco who formed the Golden Trio Jazz Ensemble that exploded in popularity with traditional jazz fused with Latin and African beats. The third member of the trio was Rafa Iglesias, internationally known as "Church." He was known for his impeccably clean yet passionate piano playing. He studied at Juilliard, and when he wasn't performing, he was also a guest advisor at the prestigious school. But it was Rey whom everyone came to see. He was the face, the showman, and the sexiest saxophonist to watch and listen.

Rey locked the wheelchair by the sofa and he pulled himself up, took a deep breath, and walked over to the rolling bar. Taking the bottle of Lismore, the single malt he knew Paco enjoyed, he poured his friend a neat drink into a tumbler. Paco took two strides and was by Rey's side to assist, but Rey quickly dismissed his help. "No, man, I'm good. Here let's toast to you for taking care of Captain for me." Handing over the glass, he also patted his longtime friend on the back.

Paco took the glass, but he had trouble talking because, from the moment he saw Rey, he was choked up to see his once imposing and powerful friend so vulnerable. He took a sip of the smooth whiskey and closed his eyes to savor the warmth of the liquor rolling down his throat. "Wow, this drink is so good. Hey, you look okay, just a little slow but okay." Paco wasn't one for small talk, but he also missed Rey and wanted to know how he was and when they could get back on the road as a trio.

Rey sensed Paco wanted to talk, so he started the conversation as he lowered himself into the sofa and propped pillows behind him to support his back. "Yeah, I'm better, but the doctors say I need a minor surgery that completes the last one, and that should do it as far as operations go. What sucks is the physical therapy because it's long and painful. Anyway, tell me about the wife and kids."

Paco walked over to the picture window after refreshing his drink and looked out longingly to the sight of the bridges and rooftops of lower Manhattan. He was a quiet and soft-spoken man who worshipped God, family, and music. He responded quietly while looking at the sky. "The kids are getting bigger and bigger. John is a senior in high school, and the twins are in their first year of middle school. Miriam is fine. She's actually amazing because I'm never really around with all the commitments, yet she never looks crazy and holds it all together. I don't know what I would do without my girl."

"Wow, you are still in love with your wife after . . . how long has it been?" Rey chuckled in amazement.

"Dude, twenty-one years together. You were my best man, and yes, I love that woman more with every passing year." Paco looked over at Rey and said pointedly at him, "It's not too late for you, man.

All of us need our other half. You can't keep up with this lone-wolf bullshit, or you're gonna end up a lonely old wolf."

Rey shifted uncomfortably in his seat, more so from the words Paco had said than the relentless and angry throb in his back. He got up with some effort and walked very slowly over to the window, where he supported himself by putting his hand on the glass while he held his drink in the other. Looking directly at Paco, he asked calmly, "Tell me, who's gonna want a fucked-up dude in a wheelchair anyway?" He finished his drink and looked out at the street.

Paco continued to stare ahead and finished his drink. He figured now was as good a time as any to bring it up. "Okay, it's been six months since the accident, you are walking when no one thought you ever would again, and you are alive. Rafa and I have been talking about recording again and going out on tour. You need this badly man, and trust me, we can't get booked as the trio without you playing Angie." Paco looked straight into Rey's eyes and saw the anxiety and pain. Looking around the spacious living space, he asked, "By the way, where is she?"

Paco was referring to Angie, the name Rey gave his beloved Seimer tenor saxophone. Everyone in the business knew about Angie and her sound and what she and Rey could create when they played together. All the sexual innuendos came from famous music magazine writers. Back in the 1990s, the cover of an international music publication showed a nude Rey in a rumpled bed with his sax draped seductively over his hairy chest. The story title read, "The Amazing Rey Aguilar and His Angie." The firestorm of sales put the Golden Trio on the international scene and solidified Rey's reputation as Mr. Sex.

"I haven't played in over six months. She's in the closet. I don't think I ever want to play again. And are you crazy? A tour? You see these baby steps I'm taking? Well, that's as good as it gets. Forget about it, man." He turned to move away too quickly and nearly lost his balance, but Paco, equal to his height, was by his side, keeping him from falling. Rey grunted angrily, and Paco understood how impotent his friend felt at feeling like half the man he once was. They walked over to the wheelchair, where Rey sat down and put his hand over his eyes as he hung his head. With a mixture of anger and sorrow, Rey uttered, "See what I mean? I'm useless."

Paco placed his hand on Rey's knee and asked, "So how the hell are you gonna walk Captain if you are so useless? That monster weighs an easy one hundred pounds, and he thinks he's a lapdog."

Rey answered softly, "Yeah, I got that covered with a dog walker. It's only until this stupid operation, and the damn therapy is done with. I figure, by late summer, I can walk my pup again."

Paco patted his knee again and answered with confidence, "That sounds great. But for now, we need to feed that soul of yours that is locked away with Angie. Come, let's play around with recording a bit. It can't hurt. I know you and Rafa have talked over the past months, and right now, he's in Australia on a gig with other musicians, and he wants our trio back as badly as I do. Will you at least think it over and take her out of the closet? That girl has cobwebs, man. Dust her off and get back in the game."

Rey looked up at his friend and knew that Paco was the brother he never had. Fighting back the emotion that swelled in his chest, he inhaled deeply and said dismissively, "Yeah, whatever. I'll think about it, but no promises, okay?"

Paco slapped both hands together and hugged his longtime friend. He got up and grabbed his jacket, and before he walked to the door to leave, he turned and said, "Anything you need, just call, and you better call me, dude." He opened the door and left Rey alone listening to Captain loudly snoring by the fireplace.

CHAPTER 5

Japan

A feverish week of sightseeing, shopping, and dancing had James and Sebastian spinning ecstatically around Tokyo. This city was abuzz with continuous excitement. Before heading out to the slower-paced culture of Okinawa, James and Sebastian decided to soak up everything Japanese but Tokyo-style. Running across busy streets with packages, they dashed into the Soba Noodle Company, where they dined on soup, spicy fish, and rice and an obscene amount of hot sake. Barely able to see straight, they hailed a cab and made it to the hotel to sleep off the drunkenness and pack for the early flight the next morning.

Arriving in Naha Airport was like entering one of those English garden mazes with creepy topiaries and confusing turns. This was not to suggest that the people or environment was scary but rather for James and Sebastian who did not know the language. Also, their hangovers were intensely dizzying. Many airport employees spoke English, but they felt helpless not knowing enough about the people, culture, and language. They followed other foreigners who looked like tourists toward the ferries that departed to other islands in the prefecture of Okinawa.

Pale foreigners looked red and blotchy in the oppressive noonday sun. Many used brochures to fan themselves or swat at annoying mosquitoes. The steamy and crowded ferry ride took a total of ten minutes before reaching its destination at Ishigaki Port. Few, if any, disembarked, as this was one of the most remote of all the islands in Okinawa.

Sebastian and James wheeled their fancy luggage and purchases off the boat and looked around as the sun beat down on the backs of their necks. Sebastian lifted his Ray-Ban sunglasses to look at the natural colors around him. He nudged James to look over to the left, where a leggy brunette was walking toward them with a slight limp, wearing a sun hat, flip-flops, capris, and a sleeveless tunic. When James turned and recognized Kate, he dropped his bags and ran to her side. Enthusiastically, he hugged and swung her around as she giggled and playfully demanded he stop. Holding her face, he looked deeply into her eyes and asked, "I almost did not recognize you, Katie. You look radiant."

"I feel so wonderful, James, almost as good as ever before." Kate gushed as her attention went toward the Adonis in neat shorts and a Lacoste shirt walking in their direction.

James reached out and took Sebastian's hand and said proudly, "Kate, this is Sebastian. Sebastian, this is my best friend and sister, Kate."

Kate and Sebastian shook hands and then hugged as they laughed at their own formality. "So how was your trip over to this very remote part of the world?" Kate asked as she shielded her eyes from the relentless glare of the sun.

"Well, it was incredible in Tokyo, but I need a shower and lunch before I can speak another word to you about anything." James pulled at his shirt, signaling to Kate that he was hot and clammy.

"Come, you will love the tiniest hotel on the island. It is very private, and Mrs. Goto is a mother hen looking after all her guests. You'll see what I mean. By taxi, it's a quick drive over. And then you can eat, shower, and put on beach outfits."

The two men stopped in their tracks as they approached the taxi. Their eyes bulged and stared at the immense animal that was the motorized part of the so-called vehicle. Kate was laughing so hard that she had tears brimming in her eyes.

"What the hell is that thing?" James approached the animal with great trepidation. In between giggles, Kate explained how this water buffalo was still the preferred mode of transportation among locals.

Sebastian looked at the driver, who sat high on a small slab of wood with the reins in his hands and his elbows resting on his knees. The wrinkly tanned driver stared ahead much the way his buffalo did and ignored the strangers. "Okay, James, when in Rome, we do as the Romans." Sebastian said calmly as he climbed the steps onto the wood carriage. They proceeded along, with James in a state of complete awe. The men gushed at the lushness around them, and within several minutes, they reached the hotel. Sebastian let out a soft "wow" as James lovingly hugged Kate. Kate was pleased that they found this idyllic place such a paradise and a unique experience.

"This is paradise," James said quietly as they walked along lush fronds down the stone path. The air was fragrant with the mixed scent of flowers and ocean water. Walking through the garden path that led to the hotel entrance, James understood why Kate looked nearly recovered from her ordeal. There was something about a remote place such as this where the locals did not concern themselves with the trappings of the modern world that could breathe life into a soul in need of such. Here, everything was timeless and pure.

Mrs. Goto and Aiko welcomed their guests enthusiastically with elegant bows and refreshing passion fruit drinks. After registering, Sebastian and James were escorted to the largest suite with a wraparound porch that overlooked the ocean. From every single room, the ocean view was the main attraction. Two older men deposited the loaded suitcases and a trunk of goodies purchased in Tokyo alongside the wall and bowed to exit when Sebastian ran over to give a generous tip. Very pleased with their gratuity, the men bowed several times and smiled, with the older man revealing numerous missing teeth. Mrs. Goto spun around showing all the ins and outs of the space efficiently as Aiko explained that there were no televisions in the rooms and that computers were only available from the little alcove off reception. That was the only location designated for such modern amenities.

Sebastian kept trying his phone, refusing to believe he could not get a strong signal to contact his office. With slight irritability, he remarked, "Well, we are definitely in the third world now."

Upon hearing this remark, Aiko defensively said, "We are not third world. This is Okinawa. Do you expect to find reception and signals in heaven?" She bowed along with her mother and left gracefully out of the suite, leaving both men and Kate with their mouths open.

"Well, now you did it, Seby," remarked James, adding, "What difference does it make if, for three days, you are disconnected from all the craziness back home?"

Sebastian looked at Kate and James and, nodding, agreed. "You are right. I will make amends right away."

Sensing the tension in the room, Kate jumped in quickly with an invitation to the beach. "I'll let Mrs. Goto know we are going to the beach for a swim. She prepares these delicious tiny fish sandwiches and can have them ready in no time."

Letting out a long yawn, James added sarcastically, "Careful, Seby, yours might be poisoned by Mrs. Goto." Rolling his eyes, Sebastian went to the bathroom to change into his beach trunks, a T-shirt, and some leather sandals.

For several months, Kate was embarrassed of the now tanned scars that ran down her thigh and calf. With her improved physical strength and disposition, these scars no longer bothered her as much. She changed into a one-piece cerulean blue bathing suit she found at a local market and threw over a midthigh white caftan Mrs. Goto bought her as a present for her birthday the previous month. By now, Kate had been a guest at the hotel well over eight months. She witnessed dozens of visitors come and go and was now one of five remaining guests at the hotel. Business had slowed due to the rainy season. Kate was a very loyal client, paying her hotel monthly rental on time and offering assistance with speaking to clients on the phone regarding their reservations. Mrs. Goto looked after Kate with her daily wellness teas and affirmation notes. The jolly older woman took personal pride in helping Kate heal, although she still had no idea why the young woman had been so depressed.

The brilliant blue and green waters were a source of delight for the three as they swam and playfully splashed around. While the sun was warmest, Kate ran off to sunbathe. As she rested on her towel, she thought back to how far she had come since the tragedy. Her body was stronger, and while she no longer felt like a dead leaf floating in the air, she missed her son with every fiber of her being.

Oliver was her first thought every morning and the last one before she fell asleep. When she first arrived at the hotel, her days were a blurry haze of memories and worries. Kate could not rationalize the point of her existence. It took months of the warm embrace of the sun and the healing waters of the ocean for Kate to feel that she could survive a life without Oliver. She decided that she would feel as she did regardless of what society norms dictated. On days when she was sadder than others, she would nurture her soul with the happy memories she had of her son; and on days when she felt strong and vibrant, she would venture out to see the world before her. She stopped caring about the ridiculous things that had mattered so much in her past. Streamlining her life helped her remain focused on obtaining physical health and a clearer perspective on the tragedy.

She turned over to tan her back when she heard James and Sebastian's throaty laughs and looked over her shoulder to catch them kissing passionately. They ran over to their towels to enjoy the warmth of the sun. Sebastian spoke first to Kate as she sat up to gather her now longer hair into a messy high bun. "Kate, we don't know each other, but I see why James does nothing but talk about you. You are so pretty, and that hair, I'm so jealous!"

Sebastian was referencing the rich golden chestnut hair that cascaded beyond Kate's shoulder blades in long loose waves. The sun had naturally highlighted it with golden streaks. As a result of her hair being lighter, Kate's hazel eyes looked like two sparkly gold marbles. All this came packed in a trimmer and slender body with long legs and honey-tanned skin. Kate was feeling good again, but there was a strong wave of survivor's remorse that often hit her, and the telltale signs of despair sat on her face in the form of horizontal lines across her forehead and a frown upon her lips.

The compliment was embarrassing and made her blush. She felt she did not deserve to be admired. This was part of the guilt she felt for surviving the accident. She looked away to the ocean and focused on several seagulls that flew overhead, making loud squawking sounds. James noticed her withdrawal and put his arm around her shoulders. Resting her head on his strong shoulder, Kate inhaled and wiped a tear away.

"It's okay, girl. I'm here to look after you."

Sebastian added, "And if you let me, I too will be a devoted friend." He touched her thigh exactly where the ugly scar started.

Kate felt the warmth of their love and let her tears flow and sniffed into a napkin left over from lunch. Laughing, she blurted out apologetically, "Now here is a fine vacation for you two watching over me." Taking a deep breath, she continued. "I am resigned to living the rest of my life yearning for my little boy. It's just that sometimes it hurts more than at other times, and I let myself cry. I'm sorry because you are not here to dry my tears."

Like an instant replay of a song, both men said the same thing, "Are you crazy!" All three laughed and cried together.

Kate looked down at the sand wistfully as she reminisced about Oliver. "He wanted to take the bike up to Bear Mountain the following weekend. Oliver was so happy because his father and I were going to share a dinner as a family. He was a boy of simple pleasures. Oliver never demanded anything and expected nothing at all. I guess I was too lucky with a perfect little boy who never gave me a moment's worry." She blew her nose into the unused napkin Sebastian handed her from his lunch.

They sat quietly, respecting the moment and breathing in the hyacinth-scented breeze. James thought it was a good time to bring up the letter and started to speak, but when Sebastian realized what he was about to tell Kate, he tried warning James with his eyes. "Katie, you remember that letter I told you about over the phone? It's from the man who was driving the SUV."

Kate looked somewhat puzzled upon hearing this. Sebastian took this as an opportunity to interject and avoid the subject. "Hey, let's get back, and maybe you can take us into the little town to help us buy more souvenirs." He started picking things up and placing them into the yellow woven bag Mrs. Goto used to organize their lunch.

Kate said, "Oh sure, we can do that because the little village is adorable. James, what about that letter?"

James looked at Sebastian and saw him roll his eyes while he continued shaking sand out of the towels, but he continued. "Well, this guy wants to donate all this money he got from the insurance company to a charity in Oliver's name. He doesn't want the money."

Kate furrowed her brows, put her sunglasses on, and threw the beach cover-up over her head. The embroidered white linen cover-up flowed down from her shoulders into a poncho, which made her long tanned legs look attractive despite the zig-zag scars that ran down the thigh and continued near the ankle. They started to walk away from the beach when Kate stopped and said to James, "Does this jerk think that by giving the money away he got at the cost of my child's life will exonerate him from what he did?" Both men were surprised at the low-voiced response that was laced deep with pain and anger.

James tried to explain as Seby continued vain attempts to discourage the conversation by giving him varied and serious faces, but he persisted. "Kate, it's a polite letter. All you have to do is read it, and if you want to, you respond or tell me how you wish to proceed. Besides, he sounds like a really decent man who is full of remorse."

Kate asked with her voice expressing bitterness, "You spoke with him? Did you also have a nice lunch or share a drink? Really, James?"

Not quite knowing what to say because Sebastian's expressions were making him nervous, James answered as nonchalantly as he could, "I never meant to upset you. Let's forget about that. I'm dying for a cool shower and drink. Anyone feel the same way?"

Sebastian jumped in. "Me too. I get the shower first while you get us some cool drinks." Sebastian hurried into the hotel and was greeted by Mrs. Goto. He wanted to continue to throw Kate off the issue of the letter and shocked Mrs. Goto with an unexpected hug and kiss on the cheek as he said loudly, "Thank you for that delicious lunch!"

The chubby woman touched her cheek where his kiss had been planted and ran inside to her office with a look of utter shock. Aiko came running out, but before she could say anything, it was Sebastian who asked, "Oh my god, your mother must think I'm crazy. I just wanted to show my appreciation for all her trouble."

Aiko covered her mouth as she giggled and said, "It's fine. She's just very shy when men show her any attention. She will be okay, and yes, she thinks you are crazy." Everyone laughed as they walked away to their respective rooms.

Inside their suite, Sebastian did not waste a moment before he reprimanded James. "Hey, what is wrong with you? Kate was talking about her kid, and you bring up the letter that the dude who killed him wrote. OMG! What is wrong with you?"

Clearly annoyed at Sebastian because he knew he was right, James said quietly, "I thought it was the right time, and I committed a major stupid blunder, but your little antics helped with distracting Kate. Thanks."

"Yeah, I know, but she is still very fragile, and something like that letter can make her depressed again. Don't you think so?" Sebastian embraced James.

"I know, you are right. It's just that I told this guy I would give her the letter and get him an answer about the donation. It's a lot of money, and maybe this gesture and a charity in Oliver's name can help Kate heal even more."

"Well, if she wants to read it, you will have to give it to her and let the chips fall where they may. Come on, let's take a shower and relax a bit." They embraced and kissed and did not mention the letter again.

Dressed in a loose and flowing linen dress the color of saffron, Kate slipped into a pair of gold flip-flops and wore her hair down in loose waves. She met Sebastian and James in the courtyard, and together, they mounted another cart led by a water buffalo with a bell fastened through the nostrils and a smiling, toothless driver. The bumpy ride took them into the tiny village where street vendors were still abuzz in the late afternoon selling everything from fish, seafood, and furniture.

The few family-owned restaurants were tiny, but they served a genuine menu of traditional Japanese food and drinks. Kate escorted her company to the aptly named Ocean Shell Dining Palace. Although it boasted a big name for a twelve-table establishment, the food was legendary. There was a full bar, and a mix of popular songs and some instrumental music piped in from a sound system. Everyone flocked to Ocean Shell, and particularly on weekends, it was impossible to get in without some sort of special connection to the owner, Mr. Kinjo. Everyone in Okinawa knew the Kinjo family because everyone of them excelled as chefs and bartenders. Nearby American military families often hired them to cater weddings and other affairs. Luckily for Kate, Sebastian, and James, the rainy season kept everyone away; and the locals were the only ones flocking the nearby places to eat. They had no trouble obtaining a seat indoors, as the weather was too unpredictable for a seat in the back garden, which had a view of the cliffs and lush fauna.

Little Lucy, Mr. Kinjo's twelve-year-old granddaughter expertly took their drink orders and explained the menu to them. The men ordered bottles of sake champagne, determined to get themselves and Kate sauced enough so that she would not mention the letter ever again. Kate ordered the Okinawan soba noodles in a soup with no meat, while each man ordered a vegetable dish accompanied by *tonkatsu*, a tenderized and breaded fried pork cutlet.

Throughout the evening, the sake flowed, but Kate had already built a slight resistance to its effects over the months, while Sebastian and James were deep in the throes of inebriation. As drunks went, they were hilarious with their off-color jokes and ornery behavior. As often happened with too much drink, Sebastian and James lost their composure and openly hugged and kissed each other without care to the stares and looks of shock upon the faces of the patrons at tables nearby. Stumbling out of the restaurant, Kate encouraged them to walk a bit to get some air, but they were silly and loud, causing people to stare at them and ultimately embarrassing Kate. She saw a taxicab nearby and signaled for it to meet her on the next corner. With a bit of difficulty, she managed to maneuver both James and Sebastian down the street and into the waiting cab.

Back at the hotel, she escorted them to their rooms to sleep off their drunken stupor but held James back and quietly asked him before he closed the door, "Do you have the letter with you?" Not wanting to entertain that conversation, James tried to close the door, but Kate held his arm and insisted. "James, give me the darn letter."

He left the door opened as he walked sluggishly over to his backpack and took out the white envelope. He walked over to Kate and held it away from her hand and said with a slight slur to his words, "You better not get all sad and go on a depression binge over this because Seby will freakin' kill me. He got mad at me for even bringing it up. You promise?"

Kate touched his flushed cheek lovingly, and with a peck on the cheek added, "Don't worry, you silly drunken fool. I promise. Now go shower and get into bed with your sexy Seby. Don't worry about me. Okay?"

"That's easier said than done. Keep an open mind, and we'll meet tomorrow for a late breakfast to discuss its contents if you like."

"Okay, not sure why I want to read it except that, since he mentioned Oliver, then I feel this pull toward reading his words. I can't explain why, just a need, I guess."

James reached over, hugged his beloved Kate, and kissed the top of her head, inhaling the pretty flowery scent of her hair. He let her go and closed the door, blowing a kiss in her direction.

Kate walked down to the garden, passing Mrs. Goto, who was yawning in her chair by reception. Kate bowed in her direction and wished her a good night as she walked toward her favorite place on the island, the greenhouse. Mrs. Goto stood up and watched where Kate went and wondered about this mysterious lady with the rowdy friends.

Entering the dark greenhouse, she flipped the light switch on and immediately turned it off again, as it gave off a garish light. She preferred the soft yellow hue given off by the lanterns that abounded everywhere. Walking carefully, Kate remembered where she had seen a box of long matches and proceeded to set alight the three closest lanterns by the deep-cushioned chair she loved. That part of the room immediately took on a romantic, tranquil feeling that enveloped her with a sense of peace.

Settling into her chair, Kate looked at the handwriting on the envelope and acknowledged the good penmanship and then carefully opened the envelope and removed the letter. Suddenly feeling a despair rising in her chest, she dropped the letter to the ground and covered her eyes with her hands. Kate moved her fingers over to her temples and gently rubbed them as she always did when feeling tense.

The door to the greenhouse creaked open, causing Kate to look up to see Mrs. Goto balancing a small tray with a tea service and flicking the bright fluorescent light. She rushed off her chair and went over to help Mrs. Goto with the tray. Together, they moved to the nearby sofa and settled in resting the tray on a small table already housing a slender and elegant purple hyacinth. Mrs. Goto smiled and went right to the point, which was unlike her character, but her curiosity brushed away all norms of behavior and gave her the bravado she only reserved for running her business. Speaking slowly and calmly and measuring her words, Mrs. Goto spoke to Kate with difficulty and in broken English. "I want to know why you so sad and cry so much when you come here." She poured tea into both petite cups and handed one to Kate.

Kate smiled at the woman with the wavy brown hair and full cheeks that always smelled like pressed powder. Her bowlike mouth was painted a soft petal pink accenting the brown in her eyes. Kate saw kindness and a genuineness rarely seen in many people. "Mrs. Goto, I came to Okinawa because I am running away from my life." Confessing this out loud caused Kate to feel a small shudder in her chest. It was as if this revelation would unlock a tidal wave of unhappiness and allow her to feel whole once again.

"What you mean run away from life? Why?"

Taking a sip of the gentle tea soothed Kate and released her fears, enabling her to feel safe in opening up to this woman who was, in essence, a stranger to her. She got up and pointed to the light. Mrs. Goto made a gesture as if swatting a bee and grunted something in her language, encouraging Kate to walk over and turn off the light. Once again, only the gentle light of candles and the feeling of peace lit the lush green surroundings.

"Mrs. Goto, my son, Oliver, was killed on his birthday." Mrs. Goto brought both hands up to cover her mouth in shock. The words were like an echo flowing through Kate. For the first time since Oliver's death, Kate articulated what had happened. "My son was riding his new bicycle on the sidewalk with me when a car lost control and hit us both. I was told Oliver died instantly, but I was badly injured and in a hospital for a long time. So after the long and difficult rehabilitation, I sold everything and bought a one-way ticket to Okinawa because this was my son's favorite vacation when he was eight years old. He was so little, and he wanted to climb the cliffs and dive off like all the professional divers come and do."

Mrs. Goto took a sip of her tea, set down the cup, and took Kate's left hand in hers. The woman understood more English than she could articulate. Shaking her head, she said quietly in her heavy accent, "You a strong mother."

Kate moved her hand away and pressed her fingers gently over her eyelids because the tears were threatening to fall. Mrs. Goto moved Kate's chin to face her, and she said firmly as if reading Kate's mind, "You will always be his mother. He is away, but you are here alive. You survived because you have more to do in this life."

Kate took the peach cotton napkin from the tea service to dry the tears that now flowed freely. Mrs. Goto got up to go around the long table that housed the calla lilies to pick up the folded letter off the floor. Kate realized she had forgotten all about the letter when Mrs. Goto came into the greenhouse. She feared Mrs. Goto would ask her to read it, but instead, she handed her the unfolded letter and returned to her seat. She drank another sip of tea and smiled up to Kate.

"Thank you, Mrs. Goto."

"For what do you say 'thank you' to me?"

"Well, you helped me heal with the teas and little papers with lovely sayings every day. I will always remember your kindness."

"Why you say this? You going away, back home?"

Kate quickly reassured the proprietress, whose face had creased in concern, thinking she was leaving. "Oh no, I love it here, and I don't want to leave. I just wanted to thank you for being such a good friend to me because this has been very hard."

Mrs. Goto closed her eyes and held both hands to her chest. She uttered what sounded like a prayer in Japanese. When she was done, she looked at Kate and took her hand. "Where is your son's father?"

"He lives in New York. We were divorced just before Oliver was five years old. Michael remarried and has a daughter."

"Everybody get divorce in your country." She touched her head as a gesture implying disbelief. Pointing to the letter, she asked, "This a sad letter?"

Kate looked down at the letter and wondered herself if it indeed contained a sad message. She shrugged and explained as simply as she knew how to Mrs. Goto. "I don't know because I have not read it yet. When I wanted to read it, I got sad and started to cry, and then you came." She took a deep breath and added, "It is from the man who killed my son."

"What?" Mrs. Goto's eyes opened wide. "Oh, how you get this?"

"James brought it to me. James is my friend, brother, and lawyer."

"Oh, I see. You must read it. Maybe he say he sorry." She smiled, and in her eyes, Kate saw a twinkle of hope.

"What good will saying, sorry, do? It won't bring back Oliver." Kate smirked and then looked straight ahead.

Mrs. Goto took her hand in her own and squeezed gently. "Oliver is gone. Nothing will bring him back, but he lives here." She pointed to Kate's heart. "If this man want to say he is sorry, then you must forgive for your son and for you."

Kate looked at the serious brown eyes of Mrs. Goto and understood on a deep level that she was right. She unfolded and started to read the letter as Mrs. Goto discreetly picked up the tea tray and left.

CHAPTER 6

New York

James and Sebastian arrived in New York on a warm, rainy day. Spring was on its last legs, and the Kelly green of new leaves abounded everywhere on trees, short grasses, and bushes alongside buildings.

Along with what seemed like an endless set of luggage was, tucked away in James's breast pocket, Kate's letter to Rey Aguilar. James desperately wanted to know its contents, but Kate had sealed the envelope and told him that it was a letter of forgiveness on her behalf and the charity she would like the monies in Oliver's name to go to. The taxi pulled up, and a skinny dark-skinned man, with the help of Sebastian, hoisted the pieces of luggage into the trunk. There were so many bags that each of them had one or more packages on their laps and on the taxi floor.

"I'm exhausted and desperately want a bath, a hot tea, and my bed," said Sebastian as he yawned.

The airplane ride took over thirteen hours, and although they had comfortable business class seats, their bodies were tight from lugging the suitcases around, along with the exhaustion that often accompanied distance travel. James agreed with Sebastian about the need for a bath, but he was too wired for sleep. He was annoyed that Kate didn't want to share the contents of the letter. Taking this personally, he was disconcerted but determined to just unload the problem as soon as possible and forget Rey Aguilar and his letter until he was back at work on Monday.

Early Monday morning, while sipping a latte in his office, James dialed Rey Aguilar's number and waited. The same gruff voice responded after several rings.

"Mr. Aguilar, James Adderley here. Is this a good time to talk?"

"Yes, of course, just give me a second to get to a quieter space."

James heard what sounded like men laughing in the background and a heavy door closing with someone complaining about a woman. James was once again intrigued.

"Okay, Mr. Adderley. What information do you have for me?"

James was a bit taken aback with Rey's to-the-point tone. Although it was polite, James understood this to be a no-nonsense sort of man. "Mr. Aguilar, I gave your letter to Ms. Connor. She has written one to you, and I need to know if your address remains the same."

"The address remains the same, but right now, I'm in New Orleans. I'll be back in New York in a few days. If you mail it today, I should receive it by the time I get back."

"Sounds like a plan. New Orleans is a great town." James stopped talking when the powerful barking of a dog came over the phone and startled him.

Rey explained apologetically about the barking. "Sorry, that's just my dog, Captain. He's clearly hungry, and I have been recording all morning, so he needs a walk and some grub. Oh and yes, New Orleans is a great town."

Just as he was about to respond, James heard another man ask Rey a question, and an exchange ensued. "Hey, thanks, Rafa. You know he needs a long walk. Thanks a lot, bro."

"No problem. I'll take a while because dogs are chick magnets, and I need to get smokes, so give us about thirty minutes."

"Yeah, sure, man. I appreciate you helping me that way. I owe you."

"Yeah, no problem."

James heard another door close and then silence. Rey proceeded to apologize for the constant interruptions. "I'm sorry about all these interruptions, but we can talk now."

James settled into his chair and hoped this man could talk because he was very intrigued. He wanted to know exactly what he did and what he was doing in New Orleans. "No problem. It sounds like you are a musician."

"Well, I play the tenor sax with my group The Golden Trio. You like jazz?"

James loved jazz, and Sebastian often played it around the apartment. They had several streamed recordings from The Golden Trio and often talked about doing a jazz cruise or traveling around the world to visit different jazz festivals. James was very interested to learn more about this man and pushed further for information. "I love jazz and have several recordings by your group. Didn't you win a Grammy just a few years ago?"

"My trio has three Grammys, and I have two for the albums *San Sebastian* and *Caribe*."

"Oh yeah, that's right, and you've been written up a lot in music and fashion magazines. Now I'm putting the name with the face. All right, this is so cool." James chimed happily as he recalled images of Rey as very masculine and tall.

"Thanks, man, I've been lying low for about two years now. First, it was lack of inspiration to write new music, and then this accident set me back a year. But I'm about 80 percent back now that I had that last surgery and can walk much better. I was in a wheelchair for a year, and that was crazy."

"I had no idea your injuries from the accident were so severe. I mean, I knew you were injured but not the extent or severity."

"I've had four back surgeries and too much physical therapy to even want to remember. Hey, you mind if I ask if Ms. Connor is okay? I know she was hurt as well."

James liked the kindness in his tone. He sounded real, like a good person who had been met with several difficulties in recent years. But despite his warm feelings toward Rey, he kept his answer as minimal as possible to respect Kate's privacy. "I just arrived Saturday from spending some time with her. She's still recovering, but it is now more emotional than physical. You know, I can't begin to imagine how crazy it is to lose a kid."

Hearing this tightened something in Rey's chest. He breathed deeply and closed his eyes. Nearly every night since that fateful day, Rey had the same recurring nightmare. A young boy looking straight at him with utter shock and fear on his face was what he saw in his dreams. He waited a minute and responded with a heaviness and sadness in his voice. "I'm sorry. I don't know what else to say except I wish it had been me instead of her kid. You have no idea how this eats away at me. I know the car was defective, but damn, I was the one behind the wheel, and I couldn't do shit." Rey's tone was heavy with remorse and despair.

James felt he needed to correct this or at least leave the conversation on a lighter note. But one thing rang sure for James, and it was that he liked this guy. There was something about Rey's voice that resonated trust and goodness. Putting aside what he already knew about the musician's good looks and notoriety, he felt deeply that this was a man who took his actions seriously. "Hey, I know there was nothing you could have done. I read all the reports and spoke with your attorneys and the car manufacturer's team of lawyers. Aside from the horror of what happened, all parties involved know you were not at fault. You should know, that this statement coming from me is huge because, besides being her lawyer, I'm Kate's foster brother. So when I tell you I know you are not at fault for killing the closest thing I ever had as a nephew, I mean it. Oliver was also my godson. I was there when he was born, and I adored that little boy. So I forgive you, man, because you were not some drunken asshole or speeding fool. What happened could have happened to anyone of us. Maybe you should stop beating yourself up about this."

The tightness in his chest made it hard to breathe. He finally let out a deep breath and sniffed loudly. Everything James had said resonated with him, and although he was grateful for the words, he had to get off the phone before he completely lost it again with this stranger. He said quickly in an emotion-charged voice, "Thank you for telling me all this. Look, I have to go, but I will be in touch. I'm good for my word. Gotta go and thanks."

James put his phone in his jacket pocket and took the letter out to his assistant with instructions and the address where to mail it. He went out for a walk to clear his head from the conversation that clearly saddened but had him asking more questions than he ever expected. He wondered more about this man and his sensitive tone, and he thought of Kate and how she was still content with living as far away from her home as possible. James thought about these two lost souls and how much they needed to heal.

Reaching for the bottle of Fiji Water, Rey drank down the twenty ounces without interruption. Collecting himself was important because he didn't have the energy or interest in any of his musician friends inquiring about why he suddenly looked so sullen. Captain came barreling through the recording studio, looking for Rey. The gigantic dog sensed immediately that his pack leader wasn't all right.

Rey took out from his duffel bag food bowls and prepared two cups of dry kibble and some freshwater from a newly opened bottle and placed the bowls in a discreet corner of the sound room. The dog ate with much gusto, not taking a moment to look up until the bowls were empty. After this, he padded over and laid his muscular body by Rey's feet and closed his eyes, content with his lot in life and being close to his master.

For Rey, seeing his dog rest by his feet was the calm that settled his mind. Picking up his sax, he played a few notes, signaling to his pals that he was ready. Rafa and Paco knew him well. They sensed that whomever Rey had a conversation with before had left him edgy and withdrawn.

Rafa interrupted when Rey was lost in thought. "Are you up for a few more hours?"

Rey was annoyed; he stopped the session and snapped, "What makes you think I'm not?"

Rafa spoke calmly yet firmly. "Hey, you aren't keeping up, you missed the last note, and you are a million miles away, that's all. No need to get pissed."

Stretching his neck from side to side, Rey looked first at Paco and then at Rafa. His eyes scanned the other three studio musicians and apologized. "Sorry, bro, too many demons in my head. Give me another chance, and if I can't do this, then it's quits, okay?" Paco was nearest Rey and gave him a friendly punch on the arm.

Rafa called out the note. "From the top. And a one, two, one, two, three." Each musician responded on cue and played in unison the notes for Rafa's newest Latin jazz composition.

The next morning was hot, and Rey wanted out of the sticky humidity of New Orleans. Captain jumped into the back of the SUV for the long drive back to New York. Making no stops, the trip would be about twenty hours, but Rey needed to stop every two hours to stretch his back and give Captain a chance to sniff around and relieve himself. He knew the trip would take longer, and that meant sleeping in the car. He could fly, but the thought of placing Captain, in a cage alone, in the cargo hold, was unthinkable.

The drive went smoothly, and they were in New York twenty-two hours later because Rey overslept. After parking the car in the monthly garage he rented, Rey walked Captain, feeling stiffness everywhere on his body and desperately desiring a shower and painkillers. It was busy on his block with summer approaching and people moving about. He glanced at pretty young legs in shorts or miniskirts walking along, and they, in turn, looked at him. Summer was his favorite season, and after a year of hellish pain and suffering, he looked forward to the warm weather and the carefree feeling that accompanied this time of the year.

After settling in, he fed the dog and stripped for a shower. Feeling the water on his back felt good, and he remained there for a long while. The early evening hours brought different sounds in the neighborhood. The tones were more muffled, and the sounds of voices were fewer.

Rey prepared a quick meal of steak, baked potatoes, and kale and tomato salad with a little olive oil, salt, and pepper. A glass of pinot noir and the beautiful *Liebestraum* by Franz Liszt completed the ambience Rey wanted to create for a relaxing end to a long road trip. Although he was no longer on any narcotics for pain, his doctor kept him on the lowest dose of Tramadol for those rare days when he would get too tired and his back would hurt to the point of delirium.

He washed down one pill and felt the effects almost immediately. Not caring that he should not mix alcohol with the medication, he relished the warm sensation from the combination.

Stretching out on his large brown leather sectional, he proceeded to open his mail. There was the new *Wine Spectator* magazine, a utility bill, a reminder from Captain's vet that his rabies vaccine was due, some flyer from a local politician, and finally a manila envelope from the law offices of Penton and Adderley. He stared at the envelope and sat up, feeling light-headed as if he had had several shots of tequila and not just one little Tramadol with wine. Tearing off the top of the envelope, he set it down to pour himself another glass of the 2013 Sea Smoke Cellars pinot noir. Drinking it thirstily, he felt his nerves spring back to life.

Rey knew he was nervous about opening the letter, and to calm down, he walked around the apartment. Feeling quite buzzed and anxious, he threw all the dirty clothes from his trip into the washer just to keep busy and not fall asleep. He then proceeded to put away his luggage, and because his movements were a bit awkward, he banged his head as he opened a closet door to put the suitcase away, ripping out a series of expletives followed by a hearty laugh. Rey laughed at the comedy of the situation. He was slightly drunk, doing laundry, and putting things away to avoid opening a letter. Reaching into the refrigerator for a glass of water, he gulped down all sixteen ounces of the Poland Spring bottle and sat back down on the sofa. He picked up the letter and opened it as if it were another bill and proceeded to read what Kate Connor had written.

Dear Mr. Aguilar,

It is with much trepidation that I write this letter to you, but I feel you deserve a response. I read your letter several times and felt different emotions hitting me at once. I sense your heartfelt remorse, sorrow, and pain as you described the events that led to the horrible accident that claimed the life of my little boy, and has since caused us both so much despair.

Although this accident has changed my life, I want you to know that I know you were not at fault in the death of my son. I understand that the car was faulty and that losing control of the vehicle did not come about through any negligence of your own.

My son was a vibrant and beautiful boy who loved dogs, bicycles, and the ocean. As a single parent, we traveled often and enjoyed trying the local cuisines of the cultures we visited. Oliver was a risk-taker, and I often found myself being a disciplinarian most of the time out of fear he would get hurt.

These past months have been a nightmare that I am too slowly coming out of. As you know, this August will mark the first anniversary of his last birthday and the same day of his death. Truthfully, I want to die before this day arrives to avoid living through it. My physical pain and suffering has not mattered much, but the deep-rooted sorrow and desperation I feel at times consumes me and makes me want to end it all.

I left New York to run away from the life I knew with Oliver. Although I have no regrets, I do feel that I am trapped in a strange sort of limbo from time to time and wish I could find that peace and strength I had before I lost him.

In regard to the matter of the award money, I would like very much for this to be a donation to the Montefiore Children's Hospital in New York. One of the most difficult things Oliver had to face in his young years was to watch his best friend, Leo Kasman, lose his life to leukemia at the age of seven. Although he did not understand what this terrible disease was, he said to me that one day he would become a doctor and make all cancer go away. To honor what Oliver could have become, I would like this money designated to this charity.

Once again, thank you for your kind and honest letter, as it did help me reflect on what occurred and its aftermath.

Respectfully,
Kate Connor

Rey reached over for his dinner napkin and blew his nose noisily, causing Captain to look up and grunt in his direction. Copious tears flowed, and he let them without shame. It was rare for Rey to cry, but between the mix of the drug, wine, and the message in the letter, Kate Connor's words released a large knot of sorrow that had settled in his chest months ago. Captain moved over to him, placed his enormous head by Rey's thigh, and rested a paw on his knee to comfort him. Once he could cry no more, Rey rubbed Captain's head and bent down to kiss him.

He got up and went to the bathroom to splash water on his face. Unsteady on his feet, he moved the laundry to the top part of the dryer and made his way upstairs to his bedroom, with Captain padding softly behind. He collapsed on the bed, and fell asleep for the first time in a long while not feeling the terrible heaviness of that knot in his chest.

The New York 1 channel, preprogrammed on Rey's bedroom television, awoke him with the weather forecast predicting a hot, humid day with temperatures in the mid-eighties. Rey lay on his king-size bed sprawled out, looking up at the ceiling and getting his bearings. His first thought was that he did not have a hangover from the bottle and a half of wine he consumed the night before, and his second was of Kate Connor and what she wrote in the letter. Stretching carefully and gently getting off the bed as he was taught to do because of the surgeries to his back, Rey put his feet on the floor and was grateful he could walk to the bathroom without the cane or wheelchair.

The coffee maker signaled that his brew was ready with a gentle medley. Freshly showered, he threw on some workout shorts and a T-shirt and stepped into his running shoes. He walked down the stairs and prepared his coffee. Captain stretched languorously and sat by the door, waiting to be taken out. This routine was repeated daily at home and whenever they traveled together.

The usually busy neighborhood was blissfully quiet at nine thirty in the morning. School was out for summer vacation, meaning fewer people and traffic to contend with in the city. They walked for a good hour around the streets, and on the way back home, he stopped to pick up oranges, asparagus, and wild salmon from Yuma's, the popular Korean market in the neighborhood.

There was something about this morning that had Rey feeling especially light-hearted and, for the first time in a very long while, happy. He walked home with an air of confidence that reminded him of when he was much younger in his twenties. Remembering himself at that time, he realized he was more of a smug know-it-all, particularly where music and women were concerned. But after Kate's letter and absolution to any fault in the accident, he felt reborn, almost as if he had a second chance at being good and whole once again.

Once home, he put away the groceries and picked up Kate's letter from the coffee table. Rey walked over to the window to closely observe the tiny print of the hotel stationery he had missed the night before. He wondered how he could have missed the raised bright blue print with a sunburst across the top, but then his eyes scanned the table with the bottles of wine and remembered all he had consumed. The address of Okinawa, Japan, was what made his eyebrows rise high on his forehead. He wondered what the devil Kate Connor could want, being so far from all and everyone she knew. Never having traveled to the Okinawa Islands, he wondered what it would be like to visit. What intrigued him most was whether or not Kate Connor could find happiness in such a remote part of the world.

Picking up his cell phone, he dialed Rafa's number. Rafa responded immediately with much enthusiasm. "Hey, kiddo, what's up? Did you have a good drive?"

"The drive was fine. Still hot in New Orleans?"

"Oh yeah, but I love it. The hotter, the better."

"Just wondering if you have set up the tour dates and locations for overseas yet."

"Not entirely, why?"

"Oh, just, uh, wondering if Japan would be on the map, that's all."

The senior man in the band thought for a moment about why, all of a sudden, Japan would be of interest to Rey. The last time they traveled there was five years ago, and it was financially and creatively very successful. He drank more coffee down and took a drag from his cigarette before responding.

Rey heard him gulp and take that drag on the other end and felt he should say more. "You know how popular we are in Asia."

"Tokyo was not one of my considerations because we were invited to the festivals in New Zealand, two in Australia, and then in Shanghai. And I wanted to hit Macau for a little gambling and fun. Okay, Rey, why the interest in Tokyo?"

Gently tapping the window with his fingernail, Rey responded, "Why not? I remember it was a lucrative deal, and we had a great time with other big-name artists. The Japanese love our music, and they have some of the best jazz clubs I have ever been to worldwide."

Putting down his cup and admiring the derriere of a pretty woman walking by in ripped jeans and high heels, Rafa said casually, "Give me a few days to see if we can add this to the tour because, from Asia, we were heading to Dubai, and then Europe. It may be too late, but let me crunch some numbers with the tour manager and accountant, and I'll get back to you. You sure you just don't want to visit some pretty lady over there?" Rafa laughed heartily.

Rolling his eyes, Rey quipped, "Yeah, that's it. My life is ruled by my dick. Shut up and try to make it happen. Thanks, Rafa."

"Yup, oh, and by the way, it was really good seeing you walking on your own again. The sax playing, well, that's a different story." Teasingly, he hung up laughing and knowing that this would piss off Rey.

"Hey, what? Asshole." He ended the call when he realized Rafa was no longer on the other end and proceeded to remove his sax from its case and practice for the new gig a few days away.

James opened the envelope that his assistant placed on his desk. Inside were two tickets for Dizzy's Club Coca-Cola at Jazz at Lincoln Center. The tickets indicated Grammy Award winner Rey Aguilar as invited guest of the Arturo Sandoval Ensemble. He excitedly picked up his phone to call Sebastian. "Guess who just scored two tickets to Dizzy's to see none other than Rey Aguilar perform?"

"Get out! I love that place, and the Manhattan skyline view is great. Remember when we went for Taylor and Robbie's engagement party, and it was snowing. The whole place was magical and so romantic." Sebastian gushed.

"Yeah, that was beautiful. This show is tomorrow so clear your calendar. Maybe you should meet me here, and we'll jump in a cab. I must go because I have to be at court in one hour. See you later?"

"Of course, can't wait. So excited. Bye now."

Nestled on the fifth floor of the Time Warner Center, Dizzy's Club Coca-Cola was packed with jazz enthusiasts and several artists who came to hear the Arturo Sandoval Ensemble play but more so to see Rey Aguilar. The terrible accident that had left him in a wheelchair for most of the past year was well publicized in local celebrity weeklies and by paparazzi taking snapshots of Rey visiting his doctor or going to physical therapy. The photographs taken of him in a wheelchair or holding a cane were too much to bear and had made Rey introverted, angry, and distrustful of photographers. Rey was thankful he was emerging from this darkness to resume his life and career.

The announcer enthusiastically welcomed all, and the jazz music began. Rey was off to the side with Paco and several other artists waiting to be introduced by Arturo himself. He felt good but was clearly nervous. He drank one neat scotch and then another and stopped. The last thing he wanted to do was to trip as he walked on stage or mess up his playing. Dressed in a black Tom Ford suit, charcoal silk T-shirt, and black suede shoes, he waited for Sandoval to introduce him. He walked confidently up to the stage, where he received a standing ovation from the musicians and audience. Several catcalls and comments were thrown out regarding his good looks, but he was already in the zone. Zoning out all the noise, Rey heard nothing around him except his inner voice and the music. Giving Sandoval a side-glance signaling his start, he ran his tongue over his lips, causing more catcalls from women, and moved the sax to his lips. He tapped with his right foot and played Coltrane's "Giant Steps" with all his heart and soul.

The audience was mesmerized as were the other musicians because everyone understood that, in selecting "Giant Steps," Rey was sharing how this past year was one of taking huge leaps medically and mentally. James and Sebastian were as enthralled as the rest of the audience, and both agreed this man was stunning as a performer and definitely someone to meet. When Rey ended his solo, the crowd exploded in applause as did the musicians.

Rey was back in the game, and he felt good inside because he felt in control of his music. Spending the year not knowing if he would ever walk again and in and out of surgeries had damaged his self-esteem and put in question his purpose for living. Returning to the music he loved and that defined him was one more step toward a full recovery. Through all the physical pain and the insecurity of whether his body would work again, Rey had reflected on his life in general. At forty years of age, he knew it was time to find that certain special person to share all his joys and sorrows with. Captain was a great companion but not all he needed or wanted. Rey wanted a life partner, someone special to call his own and share his deepest thoughts with. In the stillness of his home and when he played his sax, he often daydreamed what it would be like to have one special person by his side.

James moved along the crowd with a drink in his hand as Sebastian trailed behind. They waited what seemed like an endless amount of time for people to stop asking Rey for autographs and photo opportunities. Holding out his hand, he said firmly and businesslike, "Hello, Mr. Aguilar. I'm James Adderley." Rey shook his hand enthusiastically and then pulled him in for a manly hug. James returned the gesture and introduced Sebastian as his partner.

The crowd was returning to their seats as the Sandoval band made their way off the stage to allow the next band to set up. Piped music played, and waiters bustled about, busily taking orders and serving drinks. A large group in the center table sang out the "Happy Birthday" song to one of their friends, prompting one of the musicians leaving the stage to return spontaneously and blow out a medley of the song from his trumpet to the squeals of joy and applause from the patrons.

But Rey wanted to chat with James and suggested they move to another area. "Follow me to where the musicians hang out. It's quieter there, and we can order food and drinks."

"Oh sure. Thanks, man. I wasn't expecting to go 'backstage' at Dizzy's," James said enthusiastically, with Sebastian agreeing.

Rey escorted them through a heavy blue velvet curtain and down a short hallway that led to another door. Upon entering, they were met with a darkened room full of musicians laughing, smoking, and drinking. All were having a gregarious time. Rey shook more hands and was shown to an upholstered red velvet booth with a tiny lit lamp on the wall. Catching the elbow of Suzette, the waitress for this section, he whispered in her ear, "Bring a bottle of champagne for the table." The attractive young woman told Rey that she would put his order in right away and signaled to the roving bar to get cocktail napkins and flutes at the table. Within seconds, a chilled bottle of Cristal arrived to the enthusiasm of the three men. They relaxed and settled in for a chat.

Having to speak loudly because of all the chatter, laughter, and piped music, Rey asked James and Sebastian, "So did you enjoy the music?"

James and Sebastian looked at each other in disbelief and tripped over their words. "Enjoy the show, what? Are you kidding? This was amazing!" they gushed.

"That Coltrane piece, 'Giant Steps,' was so poignant. You had us all in a trance, man." Sebastian leaned in to say.

"Thank you, thank you. That means a lot to me. I am very grateful you shared my letter with Ms. Connor." Rey lifted his champagne flute in salute to James.

"Kate's a very special soul."

"I got that impression from her letter. Would you know if she is still in Okinawa?"

Looking surprised, James raised his eyebrows and inquired, "How did you know she was in Okinawa?"

"The letter she wrote to me was on the hotel stationery. I guess I'm just being curious."

Rey drank more champagne and started at some beef rolls when Sebastian jumped in. "I met her when we were out there a few weeks ago. It's so beautiful and tranquil, really a paradise." He too tucked into some vegetables rolls and dipped bread in olive oil seasoned with herbs and garlic.

Rey pressed gently to not seem nosy, but he was dying to know more about this woman who intrigued him through her letter. Her capacity to forgive made him want to know more of her. Never having felt this way toward a woman without a sexual intention was a new sensation for Rey. "I sincerely hope Ms. Connor is doing much better and finding peace so far from home. I can tell you both that her letter released this anxiety that had built up in my chest. I could not play the sax like I had before or enjoy anything until the words she wrote gave me that sense of peace I had lost."

Rey's honesty surprised even him. He wondered if his loose tongue was due to the champagne and overcharged emotions of the evening. Sharing his deepest feelings was not something he was known for among his closest friends or family.

The waitress came over to ask if another bottle of Cristal would be of interest to the gentlemen. James jumped in ahead of Rey. "Definitely, but run it on my tab." James was quick to add, "This time, we celebrate you for your talent and generosity in getting us the tickets."

Appreciatively, Rey responded, "It was really just my way of saying 'thank you' for getting the letter to Ms. Connor. Anyway, I accept, so let's drink and be merry."

Toasting to life and music, they also toasted to Kate. "To my beloved Kate. May she find joy once again and come back home." James choked up with the last words.

All three men raised their glasses, saying thunderously, "To Kate!"

"Have you also known Ms. Connor as long as Mr. Adderley?" Rey directed his question to Sebastian.

James interrupted. "Okay, from now on, it is James for me please. Deal?" He extended his hand and turned it into a fist bump when Rey extended his in that manner. Sebastian did the same, and now all three men were more relaxed.

"To answer your question, I met Kate a few weeks ago. She's one of those natural beauties. Wow, her hair alone makes me jealous and those hazel eyes." Sebastian shook his head in admiration.

James shook his head and added, "The most beautiful thing about Kate is her heart. Did you know that she beat up a kid when we were in elementary school for bullying me!"

All cheered and clinked their glasses to toast to Kate once again. The evening floated by on more drinks and chats relating to travel and Rey's career. They even got into some cheerful singing when the bartender broke out in song to DuBose Heyward's "Summertime," prompting the musicians to take up their instruments and play impromptu solos.

A pretty, tall woman with long golden hair walked up behind Rey and wrapped her sinewy arms around his neck. She kissed Rey on the cheek and said in a breathy voice heavily laced with an accent, "Aren't you going to introduce me to your friends?"

Rey unwrapped her arms and introduced the striking beauty to Sebastian and James. "This lovely lady is Tatiana Newman, a friend of mine." She extended her slender hand and shook hands all around. Cozying up next to Rey, she hugged him and proceeded to give him another kiss on the cheek. He promptly excused himself with Tatiana. "Tatiana, would you mind very much if we concluded our business? Your beautiful presence is very distracting. I will see you later." She pouted like a little girl and then smiled at James and Sebastian.

Before she slinked away, she added, "Don't forget about me, Rey. You have neglected me very much."

Rey rolled his eyes and apologized. "She's a sweet girl but very clingy. Sorry about that."

Sebastian disregarded his apologies with a wave of the hand and high fives, but James asked a pointed question. "So are you the kind of dude who has a girl in every town you play in?"

Bristling slightly at the suggestion he was a player, Rey sat up to clear up the misconception. "Before the accident, I guess you could say I had many girlfriends, but I haven't been with anyone since. Tatiana is a model who in the past was, shall we say, a friend with benefits. I am not interested in her." To put the subject away from his past, Rey asked James, "Tell me, how you and Kate grew up together."

Calmly and proudly, James explained to Rey, "Kate and I ended up in the same foster care home. I had just turned seven and cried over everything and wet my bed because all I had known in my life was fear and anguish. Kate had been with our parents since she was a year old. Our incredible foster parents later adopted us, and we grew up together as brother and sister." A silence grew around them almost as if all three men were in a bubble.

Rey extended his hand to James. "I understand now how important she is to you. Foster care, really? You seem so grounded."

AURA POLANCO

Growing misty-eyed, James said, "My biological mother had problems with addiction. When a crack den she was wasted in was raided, I was found in a closet, and I was just over three months old. Kate's mother was another sad example of motherhood, but as a baby, she was given up to Catholic Charities and in foster care since she was a year old with the folks who would later become our parents. I ran through a few homes where I was abused, starved, and generally ignored until I was seven, and my parents rescued me." Rey and Sebastian were transfixed as they listened to the story. Sebastian put his arm around James as he continued. "Our parents loved us unconditionally. As we got older, we learned that I was black, and Kate was white. But growing up, we never knew the difference. I was always given the same amount of love as Kate. Our parents were strict but fair, and we had to do our chores and get good grades, and college was not an option. They died more than six years ago and just months apart." Sebastian hugged James, and Rey was filled with admiration for this gentleman and Kate. They ended their evening as friends with warm hugs and handshakes.

In the cab heading to Sebastian's apartment, James reflected on the evening. "I really like this guy. He seems honest, relaxed, and just nice."

Sebastian quipped, "Hey, you falling in love or what?"

Giving him a sideways glance, James responded, "I'm really certain it's you I love, silly. I was actually thinking of Kate. She hasn't been with any man since her divorce when Oliver was five. That was five years ago, and I think this guy is sensitive enough and handsome as sin to put a smile on my girl's face."

Sebastian looked at James like he was insane. "Are you forgetting he is also the same man who plowed that SUV into her and her son and caused the boy's death? I don't know. Maybe you should stay out of this."

Looking out the window contemplatively, James pressed his lips, which was the expression he always made when pondering something. He reached out and took Sebastian's hand to reassure him that he would not meddle. "Yeah, you are probably right. Heck, Kate might even be mad that I socialized with this man. What a waste of an opportunity. I could just see them together."

"No, I don't see it." Sebastian added, "James, it's too soon, and it would also be too raw because Oliver died."

"I know what you mean. Let's get out of here and get some sleep. I'm exhausted."

The taxi pulled up to Sebastian's building on the Upper West Side, and the two went in to sleep off the eventful evening.

Rey welcomed the next morning with several e-mails all announcing his triumphant return to the world of jazz. Word spread rapidly that Rey's appearance and playing was like or better than the past. He read all the reviews on his tablet and got up to make breakfast. Smiling to himself, he cleaned up the kitchen and went over to the handsome reclaimed wood desk he used for writing music and pulled out a blank music sheet. Opening a silver box, he pulled out his favorite fountain pen, a Waterman medium point, and tested the drag of the tip and ink on a piece of scrap paper before trying it on paper. It glided across the scrap paper, indicating it was ready for writing. Sitting comfortably on his leather-padded chair, he wrote a letter to Kate on the music sheet.

July 2017

Dear Ms. Connor,

Your letter released a frustration that had settled in my heart and kept me from being a full person. After reading your beautiful words, I let go of all that anxiety that had been buried deep in my heart, and now I am able to play my music and sax once again. I have you to thank for this.

You see, Ms. Connor, it was your forgiveness that enabled me to be whole again and to allow myself to express who I am through my art. I am a musician and sometime composer of jazz music. This has been my art and job since my youth. Last night, for the first time in over a year, I opened up for the jazz artist Arturo Sandoval to excellent reviews. It took a year for the doctors to rebuild my back after the accident and enable me to walk again, but it was your forgiveness that made it possible for me to live.

I will immediately address the matter of the donation and share the outcome with you.

Thank you for the gift of forgiveness. I remain forever in your debt.

Respectfully,
Rey Aguilar

P.S. If you do not wish to correspond with me, then I will understand, but I hope this will not happen.

Putting the pen down to reach in the drawer for an envelope, Rey considered how old-fashioned it was to write letters this way. He knew of no one except himself who still respected the time-honored tradition of letter writing. Rey recalled how his mother taught him to write monthly letters to his grandparents overseas to share stories about school and hobbies and thank-you notes for gifts. As a young boy, he disliked this task immensely; but whenever he received a letter in his name, it was a wonderful feeling that encouraged him to continue letter writing.

Picking up Captain's leash, he and the dog walked out to a sunny bright day to walk to the post office and buy an international stamp.

CHAPTER 7

Farewells

The pink and purple orchid blooms were arranged to form the shape of a heart on the white sand beach. Mrs. Goto was facing the sun, and by her side stood Kate in a flowing sky blue dress, holding a photo of Oliver in her right hand and a rosary in her left. The first anniversary of Oliver's passing was here, and Kate's heart felt as if a knife were slicing it into tiny slivers. The tears started flowing days before, and she could not contain her sorrow. Mrs. Goto encouraged Kate to release herself and allow those emotions to surface. With the assistance of Aiko and Mrs. Goto, Kate prepared a ceremony to mark what would have been her son's eleventh birthday and to remember his day of passing. Facing the sun and standing before the heart-shaped flower petals, Mrs. Goto and Aiko said their prayers in their native tongue, while Kate whispered an Our Father and a Glory Be.

Together, they walked to the edge of the water, where Mrs. Goto handed Kate a large garland of white orchids with Oliver's name spelled out with tissue flowers and origami birds attached as decoration. She mimed to Kate to fling the wreath into the ocean, but Kate stared at the magnificent piece and didn't want to part with it because it had her little boy's name so beautifully shaped with flowers.

Looking at Mrs. Goto and then at Aiko, she shook her head to say no, but the two women encouraged her gently without uttering a word, as the occasion was too solemn to disrupt with conversation. Aiko rubbed her shoulder, and Mrs. Goto, with a teary grin, gestured out to the ocean by moving her arm. Taking a deep breath and shuddering, Kate stood sideways and, with all her strength, threw the wreath into the ocean. They watched the gentle movement of the waves bounce the wreath around in a watery dance until it kept flowing further and further away and it could no longer be seen.

Kate released a cry and brought her hands to her face and said aloud, "Happy birthday, my sweet baby boy." Looking out onto the creamy cerulean blue horizon, Kate wiped her tears.

Choking on her words, she added softly, "Mommy is going to go live again. I will love you forever, Oliver."

Watering the orchids in the greenhouse was an activity Kate had grown to enjoy because of the peace it brought to her otherwise tormented soul. As she watered the plants, she thought back to the previous day when she threw the wreath into the water and what she had said. She wondered what her next step would be. Moving on with her life was a complex thought and one that perplexed Kate often but not in a manner that caused any stress. She just wondered what was next for her in this life. Returning to New York was not in the cards, but perhaps she might travel around a bit. For now, Kate was content to just sit in stillness at the beach and water the orchids once a week and watch and learn how meticulously Mrs. Goto tended to them.

A month after the first anniversary of Oliver's death, Kate received Rey's next letter. Reading it over a cup of tea and a slice of orange cream cake, Kate found herself enjoying reading his letter. Aside from the elegant manner in which he wrote that was appealing to Kate, she also appreciated the fountain pen and the quality of paper Rey used. Kate considered what sort of man this was with such refined tastes and a gentle manner that came through in his writing. Surprised that she was enjoying the moment, Kate wondered if that was an acceptable feeling to have given the circumstances. Throwing all her fears aside, she went to her room for several sheets of hotel stationery and a pen and returned shortly to the greenhouse to pen a response.

September 2017

Dear Mr. Aguilar,

A little over a month ago, I held a remembrance ceremony on the beach in memory of Oliver. This ceremony came at the suggestion of the hotel owner where I have been a guest for nearly a year.

Mrs. Goto is a very clever and lovely woman who has watched over me like a mother. She prepared this ceremony, a tradition in her native village, because it was good for my soul and overall recovery. She was right. I felt an enormous sorrow lift away with the wreath I flung into the ocean that Mrs. Goto and her daughter Aiko had made. It was beautifully decorated with Oliver's name. Although it was a difficult day, the ceremony and prayers helped me overcome the sorrow.

Mrs. Goto grows the most magnificent orchids in a beautiful greenhouse, where I write this letter to you. It is here and on the beach that I have found my center once again. If I were to ever own a house, then I think I would want a greenhouse of my own. I imagine this must sound so quaint and silly to you, but this would bring me peace and joy.

I understand from your letters that you are a musician. What an interesting life you must have traveling from place to place playing the saxophone. Other than a tiny bit of piano playing, I am only creative with my hands and a camera. I taught studio arts before this past year and enjoyed it immensely. Photography was a passion and perhaps one that I will resume someday.

You also mentioned that you have recovered from this horrible accident. I am glad to hear this because I know all too well the physical pain and limitations I suffered and wouldn't desire this for anyone else.

Well, Mr. Aguilar, I must go now and wish for you continued success with your music.

Be well,
Kate Connor

Feeling surprisingly light in spirit and with a cautious speck of joy springing in her heart, Kate ventured out on an oxen taxi to the ferry to visit the large island of Okinawa for the purpose of buying a camera.

CHAPTER 8

Breathe

Kate purchased the professional and expensive Nikon D4S at Kitamura Camera Shop in Naha, Okinawa. The intention was to capture the beauty of the beach, cliffs, mountains, and daily life in the little remote island she had fallen in love with. But shortly after she started taking her pictures, she knew what she was meant to do. With Mrs. Goto's blessing and endless pots of tea, Kate practically moved into the greenhouse. Day and night for two weeks, she photographed and played with form, shadows, and nature's light and darkness to create a photographic essay on a masterpiece of nature, the orchid.

The day was bright and hot when Samu Isayama, a university friend of Aiko and the secret love of her life, came to the hotel for lunch. Mrs. Goto and Aiko opened all the skylights and doors in the greenhouse to encourage a wonderful cool breeze to move about the space. They set up a round table with their finest personal china and flatware. Mrs. Goto prepared delicious sashimi and vegetables, along with a traditional hibachi soup with mushrooms and crispy onions. Their goal was to encourage Samu to display Kate's artwork in his gallery in Tokyo.

Aiko had the same dreams as her mother for Kate, although she had a few of her own. She yearned for Samu to notice her once again and rekindle their secret admiration for each other. Efforts to express their mutual affection were thwarted while they were at university because Aiko was so controlled by her aunt and uncle. As a university student, she lived with them and was picked up and dropped off to and from school at Mrs. Goto's instructions. It became very clear to Samu that Aiko was out of reach, and he moved on with his studies, never losing hope that someday they might meet again. Already a woman in her late twenties, her mother never missed an opportunity to drop hints that she was getting old and could be childless unless she pursued a love interest. But Aiko's mother had no idea just how clever her daughter actually was by contacting Samu weeks before and luring him over to Okinawa with the promise of a free overnight stay. She prepared for his visit by freeing her hair from its tired ponytail and having the hairdresser cut it into a graceful cascade of long layers with deep caramel highlights to enhance her soft pink skin and delicate features. She looked beautiful with the addition of minimal makeup and a pouty mouth in a nude pink lip-gloss. When Mrs. Goto saw her daughter's hair with color and down her back, she responded with a smile and hug.

Kate did not understand what all the fuss was over this guest. Not thinking anything would come of this encounter; she paid little interest to her own appearance. She threw over her head a wrinkled taupe dress and slipped her feet into flip-flops. Some swift brushes along her hair and not a trace of makeup was the extent of Kate's efforts. She grabbed the folder that contained her photos from the table in her room. Samu was already in the hotel lobby when he turned to see Kate walk down the stairs with the folder tucked under her left arm. Aiko quickly introduced them and waited impatiently for him to ask to see her photographs, but he focused on Kate's eyes as most people tend to do when first meeting her. Kate noticed the look of anxiety in Aiko and instead started a conversation with the hipster gallery owner about his work.

Samu was a man of medium height and slender build, and he sported elaborate tattoos on both muscled biceps. He had a generous smile and excited eyes that kept darting at Aiko, causing her cheeks to blush feverishly with embarrassment. Mrs. Goto came bustling out of the back room to say hello to Samu when she stopped abruptly at the sight of all his tattoos. The older woman looked the young man up and down and stared again at the bleached tuft of hair on an otherwise black mane that fell straight to his strong shoulders.

"Is that gray hair on your head?" Mrs. Goto was clearly taken aback at the young man with the very urban appearance. Samu was amused at Mrs. Goto's reaction because it reminded him of when his grandmother and father first noticed his tattoos. His father walked away in disapproval from him, and his grandmother had scolded him for hours. What Samu lacked in conservative appearance he made up for in charm and politeness. He bowed elegantly and addressed Mrs. Goto, formally respecting that she was an elder. Mrs. Goto reciprocated the bow while wearing a grimace and gestured to follow her to the greenhouse.

As they walked over, Kate sped up to allow Aiko to be by Samu's side. She caught their stolen glances and Aiko's burnished cheeks and understood immediately their desire to be alone. Upon entering the greenhouse, Samu stopped and took in a deep breath. "Wow, such freshness and the lush greenery." He inhaled deeply and sat down.

Looking up and around, he admired the way the sun and trees created a sense of calm and dappled the surfaces in varying hues of green. "This is such a fresh and clean space. I love it here."

Upon hearing this, Mrs. Goto beamed and started chatting about her orchids as lunch arrived with the hotel waiters. Two teenage boys in billowy white pants and tunics carried trays of fresh sushi and udon noodles in vegetable broth. A platter of vegetables arrived later as they chatted and heard stories from Samu about his work in Tokyo and Mrs. Goto's endless chatter about the running of the hotel and raising orchid flowers. Aiko remained silent the entire time, more out of fear of tripping over her words than from having nothing to say. Not wanting the afternoon to end without Aiko contributing to the conversation, Kate gently tapped her knee against hers. "Did you know that Aiko creates the most beautiful flower arrangements?" Samu looked impressed and smiled, revealing a row of perfectly aligned white teeth. "All the flowers in the hotel and the beautiful beds along the property are cultivated by her."

Samu held up his sake cup and toasted Aiko. "To you, Aiko, the most beautiful flower of all." Aiko felt giddy from such adulation, and her mother, despite his tattoos and colored hair, beamed at the compliment her daughter received.

After they had their lunch, they were served tiny orange cakes filled with hazelnut cream and tea. As they ate, Samu looked at Aiko. He remembered the shy, awkward girl from university days and never thought she would blossom into this willowy, delicate beauty. Mrs. Goto noticed their mutual attraction, and while she was not comfortable with tattoos and other modern ways of youth, she did appreciate the gleam in her daughter's eyes.

Samu directed his attention to Kate because she was captivating to him as an artist. He was eager to see the photo essay Aiko had spoken of. "Kate, what is your back story, and what brings you to such a remote place?"

All three women darted looks at one another. Kate remained stoic and elegant, taking a gentle, barely noticeable deep breath to respond to Samu. "I was a studio arts professor in New York." Picking up her cup, she took a sip of tea. She was aware that soon she would have to answer similar questions as new people entered her life. "Did you perfect your English here or abroad?" she asked, trying to shift the attention away from her.

"Actually, I studied in the States for a while and then did my master's in a university in Melbourne. My father was a dentist in Tokyo, and I wanted to be near my grandmother, as she was very old at the time. That's what motivated my return, but my dream was always to run my own modern art gallery in Tokyo. By the way, may I look at your photos?"

"Oh, certainly." Kate reached under the table to pick up the envelope.

In fewer than five seconds, the waiters cleared the table to give Kate space to display several photographs at a time. Samu looked over the prints with care and caution. After what seemed like an eternity, he looked up and smiled. "How soon can you get to Tokyo?"

Kate's eyebrows flew up, and Mrs. Goto and Aiko beamed. Feeling somewhat insecure, Kate asked Samu, "Do you really think I'm good enough to display in a gallery?" Kate asked shyly.

"You certainly are ready, and these photographs have a beautiful poignancy to them. I also like the idea of displaying a photographic essay because my gallery has shown every media except photographs. Most artists today take their work online, but you can't see texture or feel energy online as you can in a live show. I would like to show this by the end of next week. You select which ones you want and what size you want us to project which photograph in, and I will need a minimum of thirty digital images for the gallery."

All three women sat still and focused on Samu, who reigned over the table like an ancient emperor with one hand on the table and the other upon his leather-clad knee. Kate summoned her tongue from its hiding place and spoke. "Samu, I am grateful for this opportunity because I was just taking photos for fun and to have a memory of this unforgettable place."

Samu chuckled at Kate's humility. "Fun? These are professional-grade and stunning shots. The entire essay may garner plenty of money. I'm glad you enjoyed taking these photos, but you are a very accomplished photographer. Ladies, I am going to excuse myself because I have had a long morning and would like to enjoy the rest of the afternoon at the beach. Aiko, would you be able to accompany me, as I am not familiar with this island?"

For Aiko, this invitation was akin to the heavens opening up for her. She nervously said she would accompany Samu and gave a girlish giggle that she immediately suppressed by putting her hand over her mouth. Mrs. Goto escorted her daughter and Samu out of the greenhouse and left Kate sitting there with her photographs.

A broad smile emerged on Kate's face as she contemplated the brighter future that was unraveling before her. A quiet inner joy sprung in her heart, urging her to call James and share the news. Looking up at the orchids, a tear escaped when her next thought was of Oliver. She knew with complete certainty that he would be proud of her first art show. Brushing away the wayward tear and letting out a deep breath, Kate gathered up her prints and walked briskly over to her room and called James. It was about 4:00 a.m. in New York, and James would hate it if his sleep was interrupted, but Kate did so anyway.

"Hello?" A very groggy voice came through the other line, as Kate exploded in an exuberant review of the previous events she just lived.

"What? Katie, slow down and let me get to the kitchen to not wake up Sebastian. Hold on, girl. You are just firing away, and my head is half-asleep."

She could hear James shuffling about and getting the Tassimo coffee machine she had gifted him two years ago, ready for a cup. Sinking into one of his dining chairs with a hot cup of bold French roast, James yawned noisily into the phone. "Okay, what are you displaying, baby girl?"

"Oh my god, James, I took a bunch of photos of Mrs. Goto's orchids. Remember her lush and gorgeous flowers in the greenhouse?"

"Of course, I remember, but what's this about a display?" James rubbed his face and yawned again.

"Okay, so Samu, I forgot his last name, came over for lunch. Aiko, who has a major crush on him, invited him. He is also the owner of one of Tokyo's premier art galleries, and he wants to display my photographs in his space next week!"

Kate's excitement finally helped James wake up completely as he sat there sipping his coffee. He had not heard this level of enthusiasm in Kate in a long while. She was popping out of her skin from the possibilities that lay ahead, and he could sense this in her. As he listened, he played around with his napkin by rolling it up and then moving it along the table like a rolling pin. "Katie, I am so happy for you, and I love to hear you so excited. What's the name of the gallery?"

"Oh my god, I have no idea. Well, he's here overnight, so I'll be sure to get it from him and e-mail you later. I didn't think I would be this excited over anything ever again, James. I know this is just a showing, but it's nice to be acknowledged."

"Well, it's more than nice, Kate. Your talent was always there, but you were just too comfortable teaching it instead of cultivating your own self-expression. At first, I was very upset that you went so far away, but now I understand that you had to in order to find you. I wish I could be there, but I am up to my ears in court and so much crap at work."

Disappointed but not letting on, Kate dismissed James's inability to be with her in a week's time. "Hey, no worries. I just needed to share with my brother, that's all."

Hearing the disappointment, James chimed in. "I can try and see, but it's doubtful because it's not another state or even Europe, girl. You went to friggin' Asia. I'll try but absolutely no promises."

With a huge smile on her face, Kate gushed. "James, I love you. I understand that you can't come. I'm not exactly an hour away. But thanks for trying. Okay, go back to sleep and wish me luck for next week."

Putting on a terrible Irish brogue, James said very seriously over the phone, "I send this to you from me, Mom, and Dad." He recited the following prayer to his sister:

> May the road rise to meet you,
> May the wind be always at your back,
> May the sun shine warm upon your face,
> And rains fall soft upon your fields,
> And until we meet again,
> May God hold you in the hollow of His hand.

Upon hearing this, Kate's eyes watered as she remembered their parents. She thanked James by blowing kisses over the phone several times and saying, "'Love you."

After ending the call, she was surprised and delighted with the outcome of the day. She spread the photographs all over the room and tagged each with a Post-it note and suggestion for resizing.

The next day, Aiko found Kate in the small dining room having a light lunch with the folder of photographic details for Samu. She could not contain her smile, which prompted Kate to inquire. "Okay, dish." Aiko had a perplexed look on her face. "Oh, that just means what happened. Tell me all about your beach date with handsome Samu."

Aiko blushed as she recounted. "My mother came along, so we were not alone, but when we went swimming, he took my hand underwater. And this morning, he slipped me a note with his phone number. He wants me to accompany you to Tokyo."

Kate listened attentively and sipped a dry Rośe to accompany the fruit and sashimi pieces. "Oh my god, Mrs. Goto is so old-fashioned. He definitely likes you, so I think you must come with me next week. Besides, I can't speak the language and have no idea where anything is in Tokyo."

Aiko smiled broadly, very pleased that Kate agreed she should come along. "Yes, I will come, but where will we stay?"

"Leave that to me, as we will live it up in the most exclusive place in Tokyo. This way, you and Samu can meet and chat and who knows what else." Kate's eyebrows wagged up and down, causing both women to giggle.

"Samu is ready to leave, so he is coming here to see you. Do you have everything he needs?"

"Yes, I do." Patting her envelope, she watched Samu enter the dining room and looked around for Mrs. Goto. He hurried over to Aiko and stole a kiss by the corner of her closed mouth, making her glassy-eyed and rendering her speechless. Kate admired this forward modern man and liked his style. He was more Western in his manner, making him very globally appealing.

Samu bent down and kissed Kate on the cheek. He took the package and moved over to stand next to a dumbfounded Aiko. He said loud enough for Kate to hear, "Aiko, you know we are meant to be, so stop being so shy around me. Besides, soon you will be my wife." With these words, he took her in his arms and kissed her on the mouth and held her body close to his. Aiko was in such shock that her arms remained against her sides. Then he slowly moved away from her and just stood a few centimeters from her face when Mrs. Goto walked in and interrupted with a loud pretend cough. Aiko backed away too quickly, nearly collapsing over the chair that stood behind her at the other table. He walked over and gracefully bowed before Mrs. Goto and thanked her formally in Japanese for her hospitality, and then he whispered something in her ear that made the indomitable Mrs. Goto turn a bright crimson.

Samu left the dining room, and the roar of a car could be heard from the front of the hotel. Mrs. Goto stared at her daughter and then at Kate and said, "That young man just say, 'Good-bye, future mother-in-law!' Ha! I do not like tattoos!" Leaving behind a haze of ylang-ylang perfume, Mrs. Goto returned to her office, as Kate and Aiko burst into laughter.

The post delivered a heavy package for Kate as she sat on the veranda reading the *Times* of London. The name on the box read from Rey Aguilar. As she opened the box, she wondered what he could have sent her now. She had to go through an endless amount of packing peanuts and tear off foam and tape from around the firm package. To Kate's surprise, Rey Aguilar sent her a duplicate plaque bestowed to him with Oliver's name inscribed. With her index finger, she traced her son's name etched in gold leaf lettering over a shiny burl wood background. She did not cry, as her heart was content with a strange sense of peace because other children would be helped by the donation in Oliver's name. Kate wondered just how large a donation this could have been for a hospital to create a plaque. She figured it had to be several thousand dollars. Turning the plaque around, Kate found two letters taped to it. One letter was from the hospital thanking Oliver, his mother, and Rey Aguilar for the donation of half a million dollars. Kate's eyes flew open at the amount of money Rey Aguilar actually gave away. She continued reading and learned that this money would go to support research, and to her continued surprise, the letter also mentioned how Rey set up an ongoing fund to support families that visited the hospital from afar by paying for their lodgings while in New York City. All of this would be done in Oliver's name.

Rey intrigued her with such an elegant expression and a generosity of spirit. She opened the other envelope to find a ticket to the Blue Note in Tokyo and a note on an index card. "I am touring this autumn, and Tokyo is one of our stops in late October. If you happen to be around, I would like to properly meet you. If this is too much for you, then I will understand. No pressure, but I would really feel privileged to meet you, Ms. Connor."

The clanging bell of the ox taxi startled Kate. Hotel personnel ran out to help the tourists with luggage and questions. She recognized the energetic and enthusiastic laughter and conversations in French. Kate picked up the plaque and box and went to her room to carefully rewrap it in a scarf to keep it from scratches. She placed both letters in the drawer where the other letters from Rey were kept and returned downstairs to assist Mrs. Goto with the new guests.

CHAPTER 9

First Time Ever I Saw Your Face

I t was a rainy Wednesday, and Kate was showing her photographs at Gallery Isayama. The photographs of orchids measured in varied sizes, with some as small as 4 × 6 inches and the largest being 16 × 20. Kate photographed all of Mrs. Goto's beloved orchids at different times of the day in the greenhouse, giving the delicate flowers unique personalities through shadow and light. In her right hand, she held a champagne flute and in the other a clutch bag she purchased along with the red wrap dress and nude peep-toe heels at the Ginza shopping district.

The day before, Aiko and Kate arrived at the exclusive Peninsula Tokyo Hotel. Kate insisted that she pay all expenses. She booked spa treatments for both later that afternoon. They arrived at the gallery looking beautiful with glossy hair, fragranced, and fashionably dressed. Samu was delighted at the sight of Aiko, immediately took her by the arm, and introduced her to several patrons as his girlfriend. Making a grand announcement, he presented Kate as the artist, gaining collective sounds of approval and compliments. She spent the better part of the evening floating around the room; just chatting about photography with wealthy Japanese, tourists, and foreign art collectors; and sipping champagne. The experience reminded Kate of being back in New York and going to countless cocktail parties in support of the arts except that, this time, she was there in a celebration of her talent.

By ten in the evening, Samu had informed Kate that most of the photographs were sold and that she stood to make a generous sum of money. He also gave her the card of a patron who was there earlier before the opening began. This patron wanted to commission work from Kate much to Samu's delight because he informed her that the man was well connected and wealthy. None of this impressed or mattered to Kate, as she only saw the value in her photography as a way of nurturing her soul and not her pocket.

Moving over to Aiko, she took her aside to inform her of her plans. "I'm leaving now."

"What? It's so early. Why do you want to go to the hotel and be there alone on such a special evening?"

"Well, I'm not going to the hotel just yet. I was given a ticket to go to the Blue Note Jazz Club. Besides, you need to be alone with Samu."

"I know I want to be with him, but are you sure you will be all right? The taxis are very good here, and you don't have to worry about anything, but be careful."

"Thanks, Aiko. You be very careful as well because if anything happens to you, your mother will probably kill me," Kate said with a chuckle. "Also, Samu is very busy right now, so please tell him we will talk soon." The women hugged, and Kate walked out to a moist, warm evening.

Arriving at the Blue Note, she gave her ticket to a young Japanese hostess with orange and purple dreadlocks. She was shown to a table up front, but Kate requested a table in the back instead. She wanted to have a view of the place and not be right in front of the musicians. Sitting alone in a half-moon-shaped blue velvet booth, Kate ordered the French cognac Grand Marnier. Slowly, with her eyes closed, she allowed the liqueur to ease its way down her throat. She could not recall the last time she dressed up or enjoyed her favorite drink as she glanced around the dimly lit club. The place was filled with jazz lovers from around the globe. A pianist had the house jumping with sultry ballads sung by a beautiful woman with a mellifluous voice. The beautiful singer wore a stunning weave of braids that reached down to the backs of her knees. When they completed their set, the pianist took the microphone and enthusiastically introduced the next act.

"Ladies and gentlemen, here at the Blue Note, we welcome the return of the world-famous, Grammy-winning The Golden Trio! Put your hands together for The Golden Trio!" The crowd broke out into thunderous applause and shouts. People were on their feet as Rafa Iglesias shook hands with Tony Jones, the pianist and manager of the Blue Note. He settled into his bench at the piano as Paco Nieves sat behind his drums and adjusted his equipment, but when Rey walked on stage, the crowd broke into more thunderous applause and catcalls. He strode up holding his beloved Angie close to his chest. Rey looked larger than life and polished in his dark suit and starch white shirt with a smart silver pocket square.

Although Rey felt healthier and generally good, he was nervous because he was uncertain if Kate was there. Forcing himself to dismiss these thoughts, he walked over to the microphone and spoke confidently. "It is with much anticipation and pleasure that we return to a venue that was home to us for so many years. As you all have heard by now, we have been or, rather, I have been through many trials this past year, but I am here once again with my brothers Paco and Rafa, and we will play the best music you have come to expect from us." Glancing over to Rafa and Paco, Rey took his sax and positioned it and then licked his lips and closed his eyes. The band broke into a bossa nova piece, and a hush fell over the room, as everyone was once again mesmerized watching Rey feel the music and make his sax come to life.

Kate was transfixed from the moment she saw him walk on stage. Rey Aguilar was imposing. He had a captivating air of worldliness and sophistication. But he also frightened her, and she did not know why. She noticed his stylish suit and expensive shoes. Kate observed his handsome features and liked what she saw. She liked how his body and hair moved as he played his instrument. She was captivated by everything about him. Kate ordered another cognac and just let the numbness that she had not felt for so long hit her limbs and dull her senses.

Feeling relaxed, Kate felt the music with its sultry melody. When Rey finished, the applause was deafening, with even busboys and waiters stopping to acknowledge the magic of his musicianship. Rafa counted out, "One, two, one, two, three," and The Golden Trio played the next piece, a lively Latin jazz composition, and continued until their set was over nearly an hour later.

As the crowd applauded and everyone was on their feet, the house lights went up, and that was when Rey saw Kate. She remained sitting in the booth and did not applaud. His eyes focused on her glossy chestnut hair and the red dress that hugged her body seductively in the hips and bosom. He knew it was Kate without ever having seen her before. Something deep in his core directed his attention to the woman who sat alone in the elevated booth staring down into an empty glass.

Gathering her bag, Kate got up after paying her bill and was walking through the crowded room toward the exit. Rey moved as well, trying to reach her, but people kept offering handshakes and wanting photographs with him, but he gently pushed forward, nearly missing Kate. She dropped her purse when another woman bumped into her. Squatting down to pick it up, she saw a hand reach over for it and take her bag and her hand in one fell swoop. When their eyes met, his heart was lost. Kate noticed first his honey-colored eyes, and then she felt his strong hand take hers and lead her out into the cool and rainy night.

Outside, there was a long cue of patrons waiting for the second set. When some of them recognized Rey, they cheered and called out his name. Waving to his fans, he pulled Kate into a cab and asked her, "What hotel are you staying in?"

Kate was dazed and nauseous after consuming four cognacs on an empty stomach. Muttering, she responded, "Peninsula."

He gave the driver the name of the hotel, and they arrived within minutes in a light drizzle. Paying for the ride, he watched Kate exit the cab assisted by a doorman. She started up the steps when he caught up to her and hoped she would not send him away.

"Can I buy you a drink?" Rey felt his fingers grabbing onto the sax tighter than ever. Knowing he was nervous made him feel insecure, but to Rey, this moment was too important to allow nerves to ruin it. He was intrigued with Kate and her arresting beauty and feared she would not want his company.

"I think I am done drinking tonight. One too many cognacs have me feeling a bit sick right now." Kate felt more like vomiting from the mix of the cognac and her emotions running rampant with Rey Aguilar so close.

"Are you available for lunch tomorrow?"

"Actually, my plane leaves at two for Okinawa." She placed her hand over her stomach, feeling queasy. "I don't want to seem rude, but I need to get to my room." Sensing her discomfort, Rey walked her into the hotel and through the lobby to the elevator. "Thank you but you don't need to bother yourself," Kate said softly as Rey pressed for her floor. In the elevator, Kate leaned against the wall, as she was certain she would either faint or hurl. He kept his distance but was poised to catch Kate if she fainted.

"'Just want to make sure you are safe in your room. What's the room number?"

"Oh, I don't know." She opened the clasp to the clutch and found the card with the number imprinted on it. Handing the card to him, she rushed out with Rey on her heels. When he slid the card to open the door, Kate ran into the bathroom and hurled into the toilet. He waited patiently for her to stop being sick. He set his sax upon a chair and went over to the windows to calm his nerves and take in the colorful and stunning view of Downtown Tokyo.

Minutes later, Kate emerged from the bathroom looking pale and tired. She had gathered her hair in a loose side ponytail and settled on one of the upholstered chairs with a glass of water. Rey remained by the window but faced her to ask, "Is there anything I can do or get to help you feel better?"

Kate strained her neck to look up at the very tall man. She squinted and asked him, "Please sit down. It seems that any movement of my head causes pain." He removed the sax off the chair facing Kate and settled upon it. They momentarily looked into each other's eyes until Kate glanced away.

Rey was uncertain what to do. He wanted to remain there with her, but it was now raining harder outside, and he had ten minutes to get back to the club for the second set. Boldly taking her hands in his, Rey spoke from his heart, "I feel that tonight marks the rest of my life. I know that may sound dramatic to you, but finally meeting you has been extraordinary for me. I know you don't feel up to a chat right now, and I have to get back to the club, but tomorrow, if you don't mind, I would like to take you to breakfast."

Kate smiled shyly and said, "I don't know what made me go to the club tonight, but this whole thing feels weird to me. I'm not too sure we should meet again."

Rey looked beaten but tried again. "Well, I know you might hate me or think I am the last person in the world you want to have breakfast with, but all I ask for is a chance to get to know you."

Not feeling up for further talk, Kate agreed to meet Rey the next day. "Okay, Mr. Aguilar, we can meet for breakfast around eleven? I am sorry for you having to go out of your way for me."

The sexy rumble of laughter that came from him made her feel strangely comfortable as he added, "Never think that I am going out of my way for you. Until tomorrow, Ms. Connor." Rey picked up the sax, walked over to the door, and left her keycard on the table. He turned around and looked upon her face as she returned a small smile that filled his very being with a sense of hope.

Because of the rain, a taxi was impossible to find, so he half-walked and ran the four blocks to the club, arriving wet and with several minutes to spare. He grabbed napkins to dry his face and the instrument and went on stage to the applause and cheers of the room. He looked over at Rafa, who rolled his eyes at him and started the count.

In the early morning hours in the privacy of his hotel room, Rey took extra-strength Tylenol to dull the intense backache from his earlier sprinting, but he didn't care that he was hurting. For the first time in his life, he knew with certainty that fate had brought him and Kate together. The circumstances were tragic, yet Rey knew that he was meant to be with Kate. Lying on his bed and looking up at the ceiling, he remembered the way the sexy red dress hugged her curves and showed a hint of a cleavage. Her hazel eyes with the golden flecks and full mouth brought a grin to his lips, but it was her quiet manner that captured and held his heart. That night, his sleep was fitful, as he could not relax enough in anticipation of seeing her the next morning.

Kate awoke with a slight headache that was not provoked from the previous night's drinking but instead from not eating a thing since yesterday morning. She let the cool shower wake her up and dressed in a simple sleeveless black shift that hung loosely from her shoulders. She slipped into a pair of silver sandals and finished packing for her flight. Not remembering where her keycard had been left, she looked around the suite and found it on the table by the door. Mixed feelings of her first encounter with Rey were combined with the distasteful event of retching. It was now half past eleven, and the grumblings in her stomach urged her to go have breakfast. Grabbing her bag and keycard, she headed down to the lobby. Exiting the elevator, she saw him standing before the large doors with his hands in his pockets. She approached quietly and slightly guarded. "Good morning, and sorry about last night," Kate said softly.

A handsome grin broke out on his face, causing her already sensitive stomach to flip. His shoulders relaxed because he had been tense, thinking Kate would not come. "No need to apologize. I hope you are feeling better this morning."

She smiled and said, "Much better. Thank you for making certain I was back here safely." Kate blushed, recalling how embarrassing it was for her to have been sick in front of this man she barely knew.

He saw her obvious discomfort and changed the subject quickly. "Would you like breakfast here at the hotel or elsewhere before you catch your plane?"

"Yes, I need to eat something. Let's just go to the Boutique Café. They offer a varied continental breakfast."

"You lead, my lady." Kate smiled and proceeded to show Rey where people were congregated for breakfast. They were escorted to a sunny table with an elegant spray of pink and white orchids. Upon ordering coffees, omelets, and croissants, Rey started the conversation. "So besides the invitation to the Blue Note, did anything else bring you to Tokyo?"

Kate watched him spread butter and marmalade on one half of his croissant and noticed his elegant hands and long fingers. "Actually, do you recall in the letter I mentioned I enjoyed photography?"

"Yes, of course, I remember." He wanted to tell Kate that every word she wrote was etched in his mind. He watched how gracefully she poured steamed milk into her coffee and drank lifting the cup and saucer to her lips. Kate was for him the epitome of grace and class. She spoke softly and moved gently, two qualities he admired in elegant women.

"Well, I bought a professional camera and, just for fun, started taking photos of Mrs. Goto's magnificent orchids. Her daughter, Aiko, also part owner of the hotel, contacted a gallery owner to come to Okinawa to see my little pictures. He thought they were good enough to display, and we had my first showing yesterday." Kate sipped more coffee and ate some berries and melon. "I never thought anything would come of my photography except just fun for myself."

"I am so glad to know you are being creative because, as you know, that is what feeds our souls. In which gallery are you showing?"

"At Gallery Isayama."

"Perhaps I can go and see your work later. It's too bad you have to return today. What's Okinawa like?"

"That's very kind of you to take time to go see my photos. Let's see, how can I describe Okinawa without sounding like a travel brochure?" His chuckle made her smile. Kate looked out the window and then focused on the flowers on the table. Rey saw her eyes change from clear and happy to tearful. Remaining silent, he hung on her every word. "I arrived broken and in despair, and I have been restored in the blue waters and from the love of the people around me." Kate took a tissue from her bag and dabbed the corners of her eyes.

"I am so deeply sorry." Rey looked crestfallen and felt suddenly uncomfortable being the cause of so much misery.

"May I call you Rey?" she asked.

He let out the breath he was unknowingly holding in and said, "Yes, please do. And may I call you Kate?"

"Of course, you may. I appreciate formality and decorum, but I believe we are beyond the mister and missus stage, wouldn't you agree?" Looking him squarely in the eyes, Kate firmly stated, "Rey, I have to be sincere and say that I can be forgiving because there was a defect with the car, but you must know that I'm not entirely comfortable with you right now."

The words were like a one-two punch to his face, but he took it stoically and waited before he said, "The last thing I want is for you to feel uncomfortable around me. I'm sorry for imposing myself on you, and I won't bother you again. Have a wonderful day and be well." Rey pushed his seat back to get up and leave when Kate placed her hand on his.

The last thing she meant was for him to leave. Something deep in her pulled her toward him, demanding to know more of him. Rey was easy to talk with, and she felt strangely safe with him in her presence. It was just the circumstances of how they came to be in each other's lives that troubled her. "Rey, please sit down. I think that came out a bit harsher than I intended." He looked down at her and carefully resumed his seat. He sat back and nervously stared at the cup of coffee he had before him. "I am conflicted at how easily we can chat despite what happened. But, promise me that you won't keep blaming yourself because this will only serve to hurt you. I think we have both suffered enough."

Kate kept her hand over his, and he felt goose bumps on his arm. A current ran through him, making him want to grab hold of this woman and just devour her mouth and kiss her beautiful face. Containing himself, he was thankful she wasn't sending him away. "Yes, I promise. I just wish I had been the reason for you feeling better and not the catalyst for all that happened to you, Oliver, and even myself."

Moving her hand away to serve herself more coffee, Kate hesitated midstream and placed the pot down carefully. "Rey, it was because of you that I thought about rediscovering my passion. After I read your letter, I boarded the ferry and bought the camera in Naha. Without your suggestion, I may never have ventured out. You did have something to do with my recovery. I haven't even thanked you for sending me the plaque and letter from the children's hospital regarding that enormous and generous donation. And I believe that your helping families visiting New York with expenses is thoughtful and evidence of your kind heart. My son is gone from me physically, but he will forever live in my heart."

He choked up at her words, and his eyes turned red and glassy from fighting back the tears. He drank all the water in his glass, and she noticed a tear escape from the corner of his eye. Kate knew this man was special, but it took every cell in her body to fight wanting more with him. Despite what her body wanted, her mind could never have anything amorous with him because it would be too peculiar and almost an affront to her son's memory. She could not shake the truth that Oliver was gone because Rey was behind the wheel of that damaged vehicle. By the look in his eyes, she knew he was interested in her; but besides a distant friendship, she could not see anything else in their future. Suppressing her own desires was what she had to do, and she understood that this sacrifice needed to be made.

He changed the subject when she became pensive. "Kate, when are you returning to New York again?" he asked.

"Returning to New York is not in my plans, but if this past year has taught me anything, it is to not plan for tomorrow. Besides my brother, there's nothing left for me there. And truthfully, I fear getting hit with all these memories and losing my mind all over again."

Secretly wishing she would return to New York, where they could be closer, he took a chance at asking her about other locations. "What about Europe? So many wonderful cultures and closer to the U.S."

"You sound like my brother, James. He is desperate for me to return, but for now, I will disappoint you both because I'm okay here." She smiled radiantly at Rey, filling his heart with anticipation and hope. Looking down at her watch, she noticed it was noon and had to check out, find Aiko, and head to the airport. "Rey"—he loved hearing his name on her lips—"I must go."

He could not hide his disappointment. "I understand. Would you mind if we exchange mobile numbers or e-mails?"

"I'm going to disappoint you yet again. I have neither. I disconnected from everyone and everything and left it all behind in New York. All I packed were a few pieces of clothing and photos of my son, that's all."

Rey's brow creased in disbelief. "Well, you are a breath of fresh air. No technology, huh? That leaves us with the good old snail mail. May we continue corresponding? I enjoy writing, and in this day and age, no one writes or mails letters anymore. For me, it's relaxing."

"Writing is sweet, and I would love that. I agree with you and wish we could just slow life down a bit. Everything moves too quickly, and after a year in Okinawa, I just don't want what I had before."

Pulling her chair back, the waiter was there instantly to assist Kate as she stood up. Rey came around, placed several bills on the table, and walked back to reception with Kate. His stomach was in knots knowing this was their farewell. Kate asked for her bill, and as the reception retrieved it from the computer, she controlled her own desire in facing him for what could be the last time.

Extending her hand to say farewell, Rey took hers in both his and held her there, moving closer toward her. They looked into each other's eyes, feeling mutual attraction. "I am so grateful to you for this—last night, breakfast this morning, and our conversation. You are very special, Kate."

"Thank you again for helping me last night and bringing me back to the hotel. We will keep in touch. Be well, Rey, and good luck on the remainder of your tour."

"I wish I could go to Okinawa and swim in your waters and feel the sun on my back." Lifting her hand he gently kissed it.

"Goodbye, Rey." Kate smiled, and calmly pulled away. She directed her attention to the receptionist, leaving Rey standing inches away and fighting the urge to hold and kiss her. He slipped both hands into his pockets, as he did not trust himself to not reach out and take her in his arms and never let her go.

The heat he radiated filled her senses with longing and desire, but she closed her eyes and counted back from ten very slowly. Her mind raced with thoughts about him. *Why do I feel so attracted to him? I should be repulsed and want to run away, yet I want him by my side. Why is this receptionist taking so long with my bill?* After opening her eyes, she noticed with her peripheral vision that he was still there and that his eyes were pained with the same look of longing and desire she felt in her heart. Kate wanted to kiss his mouth and inhale his cologne until it became a part of her, but she knew it could not be.

Rey stood transfixed, staring at every inch of her. He looked down and admired her silver sandals and noticed the delicate petal pink polish on her toes and hands. The black shift did not keep his memory of her curves from invading his every thought, and her hair was like a waterfall of milk chocolate cascading over her shoulders and gracefully waving toward the ends. When she did not redirect her attention to him, Rey understood that she would not engage in more than just being correspondence buddies. Reluctantly, he turned away and walked to the large doors, where he stopped and glanced one last time to look at her. Forcing her head to focus on the bill before her, Kate sighed and walked away. Rey nodded and left.

Aiko saw their final exchange quietly from the elevator banks and had watched from when Rey and Kate stood in the restaurant to leave. She sensed how much Kate liked this man but wondered why they left so sadly. Seeing how emotional Kate was, Aiko stood by her side and put her arm around her shoulders. Dabbing her eyes with a tissue, Kate folded away the bill and made a feeble attempt at hiding the sadness from her face. They went over to a leather settee to wait for their luggage and for the porter to summon a taxi.

"Who was that tall and handsome man?" Aiko asked softly. Kate shook her head and looked down, crying now into her tissue. "Did he make you sad, Kate?"

Kate shook her head, blew her nose, and searched for another tissue in her bag. "No, he was a very nice man. That was the man who drove the SUV that killed my son. His name is Rey Aguilar, and it's just sad that we could never be."

"I see. Perhaps later on at another time."

Kate smiled at Aiko. "No, Aiko, it could never be. Well, enough of my sentimentality. Tell me about Samu. I want to know everything." She faked enthusiasm, and Aiko played along if it meant that Kate would feel better.

"After the gallery closed, Samu took me out to dinner, and then we went dancing. He told me what his life was like here and asked if I would want to live in Tokyo." Aiko's excitement was palpable as she recounted the evening.

"What did you tell him?" Kate asked, acutely aware that her mind was asking questions, but her focus was infiltrated with everything Rey and her desire to be near him.

"I told him I would love to live in Tokyo if my mother had another person helping her run the hotel. He understands, so we will see where we go from here."

"Aiko, how do you really feel about Samu?"

"I have loved him for many years now, but I never thought he would love me in return."

"You contacted him for my photos, or did you use that opportunity to lure him to the hotel?"

Blushing, Aiko lowered her eyes. "I called him for you and for me, hoping he would like what he saw. He liked me at school as well, but he wanted to pursue his studies, and then life got very busy."

They were told the taxi was waiting, with their luggage already in the trunk. The drive to the airport was quiet, with each woman lost in her own thoughts of the adventures from previous days. Aiko had hope in her heart, while Kate was distraught at there not being any chance with the incredibly interesting Rey Aguilar.

Rey strode into the gallery, and as he walked around, he grew increasingly upset that every single photograph had a "sold" tag by its description card. He was anxious to find one he could purchase, but all were claimed. To Rey, looking at her artistic expression was like taking a glimpse into her mind and heart.

Samu recognized Rey from his mezzanine office and came down to welcome him to the gallery. He was a fan of jazz music and particularly instrumental saxophone and clarinet because, like Rey, he also played the sax, though on a purely amateur level. Dressed sharply in a navy suit and crisp white T-shirt, he walked up with his hand extended.

"Mr. Rey Aguilar, you honor my gallery with your visit. I am Samu Isayama." They shook hands, but Samu noticed how restless Rey appeared. Trying to relax the man, he offered him a drink in his office.

"You have a fantastic space here, but I will have to say no to the drink. I wonder if you could assist me in another way."

"Anything you need, Mr. Aguilar." Samu stood with his arms crossed over his chest and watched Rey carefully scan the photographs with a look of longing and sadness.

"I know the photographer of these works but had no idea you were displaying her art and missed the opportunity to acquire a piece.

Here's my card. Would you please contact me via e-mail or call me the next time Ms. Connor shows in your gallery?"

"It will be my pleasure. With the success of this show, Ms. Connor has been summoned for a private collection, and who knows when she will be prepared to show here again. Just the same, I will keep you in mind. I wanted to make your show at the Blue Note but could not because it was the same night as this opening. Perhaps I'll catch you next time you are in Tokyo."

"If you can make it to Macau, I have an engagement at the MacauSoul. Here is another card, and show them this number I am writing. They will know you are in my party. Bring a friend."

"How kind of you. I will invite my girlfriend and try to persuade Kate Connor, the artist, as well. She lives in the same hotel my girlfriend and her mother run in Okinawa."

"Are you kidding me?" Rey came to life as he closed his fountain pen and placed it inside his jacket. "Mr. Isayama, if you can make that happen, I will secure tickets for you throughout this entire tour. That is a promise." They shook hands vigorously and bowed in the time-honored tradition.

"I will do my best, Mr. Aguilar. Have a safe trip."

"Thank you very much. See you soon."

Rey was newly restored and walked down the streets to his hotel with a spring in his step. In his mind, he was playing out ways to conquer and win Kate's heart. He thought about how many women he had come in contact with throughout his life and how it took this accident to bring into his life the one woman he could not imagine the rest of his life without. Regardless of what Kate felt, Rey was determined to enchant her with his charm and wit and ultimately win her heart.

CHAPTER 10

Trevor Miles

Samu arrived in Okinawa a week later with two important things in his portfolio: one was a substantial check for Kate and the other an engagement ring for Aiko. He was calm as he dismounted the ferry and waited his turn to get into the ox taxi. He could have had a car waiting, but Samu wanted to experience the island as Aiko always did and not like the city slicker he was. Four weeks had passed after he reconnected with Aiko since their university days, and he knew she was the woman for him. But Mrs. Goto was front and center in his mind, as he had to win her over. His master plan included first sharing the ring with Mrs. Goto and very humbly asking her to grant him her daughter's hand in marriage. He also wanted to ask with great respect if she would also consider him a son, as his mother was deceased.

Samu's intentions were honorable, but he scoffed at the traditions and formality he had to endure to marry Aiko. He was very Western and sophisticated, but Aiko had been cloistered on an island most of her life, with the exception of the few years she attended university in Tokyo. But even when she was in that great bustling city of so much history and excitement, Aiko was strictly guarded by her aunt and uncle and never allowed to venture out or be with friends outside of school. Samu knew he had an uphill battle, but he believed Aiko was worth the struggle. Her beauty and elegance had stolen his heart, and her girlish laugh made him feel hopeful in an otherwise cynical world. He knew she wanted this as much as he did, but he had to get through to her conservative mother first.

Aiko boldly went out to the reception to welcome Samu despite her mother's reprimands that she should remain quietly behind. Mrs. Goto checked in Samu and showed him to the furthest room away from the entrance to the hotel and therefore away from the cottage where Aiko lived. Samu unpacked, changed, and prepared for executing his plan; but first, he would see Kate.

He walked along the beach, where he found Kate sitting on a boulder high above the beach with her camera focused on an endangered black-faced spoonbill swooping down to hunt for fish. With an estimated population of fewer than three thousand left, capturing one was rare, and Kate was determined to film one securing its meal. She read about them in a book she found in Mrs. Goto's office on wildlife natural to Okinawa and knew that to spot a black-faced spoonbill would make for a special photograph.

Samu did not call out her name because he suspected that whatever Kate was focused on was too important. Instead, he lay out on the sand to catch some sun and wait for Kate to finish. It was a long while later when he saw her climb down from the rocks in her bare feet, rolled-up capris, and T-shirt. When she saw him, she called out joyfully. "Samu, hey, what brings you here?" She walked briskly over to him, and that was when he noticed her wince in pain and readjust her walk. She had been sitting on that rock for too long a time, causing her injured leg to cramp up and her lower back to ache. Brushing it off, they hugged and kissed both cheeks.

"I have been here awhile but didn't want to disturb you. What was so special over those rocks?"

"I caught a black-faced spoonbill in flight catching a fish." Kate was very enthusiastic. Her smile showed the joy her work brought to her.

"You are limping. Did you fall?"

"Oh no, it's an old injury, but it will go away by the time I get to the hotel. It happens all the time. Not very glamorous, right?"

"Glamour doesn't matter. I just hope you are okay." He slowed his gait, took her arm, and linked it to his for support. She welcomed his support and appreciated the slower walk.

"So why are you here, Samu? Hmm, let me guess, you are here for Aiko. Am I correct?"

"You are like a curious child, but yes, my trip is partly for Aiko. Can I tell you a secret and you promise you won't betray me?"

"You can trust me. What's going on?"

"I am going to ask for Aiko's hand in marriage tonight." Kate squealed with delight and squeezed Samu's arm. "But first, I must do it in the very traditional way, by talking to her mother and showing the ring, and pray that tough Mrs. Goto accepts me."

"Oh my goodness, this is so thrilling and so soon. Well, your secret is safe with me. Thank you for trusting me with such important news."

"You are welcome. We have known each other for many years, and I always loved her but never realized just how much. Sometimes guys travel through life looking for greener pastures when, all along, the greatest joy was right where we started from."

Kate smiled up and whispered, "It happens to women as well."

"By the way, the famous jazz musician Rey Aguilar came into the gallery some days ago, looking quite despondent when he missed his chance at buying one of your photographs. He gave me his card and invited Aiko, you, and me to Macau to watch him perform. I want to go with Aiko, but her mother will not let her go if you don't come. Say you will come, *please.*"

Kate just stared at Samu, not knowing what bothered her most, being used as a chaperone in their little games or giving Rey false hope by showing up in Macau. Kate remained silent as they entered the hotel, and before Mrs. Goto could say anything, she whispered, "I have to think about it."

Samu gave her a look that could melt an iceberg and sweetened the moment by inviting himself to her room. "I have to give you something. I'll be up in your room in a few minutes."

Kate rolled her eyes and climbed the stairs to her room, leaving Samu going over to Mrs. Goto. She stopped at the top step to watch him give a respectful low bow to his future mother-in-law and Mrs. Goto return a shorter bow. Once Samu started to speak to Mrs. Goto,

Kate resumed her walk to her room, knowing this was an important moment for Samu to try to win over the strict Mrs. Goto.

"May I have the pleasure of your company for a very important discussion tonight, Mrs. Goto?"

"Yes, after dinner, I will be here. You may come to my office at seven sharp. I don't like people who are late."

"Of course, and thank you for bestowing me this opportunity. I shall see you at seven." Bowing deeply again, he walked backward until he reached the stairs and then ran up to his room to get Kate's check. Walking briskly down the hall, he rapped on her door and heard her say to come in. Samu left the door open to avoid any scandals or misconceptions and handed Kate the check worth $25,000 and a letter from Mr. Trevor Miles.

"Wow, what is this for?" Kate's eyes were wide open as she held the check.

"That is, as I have heard Americans say, your 'cut' from the sale of your work. Nice job, Kate. You are making a name for yourself. Now close your mouth and open the letter Mr. Miles wrote."

"Who?" Kate opened the letter hastily and read the sentences Trevor Miles scribbled in scratchy penmanship.

Dear Ms. Connor,

Your orchids have captivated me in such a way that I purchased the black and white prints to decorate a room in my house.

If you are available, I would like to invite you to stay at my cottage in South Africa, where I also cultivate orchids and calla lilies and have what I believe to be an impressive greenhouse that I would enjoy showing to you. I will cover your travel expenses, but I will only be available at the house the first two weeks of November.

I was so impressed with your photographic eye that I know you are the person to capture the magnificence of the landscape in my homeland. If you accept, which I hope you will, please contact my assistant Barbara, and she will make all arrangements.

Looking forward to our encounter.

Yours truly,
Trevor Miles

Inside the envelope, Kate found a glossy white card with a raised black engraving of the unmistakable marula tree. The name of Barbara Quincy, a number, and an e-mail completed the information. Kate could not stop rubbing her thumb over the raised engraving of the tree. Raising her eyes to meet Samu's inquiring look, she said softly, "Did I meet this man at the opening?"

"No, he had a private showing because he was leaving hours before we opened for the party. He read the advertisement about the show in the *Japan Times* and contacted me. Mr. Miles is a very wealthy man with a discriminating taste. He often visits the gallery and is well-known in the art and travel world. He was impressed with you, Kate, so now you must decide. A commission with him will put your name on the map in art circles. You know that art is a small world yet a powerful one."

"I have so much spinning in my head. First, you want me to join you in Macau and now this South African thing. What I need is a nap." Kate brought her fingertips up to her temples and rubbed gently. "How funny life can be. One minute, everything is quiet and still. And then suddenly, I'm on a roller coaster."

"That is life. Now I must go and plan my big event with Mrs. Goto. Wish me luck."

"Good luck, Samu. I'll keep my fingers crossed." She held up crossed fingers and waited for him to leave before reaching for some Tylenol and water.

After a short rest that did do wonders for the pain in her back, Kate checked the photographs she had taken that morning and smiled at how beautifully clear and serene the images appeared. She thought about the stunning nature around her, and her mind wondered about South Africa and the unique qualities she would find in mountains, plateaus, and the water. It was then she realized that all her photos were on her camera and therefore not protected. Not wanting to be beholden to the technological world, she also realized that she had to be smart about storing her work, especially now that it was steering her life in a rewarding and enriching way. She threw her woven bag over her shoulder and placed inside the hefty check Samu gave her. At the hottest time of the day, she set out to Naha to open an account in a local bank and buy a newer version of the Apple laptop similar to the one she had in New York.

The streets were busy, and at Mizuho Bank, she was directed to American Village for an Apple retailer. There was always excitement in the busy streets of Naha with all the traffic and people moving about. The traffic fumes made Kate cough and miss her clean paradise back at the hotel. An hour later, she had purchased a new Apple MacBook Air and an iPhone, both in silver. She established an iCloud account and had a new e-mail.

Looking at her purchases, she wondered how she could go from being determined to run away from the world one minute to now wanting to embrace her life. Standing at the curb with her purchases, waiting for a taxi, Kate concluded that it had to be the remembrance ceremony she had for Oliver that triggered this change. Since that day, she had felt lighter; the survivor's guilt was almost gone, and although her heart was still in pieces over losing Oliver, she felt him closer now more than ever before. Coming to terms with what she could not change in her life helped with her grieving and accepting his death, but Oliver would forever be front and center in her mind.

Samu and Mrs. Goto spoke for two hours, and in the end, she embraced him as her new son but not without reminding him that her daughter or her grandchildren were never to mark their bodies with tattoos and that perhaps he should change that tuft of bleached hair that often fell over his handsome face. He agreed to the tattoos until the children were eighteen years of age and could determine this on their own, and as for Aiko, he loved her just as she was. Mrs. Goto planned for a special and secret private dinner in the greenhouse, where Samu would propose to Aiko the following evening.

That night, Kate had a fitful sleep and awoke feeling like there was a large gray cloud in her head fogging all her senses. This feeling prompted her to go for a swim in the ocean before breakfast in hopes that her internal fog might lift. The cool water made her bottom lip quiver and her skin crawl, but after a short while, she felt comfortable.

The warm sun caressed her skin as she thought about the decisions she had to make. She wondered about accompanying Aiko and Samu to Macau to see Rey play. Her heart wanted to go, but her mind told her otherwise. Kate could not ignore the enormous sense of guilt she felt and a form of betrayal toward Oliver if she allowed her heart to rule her decision. By showing up in Macau, she would be sending Rey signals of hope. The attraction between them was there, and it was strong, and the only thing that kept her from freeing her heart to feel anything toward him was the guilt she would have if she did. On the other hand, not going would disappoint her friends because Mrs. Goto would disapprove of her daughter traveling unescorted with her fiancé. Then there was South Africa.

Diving down into the water, Kate swam underneath for as long as she could hold her breath. Coming up for air, she gasped and coughed, having pushed her abilities, and she decided then and there that she was calling Barbara Quincy to inform her of her future travels to South Africa.

Samu was discontented when Kate informed him that she was going to South Africa the following week and could not make it to Macau. To complete his annoyance at having to let Rey down, Samu had to fake a smile when Mrs. Goto announced she would be coming along to Macau for a long-overdue gambling excursion. Because it was slow season at the hotel, Mrs. Goto left the management for three days to Tsune, her head chef and longtime friend. There were only four guests currently registered, and she felt Tsune could manage their immediate needs.

Several days later, Samu and Rey met in Macau. When Rey realized Kate had not come, his face wore a mask of curiosity and sorrow. He thought she would, and knowing she went instead after a job was confirmation of her disinterest in him. Rey thanked Samu and proceeded with his playing, which was at best lackluster. His head just wasn't into the gig anymore, and he didn't care until Paco and Rafa pulled him aside in between sets and allowed him to vent his frustration in the dressing room. Paco and Rafa had never seen him this way before, and darting concerned looks between them, they let Rey blow off steam.

After the show, they got into a waiting limo to head back to the hotel when Rey served himself a scotch from the bar. "Nice ride. I love pimped-out limos," Rey said as he sipped his scotch, slowly savoring the flavors and scents in the aged liquor.

"So is the reason you are looking like a wet puppy because of that delicious Brazilian model Tatiana Newman?" Rafa chuckled, knowing this annoyed Rey.

"No way. It's someone else. This one is pure substance, but apparently, it won't matter." Rey scowled.

"Hmm, I think she is a huge deal to you because, in the twenty-plus years we have known you, you have never been this way over a chick." Rafa continued.

"She's not a chick. She's different, but I'm invisible to her."

Sensing his dark mood, Paco intervened to ease the atmosphere and avoid a blowout between the two men. "Sounds like you have feelings for this lady, don't you?"

"What difference does it make? Besides, I was stupid to think I stood a chance. Man, I plunged the car into her and her kid. Now you understand how I can't even dream."

Paco and Rafa sat with their eyes bulging and not saying a word. The silence was choking everyone in the car. They could not figure out how Rey and this particular woman had met. Rather than sit around in awkward silence, Rafa went for the jugular with his pointed questions. "What were you thinking pursuing this woman whose life you unwillingly destroyed? It's no wonder she won't see you."

"Just keep plunging that knife deeper into me, bro. I can handle all the punishment you've got." Rey glanced out the window with a look of disgust etched across his face. Despite his discontent, he knew Rafa was right.

Always the pacifier, Paco intervened. "Hey, you guys, quit it. When and where did you two meet?"

Rey didn't respond. There was a look of deep sorrow in his eyes that both his friends saw and felt uneasy around. Rafa offered him a fresh drink as a peace offering. Although he wanted to dull his senses, he refused the drink. His response came as a surprise to both of them. "She's beautiful, and she's the one. She may not know it or care, but she's the one. We met through letters. I wrote asking about making a donation in her son's name from the monies I won from the insurance and car manufacturer. When she wrote back to me, there was something about the way she expressed herself that just told me this was a special woman. I sent her a ticket to the gig in Japan, and it so happened she was having a showing of her art at a gallery. She came to the club, and without having seen her before, I just knew who she was from all the faces in the crowd."

He stopped and looked away and then looked at his friends and continued. "She wasn't feeling well, and I escorted her back to the hotel. We had breakfast the next day, and I couldn't help but show her my feelings. I think I scared her off. The gallery owner was supposed to entice her to come to Macau, but she went to South Africa on some job."

Rafa and Paco understood how Rey felt even if they had never had a similar experience in their lives. Extending his hand, Rafa playfully slapped Rey's knee and said, "So what now? Where do you go from here?"

"Nowhere, I guess. I couldn't even buy one of her photographs because it was a sold-out show. I may never see her again." He said this quietly and regretfully. "Damn, I have gone through my life always playing around with women and never thinking twice about any of them. I don't know anything personal about Kate, but somehow, I feel like I have known her all my life."

"You know what, Rey, you have to try a little harder because if she gets away, then you have only yourself to blame," Paco stated.

Rafa concurred and added, "Bro, you have to understand that she may feel that she should not get involved with you because of everything that happened. You will have to show her that this terrible thing wasn't really your fault and that you too nearly lost your life." Rafa finished the scotch he had poured for Rey.

Looking defeated, Rey responded, "You know what, she forgave me when we met for breakfast, and she told me that I should never blame myself or even bring it up again." He grunted as he ran his large hands over his hair and squeezed his palms into his eyes.

"It's too bad we aren't going to South Africa," chimed in Paco.

"I just have to continue in my own thing and let her continue her full recovery and pray that, along the way, she will give me a thought. She agreed to continue letter writing, so I guess that's something."

The car arrived at the hotel as Rafa wrapped up their conversation. "Good thinking. She lost what, I can guess, was the most important person in her life, and this is a loss she will carry forever. Maybe time is exactly what you both need." Before exiting the car, they fist-bumped one another and went to pack for their next stop, Shanghai, China.

CHAPTER 11

White Rose Cottage

Barbara Quincy had one of those infectious ear-to-ear television smiles. Her manner was gentle and professional with a direct yet soft voice. Opening an enormous golf umbrella, she jumped out of the limousine to collect Kate as she came through the airport revolving doors. There was an awful midday downpour causing chaos outside the busy Cape Town International Airport. People scrambled about, shouting for taxis in both Afrikaans and English and moving quickly to avoid the sheets of rain and gusty winds.

Kate and Barbara shook hands awkwardly under the umbrella as the driver opened the door and held it tightly to keep the wind from slamming it against the women. Starting the car, he headed out honking his horn and navigating the worse traffic Kate had ever seen.

"Well, Ms. Connor, it is so good to have you here despite our insane weather." Barbara kept that smile plastered on her face for most of the ride.

"Please, call me Kate."

"All right, Kate, are you hungry? Because we have quite the feast awaiting you."

"Oh no, I hope no one has gone to any trouble for me. So tell me a little about where I am staying."

"How humble you are. Mr. Miles likes this quality in people, so you will fit right in with his lot. You are staying, as you know, at his country estate here in Cape Town. It is famous because of the pure white roses he grows in his greenhouse. Actually, they are everywhere you look, but his 'babies,' as he calls them, are the new blooms in the greenhouse, such as the calla lilies and orchids. They are gorgeous, but his preference is the rose. He named his house White Rose Cottage, but there is nothing quaint about it, so the name is quite misleading."

Kate watched how animated Barbara was when she spoke. Guessing at her age, Kate figured she was around her early forties, impeccably dressed in a gray raincoat over a beautiful Missoni sweater dress and red Prada sling-back mules. In her hands, she held a smartphone and notepad with a pen, always poised to take down a note or two that Kate noticed she took as they rode to the house.

"Mr. Miles regrets he will not be there to greet you, but he will arrive by tomorrow evening and looks forward to showing you around our splendid city in the coming days. But you must be tired, and I'm rambling on. I do apologize." Barbara looked down shyly and did not speak again until after Kate invited her to do so.

"I have enjoyed listening to you. Have you worked long for Mr. Miles?"

AURA POLANCO

"Thank you. I have been Mr. Miles's assistant for many years now. But I'm not interesting compared with you. Your photographs are a dream. They lit up the entire room. I was instructed to show you the arrangement when you arrive." Kate was starting to like this chatty woman with blue eyes that sparkled like a sunny summer sky.

As the rain diminished to sporadic drops, the driver pulled off the main road. They drove up through a lane of overhanging trees with yellow pom-pom-like flowers unfamiliar to Kate. She stared at these very interesting trees, trying to figure out what they were. They circled a pebbled driveway and arrived at two gigantic glass-encased iron doors. Kate looked back to gaze at the trees with their bowing heads and arms full of branches and fluffy yellow orbs and thought about what a lovely photograph this image would make for her collection.

A slender woman wearing a butter-colored uniform and white sandals opened the large glass and iron doors that led to the main house. Upon her head, she had a white wrap covering her hair. Smiling with a row of pearly teeth, she waved Kate and Barbara through. Once inside, Kate was met with an enormous entryway adorned with two elegant marble staircases flanking each side with magnificently carved lion-head balustrades. The walls leading to the second level were adorned with imposing murals. One side had a painting of South African mountains and the other side an expansive painting of the sea. It was clear to Kate that the inhabitants of this home had a deep appreciation and love for their country and held its people and nature in high regard.

The graceful woman in the uniform escorted Kate and Barbara into the salon, where a butler in starchy white pants and an equally polished white shirt greeted them. He bowed gracefully and welcomed the ladies to sit upon the damask sofa and chairs. "Welcome to White Rose Cottage. I am Mr. Themba and will be at your service throughout your stay." Mr. Themba snapped his fingers sharply, and the same woman in the butter-colored uniform returned carrying a tray of sandwiches and cakes while another woman, more rotund and older, carried an elegant silver tea service.

"This is Sally." Mr. Themba waved his long brown fingers over to the smiling younger woman. "And this is Farai. These ladies work in the house and are also here to make your stay as comfortable and enjoyable as possible. Please allow me to serve you some tea." Kate and Barbara busied themselves in placing sandwiches on pretty hors d'oeuvre plates while Mr. Thelma skillfully served the tea. "If you need anything, just ring this bell, and we will come to your assistance." He bowed again, this time more exaggeratedly, and stepped backward as if he were exiting a room from royalty.

Kate looked at Barbara and chuckled, feeling somewhat out of place in such splendor and with so much attention. Being a keen observer, Barbara tried to allay Kate's concerns. "This is a champagne-and-caviar world you will be in for several days, so if I were you, I would live it up." She winked and proceeded to pop a tiny watercress and butter sandwich shaped like a flower into her mouth without disturbing her lipstick. Kate ate moderately and had some tea, although she was more eager to see the gardens and get on with her work.

"Barbara, do you live here?" asked Kate, wrinkling her forehead from the unique flavors in the tea.

"Yes, I do. I stay in one of several guest cottages Mr. Miles had built for that exact purpose. Your cottage is directly next to mine and by the pool. So we can lounge about like two girl friends and chat it up later on." Reaching over for the bell, Barbara moved it about, sending a gentle ring that ushered in Mr. Themba.

"Yes, Madam Quincy?"

"Let's show Ms. Connor to her cottage, and did Mr. Miles leave any instructions for me?"

"No instructions, madam, but I placed all the correspondence on your desk. If you are prepared now, Ms. Connor, I will show you to your cottage."

"Thank you, Mr. Themba. Kate, I leave you in expert hands. I have some work to do but will see you later for supper. This way, you can meander on your own around the grounds. Do you have any questions for me?"

"I'm good. Thank you so much, Barbara. I will see you later."

"Okay, have fun. Mr. Themba, my compliments to Farai for those exquisite sandwiches. That woman is a marvel."

"I am certain she will be pleased to hear this. This way, Ms. Connor."

Kate followed Mr. Themba back through the foyer. This time, they went past an enormous glass table with an impressive arrangement of calla lilies and lilac delphiniums. The entire home caressed the nose with a gentle scent of thyme and sage, reminding Kate of the tiny herb garden she once kept on her Manhattan kitchen windowsill. They walked along a garden path flanked by lush and pretty flowerbeds and swaying trees. The warmth of the sun and the scent of freshness were like an elixir that belied the earlier rainstorm.

Mr. Themba moved aside to show Kate her lodgings. The cottage was a small powder blue house with a porch and slanted pink tiled roof. The windows had charming white shutters with white window boxes bursting with yellow roses and creeping vine. Mr. Themba held the door open for Kate to enter. As Kate looked around at the airy and bright space with a deep and cozy sofa and two equally plump chairs, Mr. Themba moved about opening windows to let in the warm breeze. He ushered Kate through an archway to show her the bedroom and bathroom. The rooms were elegantly styled and furnished. Kate was grateful for the neutral palette, as she preferred calming colors. She particularly liked the ecru color in the bedroom with the white iron four-poster bed. Noticing the mosquito netting, she made a mental note to let it down at nighttime, as she did not want to be mosquito meal.

Being in this enchanting home with the attentive staff and her own cottage was deliciously fun for Kate. While she had lunch, Kate's clothing had been hung or folded in the drawers and closet. Her toiletries were placed upon a silver tray in the bathroom. On her bed she found a plush robe and slippers. She went out to the porch to examine the light and saw that it settled behind the main house and furthest part of the garden. Changing into some flip-flops and a linen dress, Kate made a messy top bun of her long hair and walked out to explore what lay beyond the trees that separated the gardens from the main house.

The sun kissed her shoulders, and she caught herself smiling. The trees appeared smaller as she approached them, and she noticed they bore fruit. As she turned to the right, she saw a majestic greenhouse. It looked more like a conservatory with its glass dome ceiling. Every wall was glass with a stunning stained glass door. She figured that three of Mrs. Goto's greenhouses could fit in this massive one.

The desire to enter was only curtailed when a pair of Jack Russells came leaping over some short hedges to inspect Kate. She squatted and remained still, giving the curious dogs time to sniff her out and capture her scent. Once they relaxed, she held out her palm, and they became playful. These were small but powerful dogs that loved a challenge and running after anything that moved. A low whistle set their ears up, and off they dashed toward the sound. Beyond the trees walked a young boy and an older man with the bouncy dogs by their sides. The older man bowed to Kate as the boy just stood there with a look of boredom on his face.

"Hello, I hope I'm not intruding, but I was just going for a walk," Kate said with a smile as she shielded the sun from her eyes with her hand.

"You are a guest here. Therefore all of this is yours to explore. May I show you around?" The older man was quite gracious as he swept the straw hat he removed toward the direction of the greenhouse.

"I would love that. Thank you. I'm Kate," she said as she extended her hand.

He took her hand gently in his and said softly, "Pleased to meet you. I am Ross, and this rude boy here is my son, Michael. Nature bores him, and I refuse to return his phone until he learns to have a proper conversation with another person." Michael rolled his eyes and looked away, defeated. "I am the gardener here at the estate. Come, Ms. Kate, I will show you my masterpiece." His infectious laugh bubbled from his belly.

Kate entered through two enormous glass and iron doors and was immediately overwhelmed, not knowing which way to look first. The sensation was that of being in a tropical oasis with the sound of gentle waterfalls and the movement of aromatic air. Varying shades of green and flowers abounded everywhere, and the size of the space was daunting. "Ross, this place is an oasis. There are more trees in here than outside and all this furniture. It is like a living room surrounded by nature. This space is impressive." Ross laughed again and picked a tiny yellowing leaf off a flowering potted plant.

Kate moved over to the graceful bentwood furniture arrangement complete with pillows, white upholstery, and a coffee table. She noticed the small porcelain cupids that adorned the coffee table and the pretty floating flowers in a crystal bowl, reminding her of Mrs. Goto. Walking beyond the initial living space and flowering plants, Ross showed Kate the fruit trees that sat in gigantic glossy pots. There were lemon, orange, and mango trees growing around her. A stunning replication of Aphrodite stood before the next arrangement of furniture. At the base was a circular bed of miniature yellow roses. Comfortable loungers with throws and small tables and lamps were off to the side by the floor-to-ceiling glass with a view to a pond and the forest that lay beyond. Not knowing what this space was used for, she asked Ross to explain. "What is this space for, Ross?"

"For reading, Ms. Kate. Mr. Miles reads here every opportunity he has. He says the green helps him breathe. Come, I have much more to show you."

Turning a corner, Ross led Kate through a glass door where the temperature was warmer and the air moist. It was a caressing warmth and a lulling of the senses as the scent of tropical flowers permeated the room. Kate felt like she was trapped in an exquisite perfume bottle. Everything enchanted her. The light coming in was softer, giving this space an ethereal quality that Kate wished she had caught had she thought to bring her camera. There was something about the fragrant flowers that made Kate somewhat dazed as if she were awakening from a long sleep.

Ross pointed to two long sections where endless orchids sat. "This is my masterpiece." He spread his arms out wide like a bald eagle. "Mr. Miles loves these flowers, and he could not get them to grow and survive until I came along and nurtured them. See? Come here." With much exuberance, Ross showed Kate the different variety of orchid flowers he cultivated. The selection was impressive, and Kate understood why Ross referred to the flowers as his masterpiece. It was clearly his pride and joy and work that brought him enormous satisfaction. They chatted for what seemed an eternity and did not exit the greenhouse until the sun was blazing a deep curry orange, inviting the night to arrive.

Back at the house, Kate wandered around and entered a room off the side of the salon where she earlier had been welcomed and enjoyed tea and sandwiches. Beyond a marble archway, Kate caught sight of her six black and white photographs taken of Mrs. Goto's orchids, and arranged neatly above a glass mosaic table. It was the first time Kate had ever seen her work as decor in anyone's home, and she had mixed feelings. On the one hand, she thought it was tastefully displayed; but on the other hand, she wondered if they would have been more impressive in color. Without question, the quality of her photographic skill was evident, but Kate was a perfectionist and had yet to acknowledge this for herself.

Hearing soft steps coming from behind, she turned and found Sally smiling at her. The pretty, young woman with doe eyes looked down in a subservient way and spoke quietly and barely above a whisper. "Ms. Connor, would you like me to draw a bath for you?"

Kate smiled back. "Yes, that would be lovely. Thank you, Sally."

"You are most welcome. I shall do it straight away." Sally curtsied and left the room.

Kate looked out the picture window to admire the mountains and thought of how life was indeed peculiar and unpredictable. In this house, far from all she knew and those she loved, she felt at home and welcome. As she walked back to her cottage, Kate wondered what else lay ahead.

Trevor Miles was tall and slender and in his early fifties. He sported a neatly trimmed silvery beard and an equally neat haircut. Being a businessman, he was always impeccably dressed in bespoke suits and traveled in private jets and cars. It was his business to move people. The people he moved were the very wealthy who would not conceive of ever traveling commercially. He owned and ran Connoisseur Air, servicing clients globally with fleets of jets based out of London, New York, Geneva, and Shanghai. Miles was a childless widower who appreciated beautiful women, art, food, drink, dogs, and horses. On his farm in South Africa, he had several Jack Russells as pets, Percheron horses, and an assortment of animals just because he could have whatever he desired.

Arriving early the next morning, he spoke softly to Mr. Themba and inquired about Kate. He was assured that Kate was comfortable and had walked around the gardens. After a light breakfast in his kitchen prepared by Farai, he read the paper at the small kitchen table and served himself a third cup of coffee. Miles was wealthy, but he enjoyed simplicity. He treated all his employees with kindness and was quite generous in their salaries and benefits. Cultivating an ambience of trust and respect kept his staff content and never wanting for more. This was important to Miles, as he needed consistency when he came home to rest.

Farai smiled over and softly asked him about his recent trip. "Mr. Miles, did you have a happy trip to Japan and China?"

"It is always a happy trip, Farai, when I make lots of money. The Beijing fleet is almost ready to start, and that means lots of money." Both of them broke into chuckles as Mr. Themba came in with Kate's breakfast order. She asked for one egg over easy, toast, jam, butter, and lettuce and tomatoes on the side, prompting Miles to interject. "She eats like a bird. Farai, you must fatten her up so that she is voluptuous like you." He made a woman's figure with his hands and laughed loudly as Farai dismissed his comment with a wave of her hand and laughed. Getting up, he planted a friendly peck on her forehead, causing a bright color to rise on her caramel cheeks, and then left with Mr. Themba on his heels. "Is everything arranged for tonight's party?"

"All is ready. Your guests will begin arriving at around seven this evening, and dinner will be at eight thirty, giving you plenty of time for cocktails and appetizers."

"Don't forget the musicians must be here before my guests arrive. Oh, and did you remember the conservatory?"

"But of course. The musicians are setting up at five thirty and eating by six, and the conservatory has already been fitted with additional lights and seating for the evening, and the caterers arrive at five with the musicians."

"Excellent, you are always one step ahead of me. After Ms. Kate has had her breakfast, please invite her to meet me in the conservatory."

"Will do, Mr. Miles. Will there be anything else, sir?"

"No thank you, Themba."

Kate was very hungry as her dinner the night before was not very appetizing due to its spiciness. Farai prepared a simple breakfast exactly as Kate had requested. Kate thanked Farai and ate hurriedly, as she was eager to get her camera and catch the early light of the day.

On her way back to her cottage, Mr. Themba caught up to her and said, "Good morning, Ms. Connor. Mr. Miles has asked that you meet with him in the conservatory at this time."

"Oh, that would be perfect because I was just going to pick up my camera and head over there myself. Thank you, Mr. Themba."

"Very good, madam. Enjoy your morning."

He bowed and moved along to the main house as Kate entered her cottage. Gathering her camera, she glanced at the mirror again and smoothed down her loose white cotton shift and headed to the conservatory. Kate entered to the same world of lushness as the day before except that the tiled floors were wet from numerous sprayers watering plants and fruit trees from above. She dodged a few small puddles and hop scotched her way toward the double doors that led to the roses and orchid house.

While Kate gingerly walked around puddles, Trevor watched her from above his newspaper. He noticed that the cascade of her flowing chestnut hair was parted down the middle and ended in gentle waves. Her loose dress did not show her body, but he admired her graceful arms and shoulders. He put his paper down and let out a friendly extended arm and hand accompanied by a hearty laugh. "You are quite agile, Ms. Connor. Come this way where the floor is not as wet."

Kate moved alongside a drier spot by the fuchsia rhododendron bushes. "Thank you, Mr. Miles, and it is a pleasure to finally meet you." Her voice was like a cool breeze to Miles as he also took in her stunning hazel eyes and full mouth.

"Well, the pleasure is all mine, but I must insist that we lose the formality. Just call me Trevor. You are my guest, and I want you to feel at home in my house."

"Thank you very much, Trevor. Please call me Kate. This is some property you have. I am in love with your conservatory. When I arrived yesterday, the sun was still out. But now that it is morning, the colors are brilliant in here with the morning light."

"Yes, this is my favorite place on the property. I also enjoy my house a great deal, but here I can close my eyes and somehow forget the world beyond these glass walls. Kate, I want you to have free rein over the property because I want you to catch the essence of White Rose Cottage. This place has special meaning for me, and I would like all the photographs you take to reflect different aspects of what makes it so special."

Feeling comfortable in his presence and finding Trevor's soft baritone soothing and reassuring, Kate smiled up at him and responded, "I took some shots late afternoon of the conservatory because the lushness is extraordinary, and the quality of the air reminded me of the rain forest I visited in Costa Rica some years ago. I would like to show you, if you don't mind."

"Certainly. Let's sit over by the divan. Be careful not to fall. The floor should dry soon, and we won't have to move around so awkwardly." Trevor placed his hand on Kate's elbow to guide her to the silk-covered mocha divan. They sat, and she arranged her phone to show him the photos she had taken." He discreetly admired the graceful curve of her profile and the way her dress stretched across her breasts. Taking her iPhone into his elegant large hands, he swiped right to see several photographs of the plants and flowers in the conservatory. Looking quizzically at Kate, he asked, "You took these wonderful photos with the phone?"

Chuckling, Kate responded, "Oh, I could, as this has a decent camera, but I used the professional one, and saved them on my phone and cloud to view later. I like to look at the photos or revisit an object at different times during the day to see how it changes with the light."

"How interesting. I like how you captured this window box at the cottage you are staying in, and this is precisely what I want. It is these little spaces like the window box that capture the essence of a home. Keep this up, Kate, and I will be pleased. Anything you need, just ask. Tonight I am having a gathering of friends. There will be music, and they often kick off their shoes and dance the night away."

"How fancy is this gathering?"

"Oh, it's just a few of my friends. We like to dress up a bit, and have fun. You look lovely as you are, or perhaps this afternoon, you can get into town and buy a new dress."

"I suppose I will be all right with the dress I brought along. Well, I want to take advantage of this magnificent light. Thank you for inviting me to your beautiful home, Trevor."

"You know, Kate, when I saw your orchid photographs in Tokyo, there was something about them that made me smile. I trust that you will make that same feeling happen in me again. Now I shall let you get on with your work, and tonight you are my guest of honor."

"Thank you. It certainly sounds like fun. See you later." Kate got up and moved along to the far end of the greenhouse where the roses lived. Trevor watched her leave and then picked up his copy of the *Wall Street Journal*, placed glasses upon his nose, and returned to reading. All the while, as he read, he knew Kate was a woman he would come to know better.

Kate moved along efficiently, capturing the sun's rays upon the flowers, and in no time at all had a collection of beautiful shots of just about every plant and flower in the conservatory. She moved back the way she came and noticed that Trevor had gone. Curiosity made her move out to the stables. The exuberant Jack Russells from yesterday barked happily when they saw her and joined her as she moved along through the forest that separated the conservatory and house from the fields, where the stables were housed.

Reaching the stables, she was slightly winded from the walk and heat. It was a dry, hot day, and Kate wished she had brought along some water. Accompanied by the bouncy and friendly dogs, she walked confidently up to the back of a large pitched cornhusk-colored stable. The back of the building looked well-kept with pretty orange blossom bushes surrounding it on three sides. After taking a shot of this angle, Kate rounded to the front and came upon the stalls with shutters where the horses could look out. She stood directly in front of one of these open shutters and looked out at the enormous pen and open yellow and green countryside.

Admiring the blue green of the grass, she felt a powerful nudge push her forward. Turning around, she saw the noble massive head of a Percheron staring back at her. She looked around again and saw no one and offered her hand to stroke the side of the head. She marveled at the power just in the neck muscles as the horse moved its head around at her touch. A soft-spoken voice came up behind Kate, causing her to jump and stop stroking the horse. She was met with a very thin, tall man in baggy khaki pants and a green and yellow T-shirt displaying the South African national cricket team emblem. He had short, black, and curly hair with bushy eyebrows and a broad smile, showing a neat row of white teeth. Two friendly eyes sparkled as he extended his hand toward Kate. Shaking hands, she readily added, "Hello, I'm Kate."

"Hello, Kate. I'm Rufus. I see you have met Lily."

Kate turned again to look upon the horse named Lily and smiled despite herself, saying, "Hello, Lily. It is lovely to know your name." Rufus laughed gently and went to open Lily's gate. She noticed how he graciously moved and smoothly handled the horse as he walked her out of the space. As Lily exited her stall, Kate was awestruck. She could tell the horse was big from the size of its head, but the caramel and white mare was a sight to be seen. Rufus spoke softly and made cooing sounds as if Lily were a baby. He brought her out to the pen to exercise her a bit and allow Kate to take in the total beauty of the magnificent animal.

Excited at the opportunity to capture such a horse, Kate prepped her camera and took endless photos of how Lily moved and trotted around, with Rufus leading her without a bit or rope. It was as if man and horse were one. He trotted, and she followed. She walked, and he followed. He laughed as if sharing a private joke with the beast, and she shook her glorious mane from side to side. Kate took the shot with Lily's head and neck in full view, with the mane flipping up from the movement. Instinctively, Kate knew Trevor would love this photo.

Rufus came up to her with Lily following by his side. "Would you like to ride her?"

"Oh no, I'm just happy photographing her in all her splendor. I know nothing about horses except that I love how majestic they look, but I think she is the biggest horse I have ever seen."

"Lily is the sweetest lady around." He stroked her mane as her intelligent eyes stared at Kate. "She stands at eighteen hands, but as big as she is, she is very gentle. We have only Percherons here at White Rose. Mr. Miles loves this breed. 'Sure you don't want to ride her?"

"No thank you. I'm just thrilled to be around such a beauty. You said there were more like Lily?"

"Yes, we have two others. I'll bring Lily back and give her a much-deserved treat and show you around." Rufus planted a kiss on Lily's face and led her into her space. After closing the gate, he reached into a leather bag to the side of the door. He pulled out a large carrot and broke it in two, feeding Lily one piece. He handed Kate the other piece, and Kate held it in her hand and almost dropped it when Lily pressed down hard to get the carrot. Rufus laughed at Kate's wide-eyed expression and walked her through the large stable doors and introduced her to Buddy, a glistening black Percheron around the same size as Lily. He left Kate taking photos of the impressive animal and brought out a young horse of around six months for Kate to pet and gush over.

"This is Lily and Buddy's baby, Starr. See how Lily is watching us? She is making sure we do not harm her baby." Kate gently stroked the beautiful dark brown mane and enjoyed how the yearling responded by the movement of her head. The young horse was as tall as Kate and very playful. She fed her two apples, and Rufus showed her how to brush her mane and coat.

After spending time stroking all three horses, Kate said good-bye to beasts and man alike and moved on toward the house. It was around one in the afternoon, and after such an eventful morning, Kate felt tired and thirsty. She decided that she would go for a swim and have a nap to not appear so tired at the party, where she was to be the guest of honor.

The music awoke Kate. Momentarily confused, she realized where she was and knew she was late for the party. After the warm swim earlier that afternoon, Kate's intended short nap had turned into a three-hour deep sleep, in which she dreamed of being on a sailboat with Rey. As she got ready for the party, she thought about how the blue sky shimmered like a jewel in the dream and she was smiling at Rey.

The fairy lights around the property gave the place a magical quality. Kate heard laughter and music coming from the conservatory. The path leading to the conservatory was lit with more lights, making Kate feel like Cinderella arriving at the ball. Her hair was up in a chignon, displaying her smooth, fair bosom and elegant neck and shoulders. She applied little make up, thanks to the tan she sported from Okinawa, and moved carefully over the large flat stones in her high heels. Kate was happy to have packed a floor-length halter and backless white chiffon dress she had purchased during her visit in Tokyo.

Upon entering the conservatory, she did not find a gathering of a few friends; but instead, the place was overflowing with stylishly dressed people. Every man sported a tuxedo, while the women had on jewels and varying lengths of formal dresses. Noticing her from the other side of the fountain, Trevor hurried over to Kate's side. He filled her with compliments at how pretty she looked and made a gesture to the orchestra to stop playing. Everyone's eyes fell upon Kate. She stood there acutely aware of Trevor's large warm hands resting on her naked shoulders. Escorting her over to the platform where the orchestra sat,

Trevor took the microphone and said, "Welcome, all, to my little gathering." People laughed and murmured as he continued. "And warmly welcome my guest of honor, the very talented photographer Kate Connor, who is spending several days with me." The crowd applauded politely.

The atmosphere was exciting with the ethnic diversity of beautifully dressed people and laughter ringing everywhere. Kate thanked Trevor quietly, and as the band swept into dance music, people started moving about in different manners of expression. Trevor took Kate's hand and encouraged her to dance. Reluctantly, Kate followed along, keeping her eyes on the black onyx buttons of his white tuxedo shirt as he aptly moved them about in a box waltz. Kate was not much of a dancer, nor did she care to learn, but she graciously moved from Trevor to another man with a large mustache that curled at the ends in stiff points.

After the music ended, she smiled politely and moved away quickly toward where the bartender stood with a collection of the finest liquors. She asked for champagne and watched the young man with a neat goatee and a shiny, bald head uncork a fresh bottle of Egly-Ouriet. Walking around among beautiful flowers and plants, she sipped the crisp and fresh sparkling wine and observed how Trevor's crowd of friends was quite gregarious and even becoming rowdy. At one point, she observed one man give another a piggyback ride and cringed as they came dangerously close to toppling over a marble table where a stunning collection of lilies were displayed.

Several splendid tables were arranged throughout the conservatory to accommodate guests for dinner. Elegant crystal and china adorned the tables with floral arrangements set in woven vases and resting upon rich, brown linen tablecloths The succulent menu was a South African delight of flavors. Guests had mussells or crocodile as appetizers. The main courses consisted of a choice between lamb curry or ostrich steak with a delectable dessert of coco-pine pudding. Trevor sat next to Kate and boldly rested his hand upon her thigh. He squeezed her thigh and smiled wickledly at Kate. Shocked at his manner, Kate moved his hand immediately and glared at him. Trevor feigned confusion and having had too much to drink. She dismissed it because she understood these things could happen when too much alcohol was involved.

After dinner, a group of musicians displayed their skills at traditional drums prompting, several guests to dance about wildly. As the evening progressed, many of the guests were quite inebriated and started to run out of the conservatory, encouraging all to jump into the pool. To her amazement, Kate watched men and women undress down to their underwear and others to their birthday suits and splash around in the pool.

While all this debauchery took place, Kate caught sight of Barbara giggling and running away from a man trying to catch her. She saw Trevor laughing boisterously with a group of older people and subsequently smiling over to her. Moving over to Kate, he started to apologize for the brazenness of his guests. "If any of this offends you, then I am sorry." He gently gave Kate a kiss on her right cheek, before he walked quietly back to the main house accompanied by a very beautiful red head. At that point, Kate concluded that if the host was done for the night, then she too would retire to her little cottage and get away from all this chaotic behavior. The antics of these guests reminded her of a Fellini movie she once watched with her mother.

The early morning sun was shimmering high in the sky, prompting Kate to catch the brilliant light for more photos. She trailed after the Jack Russells, who led her to the other side of the vast property. The energetic little dogs looked wildly around as they sniffed scents from other creatures. Kate took endless photographs of them frolicking in the grass and just being the adorable dogs they were known to be.

Walking back toward the main house, she noticed a larger crew of cleaning staff collecting the detritus of the previous night. By the pool, one man straightened up furniture while another fished out a soggy bow tie and a lady's shoe. Kate marveled at such behavior but shrugged and had an idea to get a photo of the house from a different vantage point.

Catching sight of Rufus as he rode Lily out by the pasture, Kate decided to ask him for guidance on her idea. She walked at least a quarter mile toward the horse stables before reaching him. When he saw her, he and Lily trotted back to the stables. "Goeie mirning, Kate."

"What?" Kate looked up at Rufus and shielded her eyes from the glare of the sun.

Letting out a hearty chuckle, Rufus explained, "That is 'good morning' in Afrikaans."

"Oh, then *goeie mirning* to you too." Kate struggled slightly with the pronunciation. "How are all of you today? I mean man and beasts?"

"We are doing very well." He chuckled as he dismounted and stroked Lily's mane. "What brings you here on this bright, sunny day?"

Stroking Lily's mane, Kate smiled as she responded, "Well, I was just walking along and wondered if you could help me photograph a different view of the property." Rufus walked Lily into the stables and proceeded to remove the saddle and tacking and give her a brush down as Kate explained. "I figured Mr. Miles already had an aerial view of his property, but I would like to capture this same view with all the people and animals moving about at their work. I guess, I mean, from a nearby hilltop perhaps."

Rufus looked up from around Lily's large body and said calmly, jutting his bottom lip out, "Well, the nearest hill is a distance away, and unless you have a telephoto lens, we will all look like tiny specks of nothing, but would you consider a hot-air balloon ride?"

Kate had never done that before, and her smile and wide-eyed wonderment gave it away. "That sounds very interesting and a bit thrilling." Kate could only imagine what a unique experience going up on a balloon would be like.

But just as soon as she experienced the thrill, her heart sank in darkness, thinking about how her son, Oliver, would never have this chance. Her sunny mood had soured, and it showed in the sorrowful look that invaded her pretty face. Rufus was keen to notice this sudden change in mood and quietly continued with his work. He wondered what could have suddenly made Kate fall silent and look so solemn, as he continued brushing down Lily. As quickly as her mood had darkened, Kate shook her head slightly and, with her left hand, stroked Lily's face. The horse delighted in her gentle touch by moving her enormous head to and fro. Rufus took this opportunity to inquire as nonchalantly as he could. "So, Kate, are you agreeable to such a ride?"

Kate moved away from the horse and walked on the other side of the stable. All she wanted to do was be alone, as the immense sorrow continued to deepen within her. Oliver was ever present in her heart, but when she least expected it, her mind would explode with images of the jubilant boy, and she would suddenly collapse in a void of sorrow that she could not control. On occasions such as these, Kate only recovered in solitude, where she could release her pain. How she wished she were back in Okinawa on the pristine and tranquil beach where so many of her tears had further salted the ocean water.

Looking up at Rufus, Kate's eyes shone with tears. She felt she owed him an explanation and quietly said as Rufus put away the brush and stood before the horse, feeding it carrots, "I am so sorry, Rufus. You must think I am crazy or neurotic. I think perhaps I'll just present the collection of photos I have taken and pass on your idea." Smiling shyly, Kate kept her head low and examined the horse's hooves.

Putting down the pail, Rufus let out a chuckle to ease the clouded tension he felt coming off Kate. "Oh, never mind, pretty lady. Lily and I understand." Winking over to the horse, he continued. "This girl knows all my secrets. I have subjected her to many moments of my own melancholy. Perhaps some other time then?" Making a gesture to move out of the stable, Rufus walked over to the door to secure Lily inside. They walked quietly outside, where the brilliant blue sky greeted them once again, and Kate quietly bid farewell to the kind man. Rufus watched Kate walk away, noticing she had a slight limp, and wondered what terrible secrets lived in her heart.

Barbara Quincy wondered what could have prompted Kate to announce that she was leaving the next morning. Trevor Miles was in the city of Port Elizabeth to meet with business associates and would not return until the next evening. She knew he would be disappointed at Kate's sudden departure, but what could she do? Kate had quickly transferred all the photos to a flash drive and left the tiny tool with Barbara for Trevor. She packed her bag and asked Barbara to call her a taxi to the airport, offering no explanation for leaving days earlier. Despite Barbara's pleas to remain, Kate graciously thanked her while pressing into her hand a sealed envelope with an apology note inside for Trevor.

CHAPTER 12

Declaration

As she flew back to Japan, Kate thought how her sudden departure would be interpreted, but it did not matter to her, as all she wanted to do was to be alone at the beach. Closing her eyes, she smelled the sea and felt the warm waters in every step she took. Her mind drifted to memories of her son at the beach and the sound of his laughter. She remembered the softness of his sandy hair and how his hazel eyes sparkled in the sun. Memories were all Kate had left of her son, and whenever she needed to embrace these, she would because nothing else in the entire world mattered.

When she arrived at the hotel, Mrs. Goto and Aiko fussed over Kate like two excited hens clucking away at the preparations for the engagement party and commenting at how busy the hotel had been. Collecting her mail, she headed to her room and changed into a flowing cotton dress. Picking through the mail, she discarded a magazine and walked out barefoot with Rey's latest letter in her hand and headed to the beach. She had tucked the envelope into her bosom and walked a while along the water's edge, enjoying the calm and gently fragrant breeze.

But Kate noticed that the tears that had threatened hours before while in South Africa would not come to surface. On the beach, she felt the calmness she needed, and that void of sorrow she had felt before was replaced with an overwhelming sense of peace. Kate understood that Oliver was with her always and that she had to channel that peace when she felt overwhelmed with grief. The tiny surf wet her dress repeatedly as she sat by the water's edge.

Reaching into her bosom, she extracted the letter and admired Rey's handwriting and noticed the return address was from a hotel in Shanghai. A sudden need to read his words made her tear open the envelope with much urgency. She closed her eyes momentarily in anticipation of what the contents of the letter might be before she started to read it.

Dear Kate,

It was truly a pleasure meeting you in Japan. I had imagined you to be kind and generous of spirit, but upon meeting you, it was clear that you are so much more. I was unhappy you could not make it to Macau. Truthfully, all my hope and happiness left when I saw your friends there without you.

I am going to take a leap of faith and let you know that I cannot stop thinking about you. Kate, your hair, your eyes, your smile, all of you is the first image that comes to mind when I awake and the last one before I go to sleep. Once I saw your face and heard your gentle and sweet voice, I knew you are the woman I want to share the rest of my life with.

I can only guess that, after my bold declaration, you won't want to continue our exchange of letters, but I would be cheating us both if I were not honest. These are words I prefer saying to you in person, but as I cannot, I am left with only my pen to share my feelings. When we said farewell at the hotel that morning, I felt like I was leaving behind a part of my heart, and it hurt like hell. As I write these words, there is an emptiness and sorrow inside me that only you can fill.

Even if you tear this letter up, you must know that I want to, have to see you again. I know that, between us, there was a mutual interest, and I ask—no, I beg you to give us a chance. Just give me an opportunity to show you my heart and then decide if this is what you want as well.

I ran around this world my entire adult life like a pirate conquering everything and everyone in sight without so much as a care to what I left behind. Upon meeting you, my life came into focus, and I finally understood what others have always told me, something about knowing when you meet "the one."

If you do not respond, then I will know your answer. But I ask of you, Kate, to please give us just one chance.

I await your response.

Forever,
Rey

Kate read the letter again and again before folding it neatly into the envelope and continued to gaze out to the sea. For the first time in a long while, her mind and heart were in agreement as she realized that it was Rey she yearned to see again. If he were right before her, Kate knew she would succumb to his love, but he was far away and giving her the space she thought she needed. Looking up, she noticed that the once-sunny skies were now veiled in fat white and gray clouds. She got up and reluctantly left the beach, knowing all too well that she would soon be drenched in a rainstorm.

Once in her room, Kate opened her laptop and typed in her browser "The Golden Trio tour schedule." The information popped up immediately. Her eyes followed down the list of cities around the world and realized they were not returning to Asia. At the present time, the tour was in Italy for two concert nights, and they were performing in Portugal in a week from tomorrow. She glanced at the envelope and noticed he wrote the letter when she traveled to South Africa.

Kate rubbed her temples and closed her laptop. She called the front desk and asked Mrs. Goto to ask the kitchen to prepare her something to eat and a tea. She also asked Mrs. Goto if she could have this meal quietly in the greenhouse, to which the jovial proprietress agreed all too happily. Kate knew Mrs. Goto's excitement came from her daughter's forthcoming marriage, and the promise of grandchildren had her overjoyed. But returning to her thoughts, she could not help but dwell on Rey's words and the urgency in his letter.

After a hot shower to soothe her nerves, Kate walked over to the greenhouse, where a meal awaited. She had her cell phone with her, and while she ate, she called James in New York. Kate wondered if perhaps James could lend some insight into the thoughts that occupied her mind. The phone rang four times before James responded enthusiastically. "Katie! You bought a phone! How are you, baby girl?"

Kate took a sip of her tea before responding. "I'm okay, I guess. 'Just got back from South Africa and the home of Trevor Miles."

"I remember the name in a profile piece in Fortune 500 sometime ago." James was directing a taxi driver to his destination as he spoke to Kate.

"He purchased some of my photographs in Japan and hired me to take shots of his property. He has a beautiful place in South Africa." She took a bite of her sandwich and sipped more tea.

"Wow, he sounds interesting. But how are you? I miss you."

"I miss you as well. Where are you going?"

"I am meeting Seby at The Campbell Apartment for our last cocktails there. It was sold, and the new owner wants to attract more of a casual crowd and renovate the place."

"Oh no! I love that place. It was such a cool lounge, and the history behind it as a speakeasy is incredible. It's so sad to see that change." Her voice held a melancholy that warmed James.

"Yeah, I know, but you see, Katie, the only constant is change. You still haven't told me how you are feeling."

She hesitated and thought of more casual talk, but Kate knew she could not pretend with James. "I called you because I'm thinking about Rey. He wrote this letter where he all but declared his love to me, and I kind of, sort of feel strongly, but I am conflicted. James, I'm confused and need some clarity."

James was silent, but internally, he was jumping out of his skin with excitement. He instinctively knew they would get along just fine and were meant to be, but instead of sharing his enthusiasm, he played it very cool. "Well, what's the harm in a dinner or even a chat over coffee? If you approach it casually, then you can get to know him a little and then decide if he is someone you want to spend more time with." James knew that, by sounding relaxed and casual, this would not frighten Kate. He was bursting and had to contain his enthusiasm, but he did ask, "So where is the globe-trotting musician now?"

"The website for the tour says they are in Italy and heading to Portugal next week." She stopped eating and contemplated what she had just said, realizing that she was probably more invested in her feelings for Rey than she wanted to admit to herself. The cloudiness in her heart forced its way in making her feel guilty and wrong to even contemplate a chance with him. Feeling a sudden rush of anxiety, she wanted to get off the phone and said hurriedly, "James, this is nuts. I can't allow this. Look, honey, have a great time and give my love to Seby. What was I thinking? We'll talk soon, okay?" Kate's tears escaped her eyes.

James firmly spoke into the phone to deter her from ending the conversation. "Stop it right now, Katie. What are you running away from exactly? We get one chance, just one, and this could be it. Oliver wants your happiness, not your sorrow. Don't let anything like guilt cloud your judgment." It broke his heart to know she was feeling this way and could use his embrace. He sank into the back seat as the cab careened down to Grand Central Terminal along Park Avenue. He waited for her sniffles to stop before he added, "I wish I were there right now to just hold you, little sis, but I'm too far away. I want you to be happy, and I know Oliver does too. Please don't lock yourself away from life. This is not what Oliver would want, and it's not healthy. Talk to me, please."

She blew her nose into the napkin and collected herself enough to respond. "He wrote those same words about *taking a leap of faith* in his letter. James, I'm just scared that maybe this is wrong because of the circumstances. I know it wasn't his fault, but he was driving that damned SUV that killed my baby!" The raw anguish in her voice tore through the phone. He thought she was over the suffering, but the pain coming across the distance was all too fresh, and he was too far away to physically comfort her.

Arriving at the Park Avenue entrance of Grand Central Terminal, James paid the fare and stepped out of the cab. He leaned against a Gap storefront window and let the sounds of the city flow through the phone. Kate heard the horns of cars and trucks navigating the busy streets and the bustling of people and felt a pang of homesickness. Silently, he hoped these sounds would make her want to return, but he also knew this would be wishful thinking. He braced himself for more tears and sent a text to Seby while waiting for Kate to speak. *Will be there in a few. Crisis with Katie. Sorry. James.*

Seby responded, *No worries. We just arrived and getting settled into a banquette. Give her my love.*

"I never had a chance to share with you, Katie, but Seby and I met Rey Aguilar here at Dizzy's a few months back," James said calmly, hoping she would not be angry that he had forgotten to tell her.

But Kate was so consumed with concern that all she asked was "Oh, and how did you guys come to be at the same place?"

James answered sincerely, knowing it was the right thing to do. "Rey sent me tickets just in appreciation for giving you the letter."

"Oh, so did you have a good time?"

"He's a very generous and kind man from what I see. Seby and I walked away thinking he was a stand-up guy. Are you upset that I met with him?"

"No, not at all, it's just that I never knew. I had breakfast with him in Tokyo, and he was really sweet and so kind. I know what you mean. He seems like an overall amazing person." She looked up at the glass ceiling and watched how the shadows of trees moved along the sides and painted a melancholy canopy. "He's also very good-looking. Come on, say it. I know you have an opinion about his looks."

"Damn, girl, he's so tall, broad shouldered, and sexy. You know I love the tall, dark, and handsome variety." Kate and James laughed into their phones as he continued. "Don't ever tell Seby because he thinks I should not get involved, but I have been hoping you two could meet and get to know each other, if for nothing else but to heal together and find some peace."

Kate spoke enthusiastically. "No worries. I asked for your advice. Therefore I dragged you into my mess. James, maybe I should come home for a little while and spend some time with you."

He refrained from shouting *yes* into the phone. Instead, he continued to play it cool. "My birthday is coming up, and this would be a wonderful gift for me to spend the holidays with you. We also have plenty of space at the loft. Please come home."

"No promises, but I will try to be there before Thanksgiving. James, I'm scared because I'm not sure if I can handle being in New York."

"I understand. How about we just take it one step at a time? No expectations and no worries. When you get here, you have us to support and love you. We can go out for dinner, movies, and remember how you and I just love our taxis. You can't deny they beat a water buffalo cart!" His laughter filled her with a deep desire to be back home.

She inhaled the heady aroma of the flowers surrounding her at the greenhouse and closed her eyes to take in the sound of the fresh rain pitter-pattering on the glass rooftop. Kate realized she had to come to terms about returning home and in giving Rey a chance. They already shared a breakfast in Tokyo, which she remembered as pleasant, so what harm could a little more food between them do? "Okay, James, I'm coming home for a little while. Are you sure I can stay with you because I can book a hotel?"

Breathing a sigh of relief and smiling up to the heavens, James kept his tone steady. "You stay with us, no excuses. Text or e-mail the details once you get it settled. You just gave me the best birthday present ever. I love you, Katie."

"I love you too and Seby as well."

"Oh yeah, he sends his love always."

"Have a cocktail on my behalf, nothing too crazy, like absinthe that will have you crawling home. Some refreshing champagne would be perfect. Go have fun and bid farewell to The Campbell Apartment. I sure will miss it."

"Champagne it is, and I will chase it with a real hard man's drink in honor of this famous speakeasy. Be strong love and come home soon."

"Bye, you crazy kid." Placing her hand over her heart, Kate could feel it beating strongly. She was clearer of mind but just as frightened of facing New York City and her feelings for Rey.

Resting in bed later that evening, Kate noticed the cell phone screen buzz with notifications of missed calls, e-mails, and texts mostly from Barbara and one voicemail from Trevor Miles. She settled into her bed to read the e-mails where Barbara thanked her for the time she spent at White Rose Cottage. The texts were about Kate leaving before she was paid for her work and prompting her to send notice of a bank to wire the amount of her earnings to. All these texts Kate marked as read, followed by listening to Trevor's voice mail. "Kate, I was surprised and unhappy to return home and not find you here. Did anyone or anything offend you while I was away? I expected to review the photographs with you and now find myself alone wondering just how to select and arrange these magnificent images. I realize that, as a host, I was lacking with all my disappearing acts due to business. For this, I humbly apologize. Please return my call. Hope you are safe and well."

The rain was now pelting the windows strongly, making the inside of her room feel eerie and dark. Reaching over, Kate turned on a bedside light. She got up to remove her clothes and took a brief, warm shower. She thought about how Trevor's voice sounded urgent and almost regretful at her hasty departure. After throwing on a long, thin T-shirt and brushing her hair, Kate nestled into the fresh linens of her plush bed and called Trevor. It was seven hours earlier in South Africa, still making it daytime for Trevor. Thinking she would leave a voice mail, she was taken aback when he came on the line with much exuberance. "Kate! Hello there. Thank you for returning my call."

"Hello, Trevor. I just need to apologize for my hasty, unwarranted departure from your home. There was nothing there that could ever bother me. I hope this did not cause confusion or concern for anyone."

"Well, I'm happy to know that it wasn't anything from here that made you leave so suddenly. Okay, so a little business and then a chat about another project. Are you up for this now?"

Kate could not imagine what Trevor could mean about another project. Curiosity made her sound enthusiastic. "Another project? I'm not sure I understand."

"First business, I owe you money for the images, and you need to help me figure out size and placement. So I want you to return to White Rose Cottage and finish the job."

She could hear him swallow down something and quickly responded, "I can do all that via e-mail, and Barbara can take the flash drive I gave her to a quality silk screen or canvas print shop and get these images ready for size and finally to a framer. As far as returning, I'm afraid that is not possible at this time, Trevor."

Trevor wanted Kate back at White Rose Cottage, as he never had an opportunity to woo and romance her. It was his intention all along after meeting her, but his opportunities were thwarted when business kept him away while she was there. He was determined not to let it happen a second time. Sounding a little desperate, he responded, "Why ever not? Kate, it would mean so much to me if you could return for a day or so. I'll send the plane to pick you up and return you safely, I promise."

Thinking quickly, Kate said calmly, "Trevor, I'm heading home for an undetermined amount of time. I haven't been back in a while and need to be near my dearest ones."

The elegant, tall man sank further into his ample leather chair. He played with a pen in his hand as he looked at the display of Kate's orchid photographs. Trevor was impressed with her work but was surprised with her beauty and casual style. Usually being confident around women made it easy for Trevor to open up quickly, but while Kate was in his home, he found himself amicable yet shy in her presence. On the night of the party when they danced, he was convinced at how she would be a perfect partner. But Trevor was experienced and cool and decided to further the conversation with more of a business approach to not put off Kate by insisting she return to White Rose Cottage. Clearing his throat, he asked, "Where exactly is home for you, Kate?"

"New York City."

"Well, that is very good. It is important to spend time with people you love. Here's an idea that just popped into my head."

"Oh?" Kate asked quietly.

"Next week, I fly to London for business. Are you agreeable to meet me in Heathrow for a chat and maybe something to munch on?"

The sound of Kate's feminine laughter caused Trevor to feel spasms of desire. He got up and walked around in his living room as she said, "That sounds like a wonderful idea, Trevor. I'll send you my flight details, and you can coordinate yours from there. Also, don't forget to let me know where to meet you in Heathrow. It will be a nice break for me after so many hours in a plane from Japan. Was there something about another project you wanted to discuss?"

Delighted at her acceptance, Trevor chimed back, "That can wait until we meet. I am looking forward to our forthcoming meet and munch."

Kate giggled again, feeling very comfortable with his humor, and wondered why she had not seen this while she was at his home. "Okay, Trevor. I will see you next week. Take care of yourself, and I will send Barbara all the details we discussed."

"Then sweet dreams, my lady, and I wish next week were tomorrow." He purred this last line sensuously through the phone and ended their conversation.

Kate's eyebrows flew up, and a small smile came upon her lips as she thought about what an eventful night this had been. She was feeling happy knowing she would see James and Seby soon and felt a tiny sense of enthusiasm at her forthcoming airport meet with Trevor. While she did not feel any sort of romantic sensations, she did appreciate his company and worldly style. Sleep finally won over, and Kate had a peaceful night without nightmares or doubts.

Several days later, Mrs. Goto reluctantly cleared Kate's hotel bill and reopened her room for other guests. Kate explained about her trip to New York and the uncertain amount of time she would be there before returning to Okinawa. Mrs. Goto called the taxi and hugged Kate tightly, followed by Aiko. With tears in her eyes, Aiko said softly, "You must be back for my wedding next summer. Promise me, Kate."

Kate wiped tears as well and said softly, "I would not miss your wedding for the world. I will return, promise."

CHAPTER 13

Touchy and Bold

The airport was busy, but Kate found Trevor at the Platinum lounge sipping on seltzer water. She thought he looked tired and a bit hungover, but when he saw her, his bleary eyes brightened up as he pulled her in for a tight hug. Releasing Kate slightly, Trevor moved in for what she thought would be a peck on the cheek; but instead, he planted a rather ardent kiss on her mouth, leaving Kate bewildered and not too pleased. She pulled away and brought her hand up to her lips and stiffened at this sudden and unwelcome move. Immediately apologizing and excusing himself, he continued doing so until Kate's eyes softened as they sat at the red leather booth. Brazenly, he raked his eyes, taking in the beauty of the woman before him.

Kate caught the desire and deflected her eyes from meeting his, all the while feeling a mixture of confusion and curiosity. While the kiss was unexpected, it was still stirring for Kate, as she had not been kissed this way since her marriage had ended over six years ago. Putting aside her own thoughts, Kate focused on Trevor, who was now so visibly nervous that beads of perspiration rimmed his hairline.

"Trevor, what was so important for us to meet here?" She placed one hand above the other and kept a respectable distance from his body to not give him reasons to misinterpret her actions.

Admiring her white dress with its print of tiny red cherries, he smiled at how Kate's femininity made his loins ache and said softly, "I feel so foolish. I asked you to meet me here to give this to you and discuss another business proposition. I hope I haven't put you off with my impulsive schoolboy behavior." Grinning sheepishly, he glanced down and drank more water.

Kate glanced at the absurdly generous check and inquired, "Don't you think that $50,000 is a bit much for taking a few photographs of flowers, a house, dogs, and horses?" She looked at him curiously and was a bit surprised at his chuckle.

"Those are not just photographs for me, Kate. They represent what I hold dearest, and you have a knack for capturing the essence of things." Taking out his phone, he quickly went to his photographs and moved closer to Kate as he scrolled down to make his point. "Look here. This is Mikey, my first Jack Russell, who is now the daddy of all those little miscreant dogs I have running amok on the property. Look closely at him. A lesser photographer would never have caught the wisdom in those eyes. Now here, look at this incredible image of Lily and Buddy. You caught them standing together admiring their baby like two proud human parents would. Their expressions are so tender, yet look how he holds his head, just like a proud man would." He closed his phone and placed it on the table as he skillfully moved in closer and wrapped his arm around Kate's shoulders. Because she was sitting at the end of the banquet, Kate had nowhere to go. He knew this and tried to quiet her overt and rising displeasure with flattery. "I have to tell you, Kate, you are a beautiful woman."

Smiling up politely at Trevor, she uttered a simple "thank you" and took a sip of her tea. Without question, Kate felt proud of herself for capturing the animals in such majestic and respectful ways. But his proximity and brazen behavior had her more than a little upset. She thought about the check he had just given her and played it as coolly as possible.

The flattery continued. "You know, Kate, you don't seem to realize or appreciate your own work. I am eager to know who you are when you are not the photographer."

Taken aback for a second time, she smiled coyly as she looked at the fashionable men and women in the exclusive airport lounge. Glancing down at her phone, she noticed she had a half hour to get to her gate for the flight to New York. Gathering her things, she said softly, "Trevor, sadly, I have to end our chat. I have to get going. Thank you for inviting me to your beautiful home. I loved the three days I spent at White Rose Cottage and for this generous check. But I have to get to my gate and haven't much time."

He quickly moved his hand over hers. "Kate, I am a businessman who's been around. What I am trying to say is that I want to see more of you. You have hit a chord in my heart that I thought would never be awakened again. Just let that thought live a little in your mind. I will escort you to your gate, and you can be off to New York." Kate stood up protesting that his escort wasn't necessary, but Trevor ignored her. He quickly moved to her right to walk her out the lounge and across Heathrow to the Delta terminal. When they arrived, he took her hand

and gallantly kissed the top of it. "Have a safe flight, Kate. Please give what I said some thought because you are very special." Without giving Kate a chance to say a word, he left quickly and walked down the corridor, never once looking back. Kate watched the spread of his broad shoulders and the elegance of his stride as he walked away, and she realized how she really knew very little about Trevor Miles and was equally smitten and disturbed with his forwardness.

New York was cold and gray, and there was an annoying drizzle making people move about faster than usual. But to Kate, it felt just perfect. She was happy to be back home and had none of those fearful feelings she thought she would have. She walked around the recently renovated loft with Seby as he showed her their large living space while James prepared his signature dish of vegetarian lasagna with garlic bread and sautéed spinach with roasted pine nuts. When they sat down to eat, they complemented their meal with a delicious and aromatic Chianti. Funky lounge music filled the space with a fun, energetic vibe. All three ate, laughed, and spent hours in good company and conversation. Afterward, they curled up and relaxed on the spacious leather sectional with cappuccinos and cheesecake.

Wasting no time, Seby pointedly said, "Okay, so now you are back, and the truth is we want you to stay. Period!" He continued gesturing dramatically toward James. "This man is always moping around about you being so far away, and frankly, I can't stand it anymore. Please stay in New York forever, sweet Kate." James gave Seby a look that could melt ice as Kate's big hazel eyes looked at them in amusement. She knew how James felt, as they were very close.

To smooth away any wrinkles Seby may have caused with his impromptu comment, she said, calculating each and every word,

"Well, I'm not sure what will happen. There's this man back in South Africa who would like to see more of me."

Seby jumped off his seat and made a little dance, shouting his delight. "Oh yeah, that's right, Katie's got a man!" James remained quietly staring into the remains of his cappuccino as Kate laughed at Seby's exuberance.

Noticing his silence, she moved closer to James while Seby went to make another cappuccino. "What say you about my news?"

James raised his eyes and sighed deeply. He then looked her straight in the eyes and spoke candidly. "South Africa is not nearby, Katie. If you and mystery man hit it off, then you will probably remain there, and I won't see you again."

Pulling her arm through his and resting her head on his shoulders, she whispered, "You know, I did a photography job for him at his estate, and he met me at the airport before I boarded the plane to New York. He kissed me, James, and you know what? I liked it. I had forgotten what it was like to be desired, and it felt really good. Can you be a little hopeful for me?"

Seby returned and bluntly asked, "What did I miss?"

James added like he was sharing the finals of a horse race, "They kissed."

In dismay, Kate looked at each of them as Seby loudly inquired, "Whoa! You guys kissed? Well, no one sleeps tonight until I get details of who this man is and that kiss." He snapped his fingers in the air before he curled his legs on the sofa and nestled in for a good story.

"There's not much to tell. He surprised me with a somewhat bold kiss, bought me tea, and walked me to my gate. I was a little surprised and uncomfortable at his brazenness, but he was really apologetic. That's all." She sipped her coffee as casually as possible, hoping Seby would drop the matter.

Both men looked at her, and James finally revealed the elephant in the room. "What about Rey Aguilar?"

Kate looked away and focused her eyes on the fireplace. Placing her cup on the coaster, she said, "Well, I never responded to his last letter, and that was a month ago, so I can assume he thinks I'm not interested."

Seby cautiously asked, "So you would not entertain something with him?" James took her hand and played with her knuckles, a gesture he always did since they were younger.

Kate relaxed and came to the quick realization that she had to be honest with herself and her family. "Yes, I might want to see him again. He is quite a gentleman and so generous and sweet."

James wondered and asked, "Was he bold like the airport guy?"

Not having compared the two men, Kate took a second to respond. She realized that both men were very interesting, but their behavior toward her was like night and day. "Actually, Rey was very caring and gentle and never made any forward advances. When I think back to our meeting and breakfast, he was respectful."

AURA POLANCO

Seby once again jumped up and sat on the edge of his seat. "Great! His band is playing at the Blue Note through the end of December. He's too fine to pass up, Kate. Isn't that right, James?"

James looked at him with very wide eyes and said firmly, "Perhaps you have had enough coffee for two days." Seby rolled his eyes as James redirected his next comment to Kate. "Katie, you owe it to yourself to just see him. He's written you and tried to contact you through me, and if I have to fib one more time about where you are in this world, I will go nuts. Let's just go to the Blue Note this weekend and see what happens."

But for Kate, the world was spinning too quickly. She removed her hand and rested it on James's knee before excusing herself to go to bed. "I have been flying since yesterday. Let's revisit this discussion tomorrow, okay?" Getting up from the sofa, she was followed by James and Seby; and in a group hug, they bid one another good night. Growing up with Kate, James understood this comment to mean that the discussion was closed.

Some weeks later, the voice mail she heard was short and to the point. "Kate, please meet me at 185 Greenwich Street on Tuesday. I purchased this property for the art gallery that will open next year. I need your artistic eye to help me finalize some decisions. Please be there, or if you prefer, call, and I will send a car."

The voice mail left her wondering about his true intentions. It was just three weeks before that he met her in Heathrow Airport. Kate wondered if this was the business proposition he had intended to share with her, but because she had to get to her flight, there was no time to chat. Kate determined she would go more out of curiosity and to look around the new World Trade Center.

Kate caught the IRT number 6 train down to Fifty-Ninth Street and transferred to the N Broadway line that took her to Chambers Street. Walking several blocks, she took in the new sights and stopped over at Dunkin' Donuts to pick up a hot chocolate and doughnut, which she wolfed down before reaching the new indoor malls at the World Trade Center. Once inside, Kate noticed how busy the place was. It was only midday, and the place was crowded. She saw the customer service kiosk and inquired about the new gallery installation. The ruddy-faced man directed her to walk down the hall and hook a left, and across from the Montblanc store was where the architects were meeting.

Before reaching the large and poorly lit construction site, she heard men laughing. After moving over the side of a large hanging blue tarp, she walked in, and the men instantly stopped their laughter and stared. Trevor boisterously, as if he were hosting one of his parties, came over and embraced Kate warmly but skipped the kiss. He introduced her to architects, a foreman, and a designer. She listened to the vision for the gallery and realized this was going to be an impressive location that would attract many important people. They were throwing around five- and six-figure amounts relating to costs and then, all at once, turned to her, rendering her speechless. "What is your projection on the size for the first installations?" asked the designer.

Before Kate could respond that she had nothing at all to do with this, the architect chimed in, "We want the height of the ceiling to be at the highest point about twenty or thirty feet. Do you plan to have structures taller than this?"

Before anyone else assumed she was involved, Kate clarified, "You had better direct these questions to Mr. Miles. I'm just here as a guest."

The project manager looked puzzled and said, "Oh, I was under the impression you were managing this gallery."

Smiling shyly, she turned and glared at Trevor for assuming she was his employee and not preparing her for the onslaught of questions. Ever the gentleman, Trevor moved by her side and, placing his hand on her shoulder, declared, "Of course, she will be the manager. She's the best in the business." Kate shrugged his hand off and stepped away.

After an hour of moving about in the construction space, Trevor suggested they have lunch. Not having plans, Kate agreed with one stipulation that she only had a half hour to spare. It was curiosity about this project that prompted her to agree, but she was not too happy with how brash Trevor was about the position he assumed she would want. They rode the elevator up to the 102nd floor of One World Trade Center. The elevators opened up to the restaurant One Dine, serving American cuisine with magnificent views of the New York City skyline. Trevor ordered the rack of lamb, and Kate kept it simple with risotto and no appetizers. One Dine, was a bustling yet small space with families, couples, tourists, and business types all eating and chatting.

Kate kept her eyes on the view, as she could feel Trevor's stare piercing through her. He sat there with a knowing smirk; the kind men wear on their faces to show they have the upper hand. Not wanting to come off insecure, Kate decided to meet his smugness head-on with questions related to the gallery. "Trevor, tell me of your vision for the gallery." She sipped more water and watched him become animated as he responded to her inquiry.

"I want this to be the best gallery in New York. I have a beautiful gallery in the Dubai Mall that opened about five years ago, and it has done quite well. Ever been to Dubai, Kate?"

"Not yet, but it's on my bucket list of places to see and experience. The gallery in Dubai, is it contemporary art or traditional?"

"I will take you there." Once again, she curdled at his forwardness. "The Dubai space changes all the time. In honor of the warm reception by the consulate general of United Arab Emirates, I devote the entire gallery to art from the Arab, Persian, and Islamic world. You will find that, for four months, there might be an exhibit of ancient Persian rugs, and in another four months, I might have installations of ruins, pottery, that sort of thing. I like to have the gallery change every quarter or six months and throw a big party for all my friends and philanthropists to come and visit." He drank down his third neat scotch and continued examining Kate's face and everything his eyes could capture, like the gentle curve of her chin and the way her sweater hugged her breasts.

When the food arrived, Kate ate gingerly while remaining focused on the view and sipping water. Trevor could bear the silence no longer and asked directly, "Kate, please say you will take this position, won't you?"

Not wanting to seem rude, Kate carefully danced around the topic. "Trevor, I cannot make this decision now because this requires much thought. I'm really just visiting in New York and have no intentions of moving back." This was not the response he wanted to hear.

Trevor summoned the waiter over and ordered another scotch. Kate noticed he was visibly bothered, and she stopped nibbling at the risotto and refolded her napkin on the table. He noticed she was done and figured she would want to leave. Moving quickly, he changed the subject and his disposition to not turn her off. Trevor had no idea that the woman sitting before him could not be bossed around. "That sounds fair to me, Kate. I'll need a decision soon, and we can arrange it so that you can be anywhere in the world and still manage the gallery. May I take you to dinner tonight?" Hoping she would say yes, he rested his hand on hers; but to his dismay, Kate moved her hand away.

She was put off by his forwardness and power, yet it was his strength of character she found interesting. There was something else about him she did not like, but she wasn't sure what it could be. "Actually, I already have plans for dinner. We will do dinner some other time. I will think your offer through and get back to you." The look of discontent returned to his face as he paid for lunch and escorted Kate to the elevators.

People excitedly went over to the observation decks, but neither of them had any interest in visiting. Instead, they stepped into the elevator and proceeded down to the ground floor. Halfway down, Trevor impulsively grabbed Kate and kissed her ardently on the mouth. He pinned her to the wall and ignored her ineffective pleas to stop. She managed to summon enough strength to move her arms between them, pushing his mouth off hers. He stepped back, and she saw that same conceited smirk on his face.

Kate glanced at the numbers and noticed they still had twenty floors to go before stating firmly, "It is obvious to me that you are accustomed to always getting your way. If you think that forcing yourself on me is a way of winning my trust and respect, then you are crazy and wrong. My answer to the gallery position is a firm *no*! And don't you ever get stupid like this with me again."

Upon hearing her angry words, Trevor moved to plea his current inebriated state as an excuse for his bad behavior. Moving toward her, Kate lifted her arm in a gesture implying to back off. Although seeing that Kate was visibly upset, Trevor pushed forward. Apologetically, he said softly, "Kate, I am very sorry for being so forward and kissing you. But you bring up these feelings in me that make me lose my mind." He put one hand to his head and continued. "I think I drank too much. Please don't make any rash decisions. I implore you to think over the job and forgive my stupid behavior. I will never be such a boar with you again."

At the sound of the medley announcing their arrival to the lobby, Kate took out $30 and threw them at Trevor's feet. The look of shock in his eyes grew to anger as she said very sharply but only for his ears to hear, as there was a crowd waiting to enter the elevator, "This is for lunch. I cannot be bought or sold." Turning and rapidly walking away, she moved across the enormous lobby and onto the plaza, where she walked to Washington Street and jumped into the first empty cab.

Trevor Miles looked ahead as people moved past him into the elevator. It was exactly Kate's feistiness and strength of character that he found so compelling that he determined to make her his one way or another.

CHAPTER 14

New York City Christmas

I t was blustery, and the air was crispy cold, but the feeling of the holidays was everywhere. Christmas decorations abounded in shops, store windows, and streetlamps. Sales were being advertised for Black Friday, the day after Thanksgiving, marking the unofficial start of the holiday shopping season.

Thanksgiving came and went, and Kate, James, and Seby celebrated with Seby's parents in Larchmont, New York. The holiday season was in full swing with the Rockefeller Center tree lighting and the feeling of cheer everywhere. At this time of the year, Fifth Avenue was teeming with people to the point where walking from one corner to the next was an exercise in patience and fortitude.

While James and Sebastian were at work, Kate busied herself with walking along Central Park; revisiting areas she had spent time with her son. The tears ran down her cheeks at times, and at other moments, a smile came upon her face. She enjoyed visiting the Central Park Zoo and the carousel, two places Oliver had enjoyed as a little boy. On a crispy and early December afternoon, she had a solo lunch at the famous Boathouse Restaurant and reminisced when she and Oliver had to be rescued from their fateful excursion on a canoe because Oliver had thrown the oars overboard. These visits to Oliver's childhood places were a test in strength, and while they were difficult, Kate felt triumphant because she realized that her fears about New York City were unfounded. Her son's life was not limited to places he had visited but rather to the lives he touched and to whom he mattered most. Kate took in a deep breath and walked out of the park, looking up to the sky through the bare branches on the trees, and smiled up at her son.

It was now mid-December, and Kate had been in New York for nearly a month. The fears had been replaced with a stronger, quieter sense of strength and calm. Being in New York was starting to become fun, and Kate discovered that she could come home again as often as she wanted. She was wrapping presents in her bedroom when James knocked on the door and asked, "May I come in?" Quickly, Kate threw a comforter over the gifts and jumped off the bed with a sheepish smile. She went over and hugged James, who kissed the top of her head. "Seby and I want to go out tonight to Iridium Jazz Club to celebrate my forever twenty-first birthday. Would you like to join us rather than stay cooped up in here like some punished child?" He pushed out his bottom lip in hopes she would take pity on him.

Smirking, she said, "Twenty-one my foot! Of course, I will join you, silly. But I should get something to wear, as I only have jeans, two sweaters, and the boots I got on sale at DSW last week."

Rolling his eyes, James rubbed his shiny, baldhead and guffawed. "You are a financially solvent woman, yet you look for sales? Really?" He threw both hands up in the air in a gesture of defeat and continued. "I have never met a woman with your sort of money who, by now, had not acquired a closet full of designer clothes and stuff."

AURA POLANCO

Kate moved away, huffing at his comment. "I'll never be one of those women who have to wear all that nonsense to feel complete. Do I need a dress for this thing tonight or what?"

Laughingly, James walked away from the door; and as he walked down the corridor, he said loud enough for her to hear, "Nope, just wear a sack of potatoes. You will look marvelous." Ignoring him, she slipped into her boots, coat, and scarf and headed out to buy an outfit.

Several hours later, Kate reappeared at the apartment as Seby and James were getting ready to go out. The music coming from the fancy and new Bang and Olufsen speakers that Seby gave to James on the occasion of his birthday rang throughout the apartment, giving the space a cool party vibe. As she finished dressing and applying a bit of makeup, Kate heard James and Seby calling out to her. "Katie, we're leaving." She emerged from the room and stood at the top of the stairs wearing an off-the-shoulder black cashmere sweater minidress and a pair of thigh-high black suede boots. Her lustrous hair fell down her back, and the claret lipgloss gave her sexy mouth a pout while her eyes looked like two marbles of varying shades of green speckled with gold. Both men just stared in awe at how stunning Kate looked. They complimented everything about the style of her clothes and at how desirable she looked. Pretending to tire of all this attention, Kate walked to the door, grabbed her coat, threw it over her shoulders, and walked out, saying dramatically, "Come along now, my peasants. Your lady awaits." They scrambled into a taxi and giggled the entire way along Fifty-Seventh Street toward Iridium Jazz Club.

The dark interiors of the club were sexy and shadowy with a smoky lounge and tables for dining. Settling into a table off to the side, the happy trio had an excellent view of the quartet playing on stage. In the middle was the dance floor with couples swaying to music. James escorted Kate onto the floor, and together, they danced to a swing piece.

When the music ended and they embraced, laughing at the fun they had just had, James felt a tap on his shoulder. Swinging around to see who had tapped him, he was surprised to find Rey. Standing slightly taller than James, he spoke with his eyes glued to Kate. "Excuse me, would you mind if I cut in for the next dance?"

James smiled, but when he turned around to look at Kate and saw the look of utter surprise on her face, he asked her, "Are you comfortable with this, Kate?" She looked at Rey's steady eyes and saw the desire in them. Those two pools of creamy caramel staring back at her had her nearly swooning, but she was certain it was from the wine and not the desire building in her loins. James asked her again. "Katie? Is this all right with you?"

Moving closer, Rey reached down for her hand and then told James while still staring at Kate, "Thank you, James, but I have this." In a graceful manner, he pulled Kate closer and swayed to the music as James walked away, a Cheshire cat grin plastered on his face. They danced slowly together and looked equally impressive in each other's arms.

What is it about you, Rey, which makes me feel like I'm the only woman alive? I want your arms always embracing me yet— Kate's thoughts were interrupted when she felt Rey move his hand further down to rest just above her bottom. The warmth that entered her body from his hand on her back gave her that sensation she had felt very few times in all her life, and it was the feeling of safety. They looked into each other's eyes, and without the need for words, they knew that whatever existed between them was bigger than either one could control.

Feeling that she should say something, Kate whispered, "I got your letter several months ago." To her surprise, he said nothing but continued to look at her, making her wonder if he had heard her comment. "Rey, did you hear me? I said—"

He spoke softly yet with a little indignation seeping through. "So you did read my letter where I spilled out my guts about how I feel about you. As you did not respond then, I guess this is now just a friendly little dance and nothing more for you, right?" Blushing and feeling like she had been slapped across the face, Kate said nothing but felt a desire to apologize and explain yet could not find the words.

The music stopped, and Kate did not move. Another song started to play, but this time, they did not dance. Rey saw a mixture of fear and desire in her eyes. His hands came up to her face, and her arms embraced him back, and all that pent-up desire spilled out in the form of a kiss. As couples around them danced and pretended not to notice, they stood still and kissed ardently. They continued doing so until they realized how they must appear.

Coming apart, he saw passion in her eyes and she raw emotion in his with enough tension to make his jaw twitch. They calmly moved around other couples to reach her table, where James instinctively knew to reach out with her coat and clutch and hand them to Rey. She kissed James and waved good-bye to Seby and walked out of the club and into a cab that drove them to Rey's place. In the taxi, he held her hand tightly like a man afraid of losing something very precious to him.

He thought nervously, *What if she bolts and wants nothing to do with me? I know she's the one, but there's so much baggage on both our shoulders coming into this that can destroy it before it even begins.*

His warm hand remained firmly wrapped around hers, but she kept her body closely against the door while her heart raced. She kept her eyes focused on the lights and scenes of the night to help remain still. Kate was scared of how strangely close she felt to this man. She kept fighting with her memory of how he was the driver that fateful afternoon that shattered her world. But her heart softened with the warmth of his body and the kiss that seemed to erase so many of these insecurities.

Closing her eyes, she prayed for the peace she needed. *God, please guide me to the right decision. I know what I feel for Rey, but what about what happened to Oliver because of him? I'm not blaming him. I know it was an accident, but could this, should this be? Is it right for me to be here?*

The internal struggle made her queasy and caused a small headache to erupt on one side of her head. She rubbed her right temple, and Rey noticed how anxious she looked. He squeezed her hand gently and then lifted it and brushed it along his cheek and kissed the top before returning it to her lap. Catching each other's eyes, they saw the unease that lived behind their looks, and their bodies moved closer together. Releasing her hand, Rey put his arm around her shoulders as she rested the kissed hand upon his thigh. The feeling was one of solidarity in their apprehension at what they were about to start and the extraordinary ways this could alter their lives.

After paying the fare, Rey walked Kate over to the door of his apartment. Before he turned the key in the lock, a deep guttural growl came from the other side of the door, making Kate jump back. Rey said calmly, "When you come in, remain very calm. Do not touch or make eye contact. Captain is a full-grown Rottweiler but a teddy bear. He has to capture your scent and get to know you first, and before you know it, he will be showing you his belly and acting like a goofy gigantic baby. Don't be afraid. I won't let anything happen to you. I promise." He bent down and kissed her partly opened lips as she braced herself for the massive dog that stood behind the door.

Captain circled, sniffed, barked, and finally rested next to Kate when she sat on the edge of the sofa. Rey prepared drinks and commanded Captain to go to his bed, where Rey had left a dental stick. The obedient dog, within seconds, had chewed up his treat, and as if he understood this meant bedtime, he stretched his body out and started snoring.

Taking the drink from Rey, Kate finally took a deep breath and felt a calm and warmth travel throughout her body. Settling next to her, Rey remained with enough distance for them to chat amicably without the pressure of their mounting sexual interests. He glanced over and saw her staring down at her drink in quiet contemplation. "A penny for your thoughts," he asked. She chuckled and sipped the scotch, causing her to grimace and Rey to laugh. "You are not much of a drinker, are you?"

She looked over shyly. "No, I'm not a drinker at all. I love champagne, but it gives me a headache. This scotch will kill me, and two glasses of wine will put me to sleep. I'm a pathetic excuse for a party girl," she concluded shyly.

Putting down both their drinks, he took her hands in his and, as he bore into the eyes he was certain he could never live without, said, "Well, that's a good thing because, you see, I'm not interested in party girls. I want what is real and solid, like you, Kate." Reaching over, he kissed her gently on the lips. "Are you sure this, being here with me is okay with you? Because I'm fine if all we do is talk or just sit here listening to each other breathe. Just being with you is enough for me."

She saw fire and concern in his eyes and understood that her insecurities about what brought them together were haunting him as well. She caressed the side of his cheek with her finger and whispered, "I don't blame you, but I feel guilt at being here in your home and in having kissed you." They sat in silence.

Rey reached over for his drink and downed it in one gulp. They sat and listened while Charlie Parker's "Yardbird Suite" played on Rey's turntable. It was several more moments in silence before Rey spoke up. "I'm sorry. I know what you mean, and perhaps you prefer to go home. I don't want you to feel any strangeness or guilt if you are with me. You have to be certain before you take the next step." She looked at his face and wasn't certain what she needed to find. His interpretation of how she looked at him was of confusion, and he understood she was not ready. For Rey, he believed that Kate's body was ready but not her mind. It was not his way to take advantage of a woman and resigned himself to nothing more.

Battling with herself, she moved closer to him and allowed her body to feel his warmth. He remained still and let her pace herself. Looking up to Rey, she whispered, "Rey, I don't know what I have to feel to be okay with us, but I know that I want you. I am okay with this."

AURA POLANCO

The green light shone brightly as he unleashed his emotions and the urgency of his desire. His arms encircled her, and he kissed her ardently without constraints and formality as his hands moved freely over her dress and breasts and ran down her legs. Barely pulling away, he uttered, "Kate, come with me." Rising from the sofa, he led her upstairs to his bedroom, where they undressed each other with deliberate care and enthusiasm. Into the early hours of the morning, they laughed and cried as they explored each other and released the anxieties that had grown between them. When emotional and physical exhaustion took over, they lay together wrapped in each other's arms and slept soundly.

Kate awoke and slipped out of bed. She quietly washed her face and wrapped herself up in Rey's robe that hung behind the bathroom door. For a moment, she inhaled Rey's scent that lingered on his robe and smiled, recalling their ardor the night before and how she was filled with a peaceful hope for her future. Standing at the bathroom door, she took in the six-foot-four frame of this massive man and grew warm remembering how his experienced hands and body made love to her. Creeping slowly back into bed, she nestled on his shoulder; and immediately, his body responded to her touch, arousing and igniting their passions once again.

Captain was scratching and whining at the bedroom door. The sounds of a morning in New York City were coming through the closed windows. Rey kissed Kate's cheek, slipped out of bed, and stretched languorously, giving her a view of the red scars running down the length of his back and reminding her of her own ugly ones on her leg. She pushed those thoughts aside and closed her eyes. Quickly, he threw clothing on and took Captain out for a walk.

It was a cold day, and at seven in the morning, people bustled around, heading to work. His head was still fuzzy with sleep, but the memories from last night were crystal clear. Rey had to push thoughts of Kate out of his mind because of the danger of his arousal. His leather jacket and jeans would be poor coverage if he gave way to daydreaming about how overjoyed he was at the touch, feel, and smell of this incredible woman. Since he first set eyes upon her, he had imagined what it would be like to make love to Kate. Rather than risk a painful and embarrassing moment out on the street with an uncontrollable erection, he focused on Captain as he tinkled all over the sidewalks and whatever grass he could find. When he had relieved himself, the grateful dog looked up and pulled Rey back in the direction of the apartment. As they got closer to home, he allowed his thoughts about Kate to return and knew he was in trouble. After two decades of endless fun and one-night stands, he was hungry for the love he felt with Kate. One night with Kate had erased years of empty, emotionless sex and replaced it with a peace and sense of joy he had never experienced with another woman.

The aroma of coffee invaded his nose before he reached the door. Kate was making coffee in his home, and that act gave him enormous pleasure. He found her standing by the window dressed in his robe, holding a coffee cup, and looking out to the street and rooftops. Smiling at him and melting his heart, she handed him a cup of coffee. Together they stood there silently looking out the window until Captain once again demanded Rey's attention.

"Okay, okay. Relax, Captain." Rey dutifully poured cold freshwater into a large water bowl for the dog, which noisily and quickly lapped it up. In the other bowl, Rey emptied three cups of kibble and poured more water into the now-empty bowl. He rubbed his dog's head and went to wash up by the kitchen sink.

Kate noticed how he moved gingerly and also saw him wince from the pain he felt whenever he bent down or turned too suddenly. The careful movements belied his powerful and muscular physique. Going over to him, she wrapped her arms around his wide torso and squeezed tightly. He returned the hug and felt himself sinking into the warmth of her body. How he wished he could carry her back upstairs as he did many other women throughout his life. Sensing something was off, Kate looked up at Rey. "Did I hug you too tightly?" She took in the soft cocoa-colored eyes, strong jaw, and aquiline nose.

Moving his head side to side, he said, "I feel that, with you, I can finally just be myself, so here it goes. I just wish I could pick you up and carry you back to my bed, but my back won't sustain the weight."

When Kate laughed, her eyes shone. She reached up and kissed Rey's mouth. She tickled him with her tongue and playfully bit his bottom lip. Pulling away, she whispered, "You think those Hollywood movie moments is what I crave? No, silly, it doesn't matter to me. I saw the awful scars on your back, Rey. Did you see mine?" Unceremoniously, she pulled back his robe to reveal her scarred left leg. The now-brown wound moved along the length of her tibia, and a shorter one ran halfway up her thigh.

He knitted his brows in guilt, and with regret in his voice, he uttered, "You can thank me for that. I'm so sorry, Kate."

She pressed her head against his chest and said softly, "I know you are. Let's not ruin our time together by thinking about that. I had not been made love to in years and years, and you have awakened a ravenous giant." Kate's brazenness had him roaring with laughter as he led her back upstairs, where they rediscovered each other with abandonment and in the light of day.

The days leading up to Christmas were busy and special for everyone. Rey had two shows most evenings and spent the better part of his days in rehearsals. His bandmates chatted among themselves about how happy and content Rey appeared. He played better music and laughed at jokes, and the brooding, sarcastic man they loved to hate was hopefully gone forever. They had no idea that these fortuitous changes in Rey were because of Kate. He was very private and moody, and he wanted to keep his personal world to himself. Rey knew how any tiny bit of information could be leaked out into numerous forms of social media, and make his life a living hell of nosy inquiries and paparazzi. He did not want to put Kate through anything like that and compromise their budding relationship.

Kate, on the other hand, had become quite a shopper. She purchased pretty outfits and accessories, much to the delight of James and Seby. On Christmas Day, they sat together around the enormous tree they had decorated and exchanged gifts. It had been a little over a week since her encounters with Rey, and for the most part, she was taxiing between James and Seby's apartment and Rey's. They did not dare ask questions because they knew she would talk about it when she was ready, and on this very day, she was.

"I believe I love this man," Kate shared. Seby nearly spilled the hot cocoa he was drinking from Kate's sudden declaration.

James looked her seriously in the eyes. He wasted no time and asked, "Really, Kate? Why do you say this? It has only been one week."

Seby punched James playfully in the arm and said loudly, "Counsel, this is downtime, please. You are not in a courtroom, so hang up your law degree."

Laughingly, Kate responded, "Actually, this man first caught my attention in the letters he wrote, and then we met in Tokyo, and I knew he was special, but it was too soon for me. Maybe it's still wrong of me to pursue this, but it feels so right." She returned to her cocoa and continued when neither man offered a response. "We complement each other in many ways and like so many of the same things. When I am with Rey, I feel beautiful, and safe."

Seby curled up next to her and needed to ask, "So, how is it with him?"

James yelled out his name. "Seby!" Seby cut him a look and returned his gaze upon Kate.

Kate continued. "He is unbelievable. I never had so much fun or felt so happy." Seby reached over and hugged Kate, but James looked at her cautiously.

James finally offered his take on this budding romance. "Okay, I'm happy for you but here's the thing. I really like Rey, but I love you. Just go slowly, get to know him, and maybe pursue the photography to keep yourself busy in your own work."

She smiled at his advice and loved James deeply for his concern. "I promise, I won't move in with him or forget myself in the fog of what we have. I know what you mean, James."

Seby asked with excitement, "So does this mean you are staying in New York?"

Kate calculated the question. "I suppose I am, but I want a place of my own far from the Upper West Side. In fact, I prefer the Tribeca or SoHo areas."

With eyebrows raised, James asked, "Where does he live?"

"He lives in the West Village, so Tribeca and SoHo are very nearby," Kate offered as she played with her holiday-themed red mug, knowing all too well that James was worried she was moving too quickly. "James, I'm not going to lose my head. I'm in my mid-thirties, not my teens." He came over, kissed the top of her head, and walked into the kitchen.

Seby asked her curiously, "He's so uptight! Has he always been this way with you?"

Kate smiled shyly. "Yes, ever since we were little kids, we have looked after each other. He's my brother, and I'm his sister. I understand him. It's just that he can be intense." She uncurled her legs from under her and stretched them before wincing at the cramp that traveled through her leg. Glancing at the clock over the fireplace, she quickly picked up wrapping paper, with Seby joining in, while James placed breakfast dishes into the dishwasher.

AURA POLANCO

Kate ran up to her room, where she showered and dressed in jeans, boots, and a cozy sweater, and ran out the door to hail a cab over to Rey's apartment. While the taxi moved south along Ninth Avenue, she received a text from Rey informing her that they were at the Leroy Street dog run. She hurried over while pulling on her gloves and wrapping the scarf closer around her throat. From one block away, she made out Captain's massive body running around with other dogs. As she walked closer, she saw Rey sitting on one of the benches in a peacoat while talking on the phone. When he saw her walking toward him, a huge smile erupted on his face. He put the phone in his pocket and walked over to sweep her into his arms. Captain came barreling across the park and nearly knocked both of them down in his efforts to welcome Kate. She very patiently and lovingly played with his ears, and to Rey's surprise, she took the powerful head into her hands and planted a kiss on the dog's forehead, causing Captain to jump around and come to stand by her side.

The air was icy as they walked hurriedly to the warmth of his apartment. Once inside, Rey kissed Kate longingly. They remained in an embrace for quite some time until his phone rang again. "My goodness, I saw you on the phone as I approached you at the park," Kate exclaimed, annoyed that the ringing intruded upon their moment.

"Well, in a minute, I'll tell you why it's been ringing off the hook," Rey hurriedly said as he moved away to answer the phone, and immediately, Kate knew it had to be about the band because Rey spoke differently when in conversation with his friends. He was courser and more street and let loose with expletives that he never used when in conversation with her.

She busied herself by filling Captain's water bowl and his food dish with dry kibble. The dog was in love with Kate, and she too enjoyed the company of the gentle giant. Curling up along the window seat, Kate checked her phone as she waited for Rey to finish the conversation. Watching him emerge from the office made her smile at how handsome he was. She was awestruck at his height and build, but it was his sensuous mouth and seductive eyes framed by thick dark lashes that stirred her emotions. It also did not hurt that he had dark wavy hair that grazed his shoulders.

After looking over at Captain eating in the kitchen, he leaned over and kissed Kate's cheek and sat next to her on the leather-padded window seat. "Kate, my love, the tour is booked for next year."

"Is that what you were on the phone about?"

"Yes, but here's the thing. I want you there with me. I can't be away for four months without you."

"I'm too old to be a groupie, love." She followed this with laughter.

"You are not my groupie or the band's. You are my muse and lady. What plans do you have here in New York?"

She glanced out the window and remembered what she promised James about not losing herself in a man. "Rey, I don't want to follow you around like a puppy. I will remain in New York and be here when you return."

Rey was not pleased with her response, but he was also too mature and careful to push the issue. Usually, women threw themselves on him and wanted to hang around like leeches. This was new territory

AURA POLANCO

for Rey, as he was unaccustomed to this kind of strength in a woman. He remained silent, which prompted her to kick him playfully on the tip of his boot. Looking up at her, he smiled sadly and shared, "That won't work, baby. If I can't see you all the time, then that will play with my head. Why exactly can't we find a middle ground? Remain in New York if you like, but will you meet me in different cities where we play?"

She thought about this and moved over to embrace him. "That I might be inclined to do. Where exactly will you be?"

Rey started kissing her face, and in between each kiss, he said, "The tour takes us through, Argentina, Brazil, Chile, and Mexico." Here he ended by devouring her mouth, causing a warm pool of desire to settle between her legs.

Seductively, she spoke in a husky voice. "Then we should go practice our tango moves if we are meeting in Buenos Aires. Come, big boy, show me what you got." His eyes opened wide as he allowed Kate to lead him up the stairs to his bed. He was rendered speechless as she removed his clothing and took his manhood in her mouth and turned him into a mound of putty.

Later that day, they exchanged Christmas gifts. Kate gave him a silk robe, which he liked very much. When he gave her a small rectangular jewelry box, she nervously opened it. Inside was a rolo-link platinum bracelet with an angel wings charm encrusted in diamonds. In the center of the charm, Rey had the jeweler engrave the letter O for Oliver. Kate's eyes filled with tears at the sensitive and thoughtful gift. He fastened it to her wrist and kissed her tears away. No words were uttered about the gift because none were needed.

CHAPTER 15

New Year's Eve

Bringing in the New Year at Blue Note Jazz Club with Seby, James, and the Golden Trio jazz band was enticing and fun for all. Rey played his heart out, much to the delight of the crowd, especially his band mates. On stage, he was filled with energy and happiness, and it showed in his interaction with the audience. Rey told jokes and poked fun at his band mates. The audience was having a fantastic time. But the star of the evening was Kate. She wore a gold dress encrusted in tiny sequins, making her eyes shine and skin shimmer with extraordinary allure. The crowded venue was buzzing with people and excitement when The Golden Trio played with other famous musicians. The dancing and partying ensued as the Grammy Award–winning band played enthusiastically.

Kate was approached by a tall blond woman in her mid-twenties in the vanity area of the restroom. She applied fresh lipstick as she said hello to Kate. "You are Kate, correct?" asked the woman with an accent. The woman slanted her big soft brown eyes in the direction of Kate as she adjusted the bosom of her dress.

"Yes, I am. Do I know you?"

She responded casually as she glanced at Kate. "No, but we both know Rey. He is my boyfriend for some years now. So I want to know why you are hanging around my boyfriend." She replaced her lipstick in her clutch and stared down to tower over Kate.

Kate glared at the woman and said calmly, "Oh really? Huh, you don't look like his type, but if you insist, then he's all yours, buttercup. I don't fight over a cock, so I hope this calms your nerves." She turned and exited the bathroom, leaving the blonde somewhat surprised but pleased. Kate marched herself through the crowd and up to the mezzanine to the musicians' room to get her coat and then returned to the table to tell James she was leaving.

Trevor Miles was surrounded by people at the deeply crowded bar, trying to put in an order for a neat scotch and failing because of the overwhelming decibel of the live music mixed with laughter and the predictable New Year's Eve revelry. He quit trying and gently pushed his way away from the bar and wondered how this enormous crowd was not a fire code violation. His height helped him to spot Kate as she stood with two other men and looked like she was having a deep conversation. It took several more minutes before he finally stood behind her and tapped her shoulder, causing her to turn and call out his name in surprise. Kate introduced both Seby and James to Trevor, as they exchanged handshakes and good wishes for the New Year. He leaned in closely to talk with Kate and put his hands on her bare shoulders, causing her to step back. Although on stage, Rey saw the stranger talking and touching Kate and nearly missed a note, but he refocused and continued with the performance. Kate barely heard what Trevor said but caught something about needing to talk to her. She whispered in James's ear, "I'm just stepping outside to hear what he wants and then getting into a taxi."

James responded with, "I'm coming."

Shaking her head, she whispered again, "No need, it's okay." Giving James a squeeze on the arm, she pointed to the front door, and Trevor maneuvered them through the crowd like a charging bull.

James looked after them and then on stage to catch Rey staring at him with a look of confusion on his face. He shrugged to Rey and pointed to the blonde, who was erratically moving to the music. Immediately, Rey guessed at what had transpired. Looking impatiently over at Rafa, who had a piano solo, he was thinking of a way to get off the stage when Paco hit his drums to begin his solo, and he knew he was stuck in his current position until the end of the number.

Upon reaching the icy street, Trevor surprised Kate with a long embrace but refrained from doing more. Again, Kate bristled and went to say how she found this to be rude when he cut her off. "You must be wondering why I'm here. Can we go to that coffee shop over there?" He pointed across the street where there was a small diner next to a tobacco store displaying an impressive variety of bongs.

The low temperatures were frigid and biting, causing Trevor to cross his hands over his chest, and soon Kate could barely feel her fingers and toes. Chuckling lightly, she ignored his request and asked, "How did you know where to find me?"

He answered very casually, "Barbara told me. She said she called to wish you a merry Christmas, and you girls chatted about New Year's plans. I hope I haven't stepped over the line."

Stomping her feet on the ground to keep from becoming numb, she responded, "Well, if I recall, the last time we met you were an asshole. As a result, you are not someone I hold in high esteem. And I'm not going anywhere with you so quickly share what you need to say." Trevor thought how much he desired to pull her into his arms but painfully kept from doing anything that might remind Kate of recent impulsive antics. "Yes, I am sorry for that. Okay, Kate, here it goes. I want you to be the director of the gallery. I know I was an ass, but I promise you that I will never behave this way again."

Heading a gallery in New York City was indeed an intriguing idea, but Kate knew what her response must be. "Thank you, and I'm flattered, but my answer must be no."

Not completely defeated, Trevor pushed a little harder. "Please, do not give me a response just yet. I'll return to London in several hours. Take a few days and get back to me directly." He reached into his wallet for a business card and handed it over to Kate's shivering hand. "Thank you, Kate, for hearing me out. I have missed you very much and hope your response will be affirmative."

At that moment, Rey appeared at the front door with James and Seby. He witnessed Kate and Trevor saying good-bye and Kate's hand in his. She turned to find Rey staring straight at the other man. They were eye to eye, and both looked like two lions ready to pounce. Recognizing Rey from the poster advertising the band, Trevor inferred immediately that this man was significant to Kate from the way Rey glared at him. Rather than be defensive, Trevor played the part of a fan and offered a handshake. "Rey Aguilar, what a pleasure." After shaking hands rather firmly, Rey pulled in Kate for an embrace, but she resisted, surprising him.

Rey asked politely, "Thank you, and you are?"

Kate chimed in, as she was eager to end the stare-down, "This is Trevor Miles. He hired me for a job at his estate in South Africa."

Rey recalled then that this man was the reason for her not accompanying her friends to Macau. "I see. Let's get you inside, my love, before you get sick. Good night, Mr. Miles, and a happy New Year to you."

He made to turn when Trevor said the same thing to Rey and added, "Remember, Kate, think about my offer and call me soon."

Kate did not enter behind Rey; instead, she walked to the curb to hail a cab with Seby and James by her side. Rey caught up to them and asked, surprised, "What's going on here? Where are all of you going?"

James and Seby remained silent as Kate said sharply, "You needed to be real with me, Rey, and you blew it by not telling me about your bimbo girlfriend. You know the giant chick inside who moves with no rhythm? She told me in the bathroom that you two were a thing and that I should move aside."

Rey rolled his eyes and laughed, aggravating Kate and causing her to look at him in shock. "That's Tatiana Newman, and I swear she is nothing to me, and I will prove it you. And in front of James and Seby, I will confess without shame that, before the accident, she and I were friends with benefits. But since that day, I have been with no other woman besides you. Please, let's go back inside, and I promise all this will be straightened out."

Moving back inside, Rey looked around and spotted Tatiana. He told Kate to wait in the musicians' lounge for him and asked James to escort Tatiana back to this same room where they were waiting.

Seby tagged along because he would not miss out on the juicy scene that was certain to unravel. When Tatiana entered the room, she was met with Kate and Rey. Rey did not hold back and demanded clarification. "Tatiana, tell the truth to Kate."

The tall woman looked around at the faces before her and felt ambushed. Instead of telling the truth, she broke out in tears and wailed. "Rey, I have waited so long for you. You always throw me aside like a rag, and I'm left with nothing. We had great sex, and you know I love you like nobody else can."

Rey sighed and handed her his handkerchief, which she took and, after drying her tears, blew into. He said, "I was always clear of my intentions with you, and you were never my girlfriend. If you loved me so much as you say, then you would have been there during my darkest days when I was recovering. Where were you, Tatiana? You were in Brazil and Europe in all the clubs with new friends. I saw you in news reports. No, Tatiana, we were just friends who enjoyed each other's company, so back off and don't approach me or Kate ever again." The sniffling blonde gave Kate a look that could kill and walked away in a huff after throwing the handkerchief back at Rey.

James jumped in and said, "Seby, let's leave these two alone. We'll be downstairs. The New Year will be here in minutes, and I need a strong drink."

Rey closed the door to the small room and leaned in for a kiss. It was a gentle one because his lips were still numb from playing the sax for two sets. Although still annoyed, Kate knew the other woman was a silly girl from Rey's past. After the soft kiss, Trevor popped into Kate's head, and she realized where the true seed of her annoyance was. She wasn't angry with Rey or with anyone in his past; it was with Trevor for throwing out her professional business like ammunition to incite Rey. She knew a cockfight when she saw one and recalled the look of suspicion on Rey's face. In the short time they had been together, she already knew Rey had a strong character with a temper to match and that he was an all-or-nothing kind of man.

As if he could read her mind, Rey asked, "So what was that about outside?"

Restlessly, she responded, "I told you already." He stood still waiting for more while looking down at Kate with no expression on his face except his questioning eyes. Leaning in for a hug, she shared everything with him. "Trevor Miles is the South African businessman who hired me to photograph his estate. He asked me to be the art director for a gallery he plans to open in New York."

Moving away from Kate, he went for his saxophone case and placed Angie inside with care. Standing tall, he looked Kate straight in the face. "He's made quite a name for himself as a businessman and also as an international millionaire playboy. He wants more, Kate. Perhaps you can't see it, but as a man, I see it clearly."

Kate stood there wondering what to say next and thought about the impromptu kiss Trevor gave her at the airport and again in the elevator at One World Trade Center. She wondered what would have happened if she had responded in kind. Despite all her ruminations, she could not help but feel a smoldering anger build within her because she believed her integrity was in question. Turning to open the door, he reached out and caught her arm. "I'm not upset with you."

Kate gave Rey a sharp look of disbelief and pulled her arm away. Her eyes flashed at him as she calmly and calculatingly reminded him, "Why would you have to be upset with me? I had a brief conversation with another man relating to work, and you don't think I am grounded enough to know who I am? Rey, I'm a grown woman with my integrity intact. Don't ever question this again. I'm going over to James and Seby's tonight." Rey made to come toward her, but she held up her hand. "No, we'll talk later. Happy New Year." She turned and opened the door, leaving Rey seething in fury at how the New Year started.

CHAPTER 16

Tiffany's and a Pied-à-Terre

D ays later, Kate walked around visiting apartments with her real estate agent. Her list of wants and deal breakers was simple. The apartment had to be nowhere near the Upper West Side, a school, or a playground. She did not want to be tormented with the sound of children playing and chatting. Also, the Upper West Side was where she had lived with Oliver and where her former husband resided with his new wife and daughter. Kate wanted a spacious bedroom, room for an office, one-and-a-half bath, with a balcony, and lots of natural light. She set the budget firmly at $900,000 in the neighborhood of Chelsea. After viewing several spaces, she signed the contract on a modern, roomy, and sunny SoHo apartment in a building with a twenty-four-hour concierge. She had views of the river and a distant view of the skyline. This would be Kate's New York pied-à-terre, a place she could call her own.

Establishing new roots in New York City made Kate evaluate the past two years of her life since the tragedy of losing Oliver. She thought about how she shifted around in Japan, where the quiet and consistent lull of the ocean helped her heal her wounds and some of her emotional anguish. It was at the beach that she came to terms with letting go of Oliver. Going to South Africa for those three days reminded her of what a gloriously beautiful world she lived in. She loved being a photographer and marveled at the majesty and grandeur of White Rose Cottage and its beautiful animals and the elegance of its staff. But Kate realized that it was returning to New York, where she was reminded of the meaning of family and friends and, more importantly, of why sometimes taking a leap of faith was exactly what the heart needed to heal. She was in love with Rey Aguilar and wanted this experience to fill her life completely. Feeling hopeful and happy, she called him. Since the New Year, he had only two aloof phone calls from Kate and endless excuses why she could not meet him. Not quite understanding what he was being blamed for, he decided to give Kate the space she needed and wait. There were no other gigs lined up until the tour started in early March, giving Rey two months to properly romance Kate. After a brief phone call, they decided to meet at Aldea, a Portuguese Mediterranean restaurant, that evening at seven to celebrate her new apartment and the excellent reviews the trio received after their engagement at the Blue Note.

The Tiffany flagship store on Fifth Avenue and Fifty-Seventh Street was quiet with several Asian and European tourists looking at jewelry. Rey walked in, and the saleswoman nearest the door looked him up and down and walked over to welcome him, but her efforts were thwarted by a sharply dressed man. Rey wasted no time in stating, "This is confidential. One leak, and there will be problems. Understood?" No smiles were exchanged, but the employee of the store knew exactly how to proceed with ultimate discretion. He escorted Rey through a private room and invited him to sit at a comfortable seat. Quietly rejecting all drinks offered to him, he described what he wanted. "Classy woman, simple ring, and the finest diamond. Platinum setting for a three-carat cushion cut diamond." The diamond expert agreed and said it would be arranged.

In a hushed tone, the manager of the store spoke into a phone, and an older man arrived posthaste with a locked box and armed security personnel. On a black velvet pad, he displayed several diamonds. Each stone had a detailed explanation and a Tiffany certification. Selecting the most perfect of all, Rey signed papers and proceeded to leave. Back on the street, he walked up Fifth Avenue feeling empowered after ordering the stunning stone and custom-made, engraved setting that would be ready in six weeks.

James and Seby were packing for a short vacation in Martinique, and their apartment was abuzz with drama, music, and laughter. Kate dressed in a pair of skinny jeans, boots, and a sexy off-the-shoulder sweater in the guest room, as her apartment was not yet ready. Her makeup was light, but she did paint her lips in a deep mauve, which brought out the gold in her eyes and looked beautiful against her pale skin and flowing dark hair. Looking closely into the mirror, Kate thought she looked younger and even happier than she ever had. The last thought knitted her brows, but she quickly erased it and ran out to hail a cab.

Rey was already at the restaurant, waiting by the bar. When he saw her enter, he moved swiftly over and embraced her like a man holding on to a lifeboat. Her response was the same as she ran her gloved hands through the back of his longer and wavy hair. Their lips touched and quivered for more, but they pulled apart. Simultaneously, they uttered, "I'm sorry," and just stared into each other's eyes filled with love and lust. They sat in a quiet corner, ordered wine, held hands, and said nothing for a long while.

Rey and Kate were in love. They had fallen hard, and after a week of not seeing each other, their desires were practically uncontrollable. When dinner was served, Kate chatted about the apartment as Rey listened. He barely touched the monkfish before him because he was entranced with how luscious and seductive she looked. He was imagining all the things he wanted to do to her and didn't worry at his own arousal, as he was sitting and hidden by the long tablecloth and napkin. Kate noticed the look of lust in his eyes, stopped talking, and put her fork down. They stared for what seemed an eternity. She said, "You have barely touched your dinner."

He responded with yearning, "You are all the food I want." After summoning the waiter, he paid for the dinner, and they quietly slipped away into a cab and headed to his apartment.

After she kissed and hugged Captain, Rey's hands were all over her. In the living room, they undressed and devoured each other like two starving people. Rey kept calling her name and saying how much he loved her. His fervor was such that it completely consumed Kate as she gave way to being lost in the magic of their passion. The outside world ceased to exist as they floated in their personal bubble of ecstasy. After they were sated and could go no further, they lay in an embrace on the area rug, panting and perspiring. Pulling faux fur throws off the sofa and a chair, they covered their nakedness and slept entwined until the morning.

Weeks later, on a blustery late February day, Rey presented Kate with the three-carat Tiffany diamond. They were walking Captain in new snow that had fallen overnight in the city. Central Park looked like out of a fairy tale, and Rey used this time to bend down on his right knee and ask Kate to be his wife. She was emotional at the sheer beauty of the moment and quietly sent a thank-you up to God for all this love. His eyes watered because she said, "Yes!"

Embracing against the chill in the air, they walked along the winding road leading to Cherry Hill, where Rey had arranged a horse drawn carriage with all its finery to wait for them. Captain was stunned at the size of the horse, but after barking loudly, he jumped into the carriage and settled on the banquet. Rey and Kate nestled on the leather bench opposite Captain and placed the wool throw over their legs. This moment was completely unexpected for Kate and one of much emotion. She thought back to the significant events in her life, such as the birth of her son, and this was the second best. The carriage moved slowly with the horse's hooves clopping along and leaving prints on the fallen snow. This enchanted little world was where Kate and Rey could express their love in the company of nature. Words were completely unnecessary and seemed intrusive in the peace and romance of the moment.

That evening, they gathered in Rey's apartment those nearest to them to announce their engagement. The music played, and the champagne flowed. Rafa chided Rey on finally being hooked, and Paco patted him on the back, affirming this being the best decision of his life.

After the evening winded down, Kate heard her phone ringing in her bag. She saw it was Trevor Miles and turned it off, preferring he leave a message and not disturb her joy. The next morning, she went to hear her messages and remembered Trevor had called. Scribbling a quick message on a pad for Rey, Kate left the apartment and headed back to her brother's place. She had to think in a space of peace with no dog or her man around to meddle in or distract her decisions. A huge part of Kate knew that taking this job was, one, unnecessary and, two, dangerous because of Trevor and his touchy-feely hands, but her selfish side told her to go with the flow and take the position. She figured it would lead to more photography jobs and high-powered clientele. Kate had always worked, and sitting around or having lunch with friends was not her idea of a life. She wanted to be recognized for her talent, and directing this gallery would do just that.

She listened to the message as she prepared for a shower. "Kate, hope you are well. Why have you not called me? Just give me a ring about the idea of you being the art director for the gallery. It opens soon, and I must have art installations organized well before that for the grand opening. Call me, please."

Not knowing where in the world Trevor was, she took a chance and called. He was having lunch in London when he saw her name pop up on his screen. "Kate, my darling, how good of you to call. I was starting to get worried."

"Hello, Trevor. I have been busy buying an apartment and decorating it. So about your offer, I may be interested. But I need more details."

"This is wonderful! You will make an outstanding art director for what, I can promise you, will be the premier modern art gallery in all of New York City."

"I haven't said I will do it, just that I'm interested and need more details." She sounded somewhat curt as she spoke. Somehow she felt this man always got his way, and she wasn't going to be another "yes" person in his life.

"All right, Kate. I like your feistiness." That expression made her cringe. "Barbara is in New York, and I will let her know you are interested." He said the word *interested* slowly and mockingly. Kate wasn't certain what to make of it. "She has all the little details that you need answered. But I know that once you hear the perks and what's involved, you will be very encouraged to join my team."

"You have a team?" Kate asked, sounding skeptical.

"Yes, I could not function without the brilliant people I have around me. You shall see very soon for yourself." He sounded arrogant enough to put her off.

Kate added quickly and curtly, "For the record, if you want me to accept this position, you will have to be respectful at all times. Keep your hands to yourself. Are we clear, Trevor?"

Despite her tough tone, Trevor smiled and saw her demand as a challenge. "Yes, Kate. You have my promise that I will be a very well-behaved boy."

Kate said, "Okay, I will wait for Barbara's call, and we shall see. Have a good day, Trevor." Kate was all business in her tone. She did not give Trevor an opportunity to say good-bye because she knew that ending the call quickly would give him the clear message that she was to be taken seriously. Remembering South Africa, Kate recalled a gentler, almost shy man that was much more likable than the jet-setting, smart-talking, wise guy who was persistent and obnoxious.

Ignoring his beautiful strawberry blond dinner companion, Trevor looked down at his poached salmon and asparagus at the posh Savoy and thought to himself, *I won't stop until you are mine, Kate.*

Within minutes, Barbara Quincy called Kate. "Hello, Kate."

Kate put the phone on speaker a second time and started removing her robe for a shower. "Incredible. You guys act fast. I was just on the phone with him."

Giggling, Barbara said, "That's technology for you. Trevor just called and wants you to know details regarding the art directorship." Barbara's chirpiness was annoying to Kate. The animated woman continued. "So can we meet today? I'm staying at the W Hotel in Union Square. Are you familiar with this area?"

Kate snorted and replied, "Really? Are you forgetting I'm a native New Yorker? Anyway, what time works for you?"

Barbara was embarrassed and offered an apology. "How silly of me to just assume you would not know. My apologies. Would one this afternoon work?"

Kate walked into the bathroom and turned on the water to steam up the room. "One works. Do you want to eat at the Irvington Restaurant in the hotel? The food is good, and we won't have to deal with traffic getting to and from a place."

Laughing into the phone, Barbara said enthusiastically, "You do know your town. Good for you. I love that idea. I will meet you at the Irvington at one this afternoon. See you then."

Kate threw her robe on the velvet bench in the bathroom and uttered into the phone, "Okay, see you then." She proceeded to take a hot steamy shower, and in her mind, she ran down a list of stipulations that, if met by Barbara and Trevor, would seal the deal for taking the position.

Kate met with Barbara and had an enjoyable afternoon recalling her visit to South Africa. She learned from Barbara that working for Trevor was at times demanding because he expected nothing less than excellence from his employees. Barbara also informed Kate that he was very generous and understanding when it came to personal matters. They got into the details of what the art directorship would entail, and it did not seem like anything out of the ordinary for Kate. The yearly salary would start at $175,000 per year, and the perks included having access to a private jet and all expenses paid when traveling for work.

The position was a dream for Kate, with the salary being the highest she had ever heard of for such a position. But the nagging question she had running around her head was whether she really wanted such a commitment in her life. She wanted to keep busy but not be in a nine-to-five grind. She asked Barbara the exact hours involved, and to her surprise, the bubbly woman responded, "You will have your office in the gallery, of course, but you can easily work from home. If you show up once or twice a month, it would be fine. You see, Kate, the reason why Trevor wants you and not anyone else is because you have such a particular eye for details that is needed in this position."

As they sipped coffee, Kate informed Barbara that she would think it over and give her a response in the next forty-eight hours. Pleased with this answer, Barbara turned the conversation around to private matters. She was itching to ask Kate about the brilliant ring on her finger. Kate noticed the interest in Barbara's eyes and placed her hands on her lap. Not one to shy away, Barbara asked more pointedly, "Kate, that ring is simply gorgeous. Are you engaged?"

Looking into Barbara's eyes and keeping her hands on her lap, she responded quietly, "Yes, I just became engaged, and thank you for the compliment."

The curious woman persisted. "Do tell, who is the lucky man?"

Kate shifted in her seat and picked up her bag before responding, "Oh, he is a really nice man. No one you know, I'm sure. Well, Barbara, if you don't mind, I must move along. Thanks for the details, and I will get back to you within the next two days." They rose from their seats, embraced, and air-kissed each other's cheek. Kate instinctively knew this woman was Trevor's spy, and she would not allow her personal life to become an open book.

Rey met Kate at her new apartment. She was pleased to see the new satiny bamboo floors installed, as well as the windows replaced. The second bathroom was now tiled, but the fixtures were missing. Her new chef's kitchen was ready as was the master bathroom. Rey grabbed Kate by the waist and, nibbling on her neck, whispered, "Get ready because we will have to christen every room."

Pretending to be horrified, Kate pulled away and touched her chest in a display of shock. "Oh my. Why, I couldn't." They laughed and proceeded to dinner.

They enjoyed a quiet meal at Rey's apartment, where Kate shared the conversations she had had with Trevor and Barbara. He listened quietly and kept reminding himself that she was her own woman.

Kate finally explained the job and perks involved and the salary. Rey's eyes flew up and asked, "What are you not telling me, Kate?"

She looked puzzled and said, "I told you everything Barbara shared with me. The best part is that I can work from home mostly and just pop into the gallery once or twice a month."

He put his fork down and picked up the wineglass. After a sip, he asked, "How much travel is involved?"

Kate shook her head as she chewed her food and said, "There was little mention of travel."

He sat back and took in a deep breath to add, "Well, if there was little mention of travel, why is the private jet necessary as a perk?" He looked directly at Kate and realized from her eyes that she had no idea.

She took another bite of food and shrugged in a dismissive manner, realizing he had a point. "You are away months at a time, so what if I have to be in another city for a few days?"

Rey laughed when her green eyes flashed at him and her brows came together. "Let's not fight, my angel. Just make sure that wolf is far away from you. I know his kind. I was his kind until you conquered my heart." Kate looked at Rey with a side-glance and wondered about his past. He continued hoping for a negative response. "So are you taking the job?"

She waited a few moments to respond, "I will put in a call to Barbara regarding how much travel is involved and then make my decision. It looks like I am definitely leaning toward a yes."

Knowing her to be a woman who enjoyed work, he asked with caution, "Why do you even want such steady work? You can write or be a freelance photographer."

Kate stopped eating and looked Rey squarely in the eyes and calmly stated, "I have taken care of myself my entire life. My first job was at fourteen at a bookstore, and I have always worked. Being financially independent does not mean I should go away and vegetate as I spend money. I prefer being busy and productive."

Chuckling, he reached over and took her hand with the stunning diamond dazzling on her finger. His words made her very happy. "I have faith in your judgment, and if you decide to take this position, I will be very happy for you."

Kate smiled and mouthed the words *thank you*.

CHAPTER 17

Enter Mr. Wolf

It was late March when the Trevor Miles Gallery had its grand opening. The bleached floor and white-walled space was airy and sophisticated with a minimalist design. An international crowd filled the two-leveled gallery as caterers moved about serving drinks, and lounge music came through invisible speakers. Trevor held court by the enormous Fernando Botero sculpture on loan from Colombia. He shook hands and took endless photographs with his guests as different press outlets clamored for his attention. Kate quietly answered questions from critics and offered details on the installations she had selected for the opening. Impromptu interviews with her were held throughout the eventful evening, but unlike Trevor who lived for all the attention, Kate just wanted to be home in her new bed, reading a book.

Late February, she had decided to take the position of art director with a stipulation in the contract that this would only be a one-year residency. Kate was no longer interested in long-term work commitments, as she preferred cultivating her own photography and building a new life with Rey. His tour throughout Central and South America ended in June, where they agreed to meet in Okinawa for Aiko and Samu's wedding. Kate yearned to be back on the healing beach, which a year ago embraced and helped her through the most difficult moments of her life.

Having little to no interaction with Trevor was not a problem for Kate. The fleeting interest she thought she had felt for him had disappeared when Rey entered her heart and asked her to be his wife. Barbara must have told Trevor about her engagement because, every week, Kate received expensive floral arrangements with little notes at the gallery. She sent him several texts to stop with the flowers, but he disregarded her requests and instead wrote more generic notes thanking her on her work. He gave her free rein over the installations and admired her selections. They had business meetings via FaceTime and through e-mail, which suited Kate just fine. There was something about him now that made her skin crawl. Perhaps it was the wise-guy look he had when he chatted on FaceTime or just his obvious interest in her. She knew one characteristic of his she detested, and that was how loud he became when he wanted to make a point or show off. This behavior came to a head the night of the grand opening.

Trevor had not seen Kate face-to-face since she took the position. His other projects in Africa and Europe had kept him from traveling west while the New York gallery was going through a renovation in preparation for the grand opening. Weeks before the opening, Kate traveled to Colombia and secured the Botero sculpture. Always respectful and supportive of unknown local artists, she also secured several works to display at the grand opening.

Teetering on high heels, Barbara came over to Kate, enthusiastically waving her phone in her hand. "Kate, this is a huge success, and it's all because of you." Kate was amused at Barbara's enthusiasm and obvious inebriated state. Standing closer to Kate, she positioned her phone out to take a selfie and immediately posted it on her Instagram, Twitter, and Facebook accounts, all while chatting away about Trevor. "You are his star, Kate. Oh yes, he is very impressed with you." Grabbing Kate's left hand, she stared at the obvious engagement ring and exclaimed loudly, "OMG! You're a lucky girl to have a musician in your pocket. Does he have a brother?" Kate's eyes flashed furiously and pulled her hand away. Barbara's drunken chatter and giggles continued. "You know, Trevor was devastated when I told him you were snatched up. He said he would find out and make him go away. Imagine that, Trevor jealous." Barbara cackled loudly and spilled a little of her drink as her weight shifted clumsily on the high heels. Kate moved away several steps and busied herself with straightening out the gallery brochures. Barbara would not relent and came after Kate with more inquiries. "Oh, won't you tell me? You can trust me, Kate. Tell me how is Rey Aguilar? He's such a hunky guy. I just love a good love story." The woman plopped on a club chair and fanned herself with one of the brochures Kate had just organized.

Looking around, Kate noticed the crowd was dwindling, and Trevor was still shaking hands and taking photographs with people he knew. Spotting Kate, he called out to her. "Kate, come here please." She reluctantly went over and smiled as the cameras clicked away. Trevor put his arm around her and shared with the press Kate's role in the gallery. Earlier in the evening, this had already been done, and she was subjected to the same cameras and the interviews that followed. She figured he must have forgotten as the evening progressed and the level of alcohol increased. He became distracted when some leggy models came over to him, prompting Kate to slink away to her office to gather her coat and bag and leave. She was physically tired but felt proud of the excellent work she had accomplished with the installations and in exposing new artists.

Just as she was ready to exit the office, Trevor opened the door and stepped inside. He held a drink in his hand, made himself comfortable on a leather chaise, and looked at Kate up and down as men do when they are interested in more than a friendly chat. Standing tall, she moved over to the door, opened it fully, and said, "Congratulations on the opening. It is a great success, but I am very tired and going home." He did not move off the chaise but instead spoke quietly. "Kate, tell me something. Why Rey Aguilar?"

She bristled at the personal inquiry. Looking toward the door, she responded blankly, "My personal life is not your concern." Kate did not feel she was under any obligation to divulge personal information on events in her life.

Trevor got up slowly and stood before her. She held her head high and moved to leave when he held her arm. He grabbed her and kissed her hard on the mouth. Inhaling the liquor on his breath made her stomach roll. Instinctively, Kate crashed her heel onto the top of his foot causing him to grunt and pull away. She lunged forward enough to slap him hard across his face sending him stepping back awkwardly and falling onto the chaise. His surprise was only momentary. Instead of moving forward and apologizing for his unwanted advance, Trevor laughed and saw her refusal as a challenge. He jumped up and grabbed Kate by both arms to kiss her again, but this time, she fought him off. His body was blocking the now-closed door, and Kate felt fear rise in her stomach.

Speaking slowly and steadily, she uttered, "Trevor, step away from the door and let me get out."

Trevor stepped away but not before he shared his views on her engagement. "I had my people do a little investigation on Rey Aguilar."

Kate was incensed at the idea of someone investigating Rey. The look of disgust on his face prompted her to ask with a tone, "What?"

His next remark was a dagger in Kate's heart. "The man who murdered your son does not deserve a life with you. I am disappointed at how little you value yourself." The words pierced her deeply, and he saw their effect on her face as it melted into a mask of shock and disbelief. To Kate, the words hurt; but to Trevor, they were triumphant, knowing that at the very least he had given her some serious food for thought.

Infuriated, she snapped back, "Who do you think you are to question my choices and meddle in my life?"

He continued with another series of unwelcome comments. "Kate, you cannot be serious about this man. He should be in jail for what he did to your son and you. I don't believe for a second that he could not control that vehicle that destroyed the life of your only child and seriously injured you. I only want you to think this through. Here I am before you with open arms asking you to give me a chance. With me, you can start a new family and a life you could only dream of." Kate fought the tears that threatened to erupt, but her anger was mixed with an immense sorrow as Oliver's face came crashing into her memory.

Trevor moved closer to meet her as she stood behind her desk. Seeing an opportunity, Kate moved carefully toward the door until she was standing before it. Knowing her intention, Trevor sat calmly on her chair, placed his feet on her desk, and took out a cigar. He looked her up and down and said with disgust, "Go, run to your jazz man and the murderer of your son. You are making an enormous mistake. What a waste."

Kate flung open the door and nearly knocked down Barbara as she fled the office and ran through the mezzanine. The lump in her throat was causing her airways to constrict as fat tears finally poured out of her. Once outside, she jumped into a waiting cab meant for another couple and shouted at the driver, "Go now!"

The driver hit the accelerator, and after driving past three lights, he asked the crying woman in his back seat, "Uh, lady, where do you wanna go?"

Kate heard the voice and gave her address in a near inaudible tone. Her phone started to ring, and with disgust, she saw that it was Trevor and Barbara calling. Rey had also called and left a congratulatory message regarding the gallery opening. He also left her a text asking her to call back. She turned off the phone and threw it back into her bag. Looking down at her engagement ring, she heard Trevor's words echo in her head. *You are engaged to your son's murderer.*

Sleep never came for Kate that evening. What should have been a successful night for her budding career ended in her realization that she had no future with Rey, as others would also see him as the man who killed Oliver. She did not think she could rationalize this truth to justify a life with him. Once home, Kate threw off her clothes and showered, scrubbing her lips hard and brushing her teeth to get the taste of Trevor's liquored breath out of her mouth. She cried in the shower and called out Oliver's name.

The next morning, James called to invite Kate for a walk in the park to recount the successful evening. Instead of waiting for her response after hearing the sound of her voice, he told her to stay where she was and wait for him. Forty minutes later, Kate cried into his chest as she recounted everything Trevor had done and said to her about Rey. He listened patiently and stroked her hair much the same way he did when they were younger and boyfriends betrayed her. The morning lagged on with Kate in a comatose state on her bed, just staring at nothing. With much encouragement, he managed to make her sip some chicken broth he found in her fridge and eat a few crackers.

James was confused at her sudden change of heart toward Rey. He wondered how Trevor Miles could influence her decision so deeply. For months, Kate was happy and hopeful at the start of a new life with Rey, who complemented her tastes and zest for life. Yet it took Trevor Miles and his obvious ulterior motives to say hurtful words and have her world come crashing down into a million shards of glass. Her hurt and feelings of guilt were palpable, but James had to know exactly which of the two burned her more to help her confront the problem. He sat on her bed and went straight to the point. "What are you most hurting over, the feeling of guilt or the words that fool used to describe the man you love?"

She stared at him, and in her eyes, he could see the battle within her mind. Tears streamed down her cheeks as she responded. "I think it's both."

He was determined that she should rationalize this as best she could. "Katie, remember when I told you that when making decisions in regard to a case, we keep emotions and impulsiveness far away? Well, the same applies for anyone in the middle of a crisis. Trevor Miles is obviously interested in you and would be happy to see you return your engagement ring to Rey. Therefore he hits you where it hurts most by using Oliver as bait. That, baby girl, is a cheap move." She shifted and sat up, thinking over what James shared. He continued. "Furthermore, while he has the right to his opinion, what is important here is how you feel toward Rey and your future with him. That is independent of what anyone else may think regarding the circumstances behind your relationship."

To his surprise, Kate made a sudden decision. She pulled back the comforter and walked over to the walk-in closet. He heard her rummaging around and struggling with a suitcase. Throwing it on her bed, she stood straight and said, "You know what, James, I am sending that little bitch Barbara a text. She ran to Trevor with news of my engagement. I'm following this with a formal e-mail straight to Trevor Miles resigning from my stupid gallery position. Then I am going to leave this ring with you to return to Rey. I need a little space from everyone and can't think with this on my finger. And before you say it, I am not running away."

James clapped sarcastically as he snapped, "So this is you not running away? Really? Go ahead and throw away all this really good love you have because of some jackass and his disrespectful comments. But when you come to your senses, don't be surprised if Rey isn't there anymore. This is a huge mistake, Kate. I know you love Rey, and that should be enough to combat any bullshit that should try to keep you two apart. Why haven't you called the cops and charged this guy with sexual aggression?" James waited for a response that never came.

He rose from the bed and picked up his things, and just as he was walking to the door, Kate ran after him and hugged him from behind. They embraced, but Kate had made her decision. She placed the engagement ring in his hand and said, "Safeguard this, okay, and give it to Rey. I will contact him and tell him I just need some space. He'll understand, I'm sure. James, don't be angry with me. I don't think I can stand it if you and Rey are both angry with me."

Hugging her, he whispered, "No, dummy, I am not angry, but I cannot promise you that Rey will be so understanding. You are going to slice up this poor guy's heart into little pieces. When a woman says she needs space, it's code for she wants to break up. Where are you going? Oh wait, let me guess, Japan?"

She looked up and kissed his cheek. "Yes, just to think clearly. I promise, I will be back home soon. Besides, Aiko wants me to be at her wedding, and I want to be there to help."

As he walked down the hall, he stopped and looked back at Kate and said, "I hope you don't regret this choice, Katie. Be safe. I love you."

She stood at her apartment door, certain Rey would understand.

CHAPTER 18

Guilt

An early Spring dusting of snow had fallen as Kate finished packing. Sitting at her desk by the window, she purchased a one-way ticket to Tokyo on American Airlines from Kennedy Airport, but the flight was leaving the next morning. This gave her plenty of time to formally write a resignation letter via e-mail to Trevor and Barbara and make the dreaded call to Rey. This last part had Kate shaking at how Rey would receive her idea of "needing space." She recalled what James had said but refused to believe that Rey would take the news so dramatically. Finishing up the e-mails, she sent them and waited. Within seconds, the phone rang. It was Barbara, followed by Trevor. She ignored Barbara's calls and blocked her number, but she listened to Trevor's voice mail. "Kate, I am so very sorry for my drunken behavior yesterday. I was wrong to say those words. I have to see you. Please, don't make any hasty decisions and let's talk. I'm staying at The Peninsula and would love to take you to dinner. I am waiting for your call. You know you mean so much to me."

Kate thought to herself, *This man has some nerve. James and Rey were right about him having ulterior motives. I don't want to talk to him, and he'll just have to deal with getting a new art director.* Rapidly, she blocked his number as well and erased all his voice mails. She had

had enough of these people, particularly Trevor's sense of entitlement and control.

Calling Rey was going to be difficult. She did not want to think too much about it, so she dialed the number and waited. Rey responded groggily, "Hey, my love. God, I miss you."

Kate asked, "Did I wake you?"

He coughed and moaned. "Yes. But that's not a problem. The show ran after midnight. How was the gallery opening?"

Kate walked around the living room. She stood by the window with the view to shops and a busy street below and said, "Rey, the opening went well. Actually, we need to talk."

He struggled to focus with a hazy head as he warily asked, "So when do you arrive? I miss you so much."

Kate was in turmoil as to how to say what she needed to say. Her heart wanted one thing and her mind another. Taking a breath, she closed her eyes and said barely above a whisper, "Rey, I'm not going to Buenos Aires. I feel I need a little space."

Her last seven words awoke him. Rey felt a shiver in his spine as he walked around the hotel room trying to understand her cryptic message. There was a hollow and cold feeling growing in the pit of his stomach. He opened the window and took in some air feeling like a man who was slowly being strangled. "Space? You want space. What is going on, Kate?" he asked calmly yet fearfully.

"I just want some space to think, that's all."

AURA POLANCO

It was an eerie feeling that came through the phone when Rey spoke again. "You are asking me to understand your need for space? But in order for me to understand this need, I have to know what has happened." He kept his eyes focused on a decorative light post outside his window, to keep his voice steady because what he wanted to do was go through the phone lines and shake her to get the truth out.

"Rey, I just feel like perhaps we rushed into things, and it would be best if we took a little break."

A sword would have done less damage to Rey's heart as he stood in disbelief listening to Kate's words. His panic was now unleashed, along with a fury he could no longer contain. Raising his voice in desperation, he said, "We have not rushed into things as you say. You and I knew exactly what we were doing. I have given us a lot of thought. We did not rush. I never pushed you."

There is never an easy way to say "it's over," but Kate tried. "I am conflicted. I need time to think. Why can't you understand this?"

To Rey, these words were like knives coming his way. He reached for questions. "Why can't I understand this? I am in love with you, and I asked you to be my wife and share my life with me. Kate, I cannot see my life without you in it. Why are you doing this? Oh my god, Kate, please don't do this to me. Don't do this to us." He fell upon a chair, unable to hold himself up as the fear and pain took hold. He put the phone on speaker, thinking that perhaps if her voice filled the room, it would not seem so real or as painful. She said nothing. "Kate, Kate, talk to me, my love. What has happened to make you want to throw away such a beautiful love? We love each other, and you can't tell me it isn't true because . . ." His voice cracked, and he muffled his pain into his hands.

"Rey, please understand." He heard her muffled cries coming through. "James will return the ring to you. I'm sorry."

Returning the engagement ring made her decision concrete for him. Furiously, he shouted out words to hurt Kate. He wanted her to hurt as much as he was hurting. "You don't love me, Kate. When you love someone, you don't throw that love away like garbage. That's what I am to you, and now I know it. You know what, Kate, I don't give a shit about the ring because I'm nothing to you. Thanks for the months of pure happiness that I had with you and had never felt before in my fuckin' life." He sank deeper into the chair and let out a cry sounding like a cross between a wounded animal and a grown man wailing.

Kate trembled and cried on the other end and said desperately, "Oliver is dead, Rey, and I thought I was free from the guilt, but I can't come to terms that you are the reason for this." She hung up the phone.

The last words she spoke emptied Rey's chest of its heart. His breathing halted, and he felt the room spin before him. He cried out, "Kate! Kate! I'm sorry. It was an accident. Please don't do this!" He realized there was no one on the other end, and in one quick move, he propelled the phone into the wall, shattering it to pieces. Rey's world came to an end. He remained prostrated in the chair and cried until, from sheer exhaustion, the tears ceased.

After that terrible exchange, Kate felt worse than ever. She knew her final words were devastating to him, but her life without Oliver had been painful. She thought he would understand that all she needed was space and could not fathom why he had to be so melodramatic. Kate did not understand that men, at their deepest core, were simple creatures. For the most part, men see things in black and white, yes or no. Gray areas are confusing. Her life was now as uncertain and blank as when she started out to Japan nearly two years ago. Only this time, Kate had not lost something important; she had thrown it away. Her emotions were raw, and all she wanted was to swim in the warm waters of the beach in Okinawa.

After what seemed like an eternity to him, Rey booked the next flight out to New York. He had to be with Kate and change her mind regarding their relationship. No longer having a cell phone, he went directly to her apartment, and the doorman advised him that she had left earlier that morning with her luggage to the airport. Hailing a taxi, Rey went to the law offices of James Adderley, where he walked right in and demanded to see him. The harried secretary announced him, and James shook hands and observed the pale hue and crazed look in Rey's tired and reddened eyes. He gave him water and offered coffee, but Rey refused everything and directly asked his question. "What the hell happened, James?"

Sitting back on his chair, James buzzed his secretary and advised her to hold all calls. Lacing his fingers, he spoke truthfully to Rey. "I tried, Rey, to talk her out of this, but she was determined to leave. Trevor Miles said some things about her engagement to you, and he referred to you as the murderer of her child." He watched how Rey twitched in his seat and fisted his hands. The silence was deafening as both men looked at each other. Rey tasted blood and wanted nothing more than to destroy Trevor Miles. Suspecting his desire to be confrontational, James readily offered advice. "If you approach this man and swing first, you will end up in jail. This will work against you financially, with your career, and in winning back Kate. She's confused, scared, and hurt. But I know she loves you."

Rey shifted in his seat and laughed. The sharp guffaw had a cruelty to it that made James's skin crawl. Rey shook his head and said sarcastically, "Yeah, she loves me, all right. This is what I get for being honest and nothing but genuine with her. I warned Kate that this jerk was a snake, but she thought I was being jealous. Did she run off to Japan?" James confirmed this with an affirmative nod as Rey continued. "She can stay there and sort all this bullshit out in her head, but I'm not chasing her. She wanted space, and that is exactly what I will give her because I have nothing else left to give." He stood up and extended his hand to offer a handshake. James came around and shook hands and pulled Rey in for an unreciprocated hug.

Before he let Rey leave, he asked him, "When I speak with her, do you want me to share anything?"

Rey shrugged and spoke like a man who was beat. "Share what? She already knows how important she is to me. If another man's words can influence her so much, then her love for me was just superficial. She never really felt love for me. I know this now. This is her punishment to me for what happened."

Those words were so heavy with bitterness and pain that James put his arm around Rey. "Do you want me to keep you posted on what's happening?"

Rey chuckled. "What, so I can keep hurting each time? No way, she has to figure out for herself what she wants, and I have to fulfill the commitments I made in South America. Good-bye, James." James watched Rey leave his office looking weary and worn.

CHAPTER 19

Starting Over

Aiko and Mrs. Goto were ecstatic at Kate's return and prepared her room with fresh flowers. Upon arriving, it was evident to both women that Kate was in trouble again. They embraced her, took her up to her room, and gave her some tea with orange cake and sliced persimmons. "Tomorrow we will talk. Now you sleep," Mrs. Goto told her as she hugged Kate and left her in the quiet of the room that had before been witness to her suffering and embraced her gently for more of the same.

In the days and weeks that followed, Kate busied herself with swimming in the warm waters and in helping Aiko with the preparations for the early summer wedding. Walking back from the greenhouse where Kate had spent some time meditating, she was surprised to encounter Trevor and Barbara in the foyer. Their backs were to her, but Trevor noticed how Mrs. Goto smiled past him toward Kate.

"Kate, you have friends visiting you." Mrs. Goto, seeing an opportunity for more business, invited them to stay the night. "It is late now, and you should stay in my hotel."

Upon hearing this, Kate's voice rose sharply. "Mrs. Goto, they will not stay. These are not my friends. Mr. Miles employed me for a short while in New York, and this woman is his assistant. They will not remain long."

The chill that settled in the room made for a very uncomfortable atmosphere. Kate turned and walked out to the veranda, knowing that Trevor and Barbara would follow. To her surprise, it was only Trevor who came; and when she reached the side garden, she stopped and turned to face him. He looked around him, pressed his lips, and shook his head as he proceeded to say, "Nothing I say can express how sorry I am for hurting you the night of the opening. Kate, I was wrong."

Trevor Miles was repugnant and an affront to her senses. The gentle, almost shy man she met in South Africa was quickly replaced with the sly opportunist with a mean tongue. She felt bile rise in her esophagus but contained herself enough to end this connection to him. His hand reached out to touch her arm, but Kate pulled back and in a strong tone stated, "Nothing you say will matter to me. Leave this place because you are not welcome here." Kate moved toward the door to reenter the lobby when he grabbed her upper arm and drew her to him. She was close enough to smell his expensive cologne, which miserably failed to mask the liquor on his breath. His eyes were bright and with tiny telltale red veins, disclosing either too much drink or lack of sleep or both.

Pulling away, Kate rubbed her arm as he said in a sneering manner, "Funny thing, Kate, you hate me for telling you the truth. You have no future with that two-bit musician. He has all these strikes against him, and here I am with no blemishes or transgressions toward you. Why do you reject me when I can give you the world?"

Kate swung her hand and struck him hard across the cheek. He stood steadfast and clearly infuriated but said nothing else while she whispered firmly, "I reject you because you tried to impose your will over me. You think that because you are a man, you can grab, kiss at will, and bully your way with me. Well, you will never do that. You may be wealthy and appear to have it all, but you are not half the man Rey is to me. Do not make any further efforts to see me, and as far as I am concerned, I never met you."

Turning to leave, he spit out a last recrimination. "Have it your way, Kate, but you can't deny that you are childless, thanks to your precious Rey." He moved off the steps, and Barbara followed like a silly lapdog. Kate stared away with tears running down her cheeks at his cutting words.

When she entered through the large wooden doors, several guests, Mrs. Goto, and Aiko remained still, as they had heard the final remarks said by Trevor Miles. Mrs. Goto rushed over to console her, but Kate waved her away and proceeded to her room. She entered the shower to muffle her desperate cries over her loss of motherhood and for the only man who had made her feel alive again.

CHAPTER 20

Farewell, Angie

Instead of the predictable drunken binge Rey would have fallen into when a crisis occurred in his past, this time, he became withdrawn and sullen. His playing remained sharp, but gone was the passion and zest he was known for. By late April, he approached Rafa and Paco with news that would upset the remainder of the tour and change the face of the renowned jazz band.

They had just completed a long morning of rehearsals in preparation for a special performance for the visiting dignitaries at Viña del Mar. This venue was not originally on their tour schedule, but they took the gig when it came as an invitation. International notables from the celebrity and political world would be there for the evening of song and dance. The other musicians had left to have lunch and rest before the star-studded performance as Rey, Paco, and Rafa remained in the studio to talk. Rey was notably edgy and short-tempered. He had lost weight and looked gaunt. The man they loved to hate had returned weeks ago, and because he was silent about his problems, his friends had no idea what was bothering him.

"Uh, you guys need to know that after the tour ends, don't sign me up for any others. I already looked into a replacement. Either

Johnny Holmes or Mike Diaz is ready to take over. You guys just have to try them out and choose the one that is the best fit." Rey's voice was filled with emotion as he tried to sound casual. He kept his eyes averted by fiddling with Angie and fitting her in the case.

Rafa was rendered speechless. The pain he saw in his friend's face hurt him as well. It was Paco who spoke and showed unusual emotion and frustration. "Rey, we are like brothers, dude. You need to give us more than that. We just got back a year ago, and look at us. We are off the charts with success, and now you want to walk away? Come on, what the hell is going on?" He was on his feet, eye to eye with Rey, when he saw the hurt Rafa had already seen from where he sat at his piano.

Softly, Rafa said, "Kate. This is happening because of Kate. I saw something change in you when we were in Argentina, and ever since then, you are like a dead man. Paco is right, bro. Talk to us."

The mention of her name made Rey sick to his stomach, and the pressure that had settled in his chest, caused him to give out a cry so feral and haunting that both men stood frozen. He had closed the case and held it tightly against his chest when he exploded in a rage unlike anything they had ever seen. They saw the fury and sorrow mixed up together as he knocked down music stands and beat the case against the wall until the sax fell out. The beautiful brass instrument continued to receive punishment. Rey smashed it against the floor and walls of the studio until pieces lay askew and bent parts looked like a sad reminder of what had been a thing of musical beauty.

Rafa ran over and threw his arms around him in an embrace. Hugging him, he said, "Get it all out! Just get all this shit out." Rey collapsed on the floor and wiped his face with the handkerchief Paco offered and told them what had happened. In a mix of rage and muffled cries, he left nothing out from the last conversation he had had with Kate. Together they helped Rey get up and pick up the wrenched and badly dented pieces of the once-famous instrument. They slapped him on the back and gave him encouragement. Never had they seen this strong, proud man so broken and disillusioned. It affected them because they knew that, for Rey, Kate was the real thing. He gave off that macho facade, but deep down, he had always wanted and yearned for the honest and true love he had found with Kate.

They decided to walk back to the Gala Hotel, where they were staying, instead of taking a car. Everyone needed some air, and walking the several hundred feet would help clear Rey's torment and enable his friends to support him. Paco spoke up first, anxious to know the answer to his question. "Have you thought about going after her, Rey?"

Rafa slowed his pace to light up a cigar and backed up Paco's question with his statement. "She's an amazing woman. Take all that she has been through before you make any rash decisions."

Paco added, "And why quit us? This is still great money, travel, and who knows what could come from meeting new people."

Rey stopped walking and looked at his longtime friends. He listened, but he had already made up his mind. "You don't think I know how I'm playing. It may be pitch-perfect, but you know that it has been flat. I'm not feeling this anymore. I having nothing left in me." Rey pressed his palms into his eyes and rubbed his hands over his hair. Taking a deep breath and furrowing his brows, he added, "I'm not chasing her. She will have to come to me, and even then, I don't think my heart can take another beatdown like this again."

Paco's and Rafa's eyebrows went up at Rey's surprised surrender. They walked the rest of the way in silence.

The star-studded evening was successful, as all the performances were rich and varied. The music hall overflowed with excitement, and people were animatedly chatting and cheering throughout the night. As the concert came to a close, The Golden Trio ended their set to a standing ovation despite Rey's less than enthusiastic performance. He returned the borrowed sax to one of the musicians in the house orchestra before joining his friends.

The three friends left the venue to have a late dinner. They walked through the hotel lobby and stopped numerous times to sign autographs, shake hands, and pose for pictures with fans. Rey was signing an autograph when he looked up and spotted Trevor Miles not ten feet away, standing with a group of men and several beautiful models. Both men glared at each other when Trevor brazenly took the first steps to approach Rey. Paco and Rafa came to stand on either side of Rey, who stood as tall as Trevor and looked ready to pounce like a lion. The South African businessman, dashing in a tuxedo, extended his hand in exaggeration and loudly proclaimed, "Why, look who is here. My friend Rey Aguilar."

Rey was disgusted with the phoniness coming off this man. He grabbed Miles by his lapels and pushed him up to the wall, but Paco was there to keep him from landing a fist on the nose of the millionaire with dozens of eyewitnesses looking on. It took all his self-control to release his hands away from Trevor's chest. Keeping his breathing steady, he could feel the blood racing through his veins and his temples pulsing.

Hotel security approached the men as Rey stepped back and started to walk away with Paco when he heard Trevor say loudly to another man, "Kate will make a fine wife for me," ending this comment with a laugh as he held up his drink in Rey's direction. Rey turned around, and stared at Trevor, but at the urging of his friends he turned around again, and walked out of the hotel.

They entered their waiting car and drove to the popular German restaurant El Austriaco in silence. At the lively restaurant, the mood was depressing with Rey focused on drinking enormous amounts of wine and not ordering any food. After two hours of eating, drinking, and mostly listening to Rafa recount exploits from his youth, they paid their bill and left. They waited outside for Rafa to light a fresh cigarette and walked behind the restaurant, where they could look out to the water.

The night was cool, and in the air, there was a crispness that made everything appear shiny and new. The natural beauty surrounding Rey did not keep his head from spinning like a broken record, as it played back Trevor's final words. He loosened his tie and undid the top button of his shirt. Breathing in the salty air, he looked out to the vastness of the ocean. Feeling his friends around him, he uttered, "Thank you for being the best bros any guy could ever have." Looking out, together they stood there and let him talk. It was rare when Rey did talk, but after the day he had had, they knew this would help him. "I'm going back home and putting the apartment up for sale. Then I'll fly down to Florida and pick up Captain from your house, Paco.

I don't know exactly where I'll go, but I will give you guys a call as soon as I figure it out."

Paco nodded in affirmation of what he had said and asked, "If you are going to New York, would you see her just to find out what the hell is going on?"

Shaking his head, Rey responded, "No, she's not there, and besides, she wants space, and we all know what that really means. I love and need Kate, but I believe this is her way of punishing me for what happened."

Rafa added with assertion, "I can't believe that she's capable of such a thing. But that punk was bluffing about Kate being his wife. She would never be with that fool. He wanted to get you into a brawl and then arrested. Who would win that fight, the nice guy who went to say hello with a handshake or the one who swung first?"

Rey never took his eyes off the horizon to say, "I guess we'll never know."

CHAPTER 21

Aiko and Samu

The beach was set up with white-muslin-covered chairs adorned with creamy tea roses strung together and forming an arch. They flanked either side of the large and impressive white hydrangea and freesia archway. Yards of elegant fuchsia azaleas bloomed along the corridor that served as a demarcation between the beach and the hotel. At Aiko's request, she wanted every female guest to wear an orchid in their hair and the gentlemen boutonnieres on her wedding day to Samu.

For as long as she could recall, Mrs. Goto wanted to see her daughter wear the traditional white kimono and hat, as they implied purity and mourning. The hat symbolized sorrow in the bride leaving her family. Aiko held strong on her modern ideas for a simple yet elegant beach wedding. It had been a difficult task convincing a traditionalist like Mrs. Goto, but after a conversation with Kate, Mrs. Goto caved to her only daughter's desires. Going about the subject with care and respect, Kate sold the idea of the beach wedding with a simple Western dress instead of traditional garb by negotiating that the prayers all be recited in the Shinto tradition. Mrs. Goto agreed, as the couple was respectfully keeping the important and traditional component of the ceremony. Everyone was delighted.

The morning of the wedding, people were crazed with excitement. The hotel restaurant set up eight large tables in the dining room, each dressed with white damask tablecloths. Silver chopsticks and flatware for Western guests were set out. Each table had as a centerpiece an intricate statue of carved ice that Kate ordered from a wedding caterer in Naha. As guests arrived, musicians playing traditional Japanese music welcomed them as they sat on the warm, breezy beach while girls from the nearby village dressed in kimonos handed out the flowers.

In the quiet of the cottage, Kate helped Aiko dress as Mrs. Goto stood quietly praying and watching her daughter. When Aiko was ready, Kate and Mrs. Goto stood back and hugged each other as they appreciated the beautiful bride in the Monique Lhuillier wedding dress. Aiko stood elegantly in her floor-length white lace dress with an equally impressive lace cape that gathered at the neck and flowed to the floor. White orchids that her mother cultivated ran alongside the chignon as wisps of hair escaped and settled on the nape of her neck. Aiko looked glorious and was equally thrilled to finally become Samu's wife.

The gong for the ceremony to begin rang, and the three women left the cottage and walked over to the beach. At the altar stood the Shinto priest, along with Samu, dressed in an impressive Armani suit. When Aiko reached the altar, the priest purified her, Samu, and the congregation. This was followed by the reading of the formula to announce the marriage to the deities and seek their protection and blessing of the kami for the couple. Instead of traditional dances, the ceremony moved along with the bride and groom exchanging nuptial cups. They took three sips from each for a total of nine sips of rice wine.

As Samu read the traditional vows in Japanese, Kate rested her hand on her abdomen. It was late June, and she was four months pregnant. It was sometime in April when she could not keep anything down and felt exhausted that she suspected she had caught a stomach virus, but Mrs. Goto told Kate she was probably expecting. Initially, Kate refused to believe this until she missed her period for a second month and went to a doctor in Naha to confirm what Mrs. Goto already knew. She was carrying smaller, and this surprised her, as she expected to be larger in a second pregnancy.

But despite all the unique circumstances of her pregnancy, the one truth that kept her up at night was how much she wanted to see Rey. Kate desperately missed him and knew he deserved to know about his child, but when she tried to call his number, it was disconnected. Not a second of her days were without thoughts of Rey. She wondered where he was and with whom, where he was playing, and how he felt. Her e-mails went unanswered, and she concluded he hated her for leaving him so abruptly. Their last conversation was explosive, and she knew she had hurt him deeply. In the warm waters of Okinawa, she realized that her fears were unfounded and her decision immature and impulsive. Now all she desired was to find him. The baby was one reason, but the greatest of all was that she needed to apologize and ask for his forgiveness. James was overjoyed with her pregnancy news, and then he was equally thrilled when she said she was coming home to have her baby.

The chanting tore Kate from her thoughts. She looked up and saw that the couple was now exchanging rings, and rice wine was being given out to the congregation to share the blessings offered to the kami. Hugs and kisses went on throughout the afternoon and evening with joyful and sometimes boisterous traditional dances and songs.

By late evening, Kate went over to hug and say good-bye to the three friends who were now an extension to her small family—Aiko, Samu, and Mrs. Goto. Aiko, now dressed in an enchanting Oscar de la Renta fuchsia ball gown, floated around the room chatting with her guests. Hugging enthusiastically, everyone said good night and farewell to one another. The next morning, the couple left on a honeymoon safari in Kenya, and Kate flew home.

CHAPTER 22

Lonely Planet

The elegant New York City apartment now seemed claustrophobic to Kate as she served James and Seby coffee and each a piece of home-baked berry pie. They gathered in Kate's artistic and glamorous living room, where her photography gracefully adorned the walls. Next to a tufted white sofa and clear Lucite chairs covered in white sheepskin stood a magnificent pedestal mirrored dining table. Kate had the walls painted a soft light blue using a stripping technique that gave the illusion of wallpaper. In the evening, the light bounced off the walls and created a warm, cozy atmosphere in the open concept space. Her kitchen was small but well appointed. The cabinets were white Italian, gloss lacquer and the doors folded up to reveal intelligent storage solutions. With the guidance of a designer, Kate selected a white Carrara marble backsplash with a soft gray quartz countertop. All the appliances were in matte stainless steel and of the finest quality.

Returning home was the first time Kate felt uncertain in her apartment. Just under one thousand square feet, she wondered how a baby would fit in the space. Listening to her concerns, James and Seby tried to allay her fears about the baby with jokes and stories. They also knew that her fears were compounded by her need to know about Rey. She had been home for over a week with a cold and was impatient to see him. "Tomorrow I'll take a chance and stop by his place. If he hates me for what I did, then I will have to deal with it, but he is entitled to know about his baby," Kate said before picking up a tiny piece of pie with her fork.

After James and Seby darted questioning looks to each other, it was Seby who spoke up gently. "Kate, I hate to tell you this, but Rey's loft was listed by the Corcoran Group and was in contract within three days. He's no longer there, honey."

Her face furrowed into a large frown as a small gasp escaped her lips. Despising nothing more than to see Kate cry, James jumped in with an idea. "What if we look him up and see if the band has a tour schedule or a gig coming up and track Rey this way?" Kate got up to retrieve her laptop from the soon-to-be nursery and returned to nestle between the two men on the sofa. Her hands were unsteady as she typed the name of the band using Google. Their website came up first, along with several other venue sites. Clicking the first site, the image of Rafa, Paco, and an unknown man popped up on screen. Rafa was at the piano and Paco on percussion, but the man holding the saxophone was a stranger.

Kate let out a cry as she exclaimed, "Oh my god, where is Rey?" Anguish disguised her face as Seby's arms comforted her.

Taking the laptop, James scrolled down and read to himself the most recent information available. He wanted to know if there was any mention of Rey leaving the band. His smile was a welcome relief to Kate as he read aloud, "Riding on the heels of their successful Central and South American tour, The Golden Trio welcome their newest member Johnny Holmes, who will replace Rey Aguilar. Rey is on an extended sabbatical and wants fans of the jazz band to welcome Johnny with open arms." They sat silently in their own thoughts about what James just read.

Reading the tour dates to himself, James said, "Well, mid-September, they will be playing throughout Connecticut and Rhode Island. We can go see them play there." He pointed to the closest location. "They are playing at a jazz club called Firehouse 12 in New Haven in only two weeks."

Kate shook her head and rose carefully as she felt heavier now in her fifth month, and although barely showing, she was uncomfortable. Seby moved about quickly, picked up the dishes and coffeepot, took them over to the kitchen, and settled them into the dishwasher. Kate nervously paced by the balcony door and looked out at the view of the Chrysler Building up ahead as she wondered, *Why isn't he there? A sabbatical? No, something isn't right.* She wiped another tear that escaped down her cheek and bit her thumbnail.

Seby suggested from the kitchen, "Well, all we can do is try. Hey, what about Facebook, Instagram, and Twitter? You said he was on all these social outlets, so let's see."

James nodded and proceeded to search him first with his name, and when that failed to turn up any information, he typed in the band's name. "So if Rey had accounts, then they were discontinued, and the band sites just have tour dates with the same stuff about the new guy."

James looked up at Kate, who looked at him with questioning eyes and said softly, "He doesn't want me to find him ever again. I really screwed things up."

Not one to take defeat easily, James offered another idea. "Look, Seby and I will go see the guys play in Connecticut. I am sure they know something. Then you decide how you want to proceed from there, okay, Katie? But getting all upset does you and my future godchild no favors, so chill out." She sighed and pulled a tiny smile to appease James and Seby, but inside, her nerves were rattled, and her head was spinning as to where the man she loved could be.

The night was warm and sticky for mid-September. People crowded outside the entrance of the popular jazz club, Firehouse 12. Some huddled and smoked, while others recounted the evening they just enjoyed. Among the gathered patrons were Seby and James as they waited outside for Rafa and Paco to appear. They were hoping to spend a few minutes or even share a drink to get the information Kate so desperately needed. She told James not to mention the baby under any circumstances. It was Rafa who spotted James's tall frame and, with open arms, exuberantly said hello as if seeing a friend after years apart. After much hugging and handshaking, James complimented them on the show. "You guys were great."

Paco responded quickly, "Thank you. We have had some growing pains without Rey, but it's getting better. But what brings you guys over here?"

They walked over to where the cars were parked for more privacy, and James jumped right in with his question. "We need your help in finding Rey."

Both men shifted on their feet, and Rafa lit a cigarette and said, "You, us, and the entire world wonder where he is hiding. He disappeared and told us that, eventually, he would let us know but nothing yet, and it's been five months." He took a long drag and let out smoke through his nostrils first, and then the vapor from his mouth filled the air with little clouds.

Cracking his knuckles, Paco asked, "So what's up? Is Kate all right?"

Not wanting to linger in a dead end, James responded, "Kate is okay for now, but we really need to find Rey." He said this with emphasis. "Did he have another home where he could have gone?"

They walked along toward the parking lot, and it was quiet for about a minute before Rafa said, "Listen, why don't you give me your number, and when I know something, I'll call. But let me tell you." He pointed to Paco and them himself. "We adore Kate, but she really messed up Rey."

Paco added, "It was rough for him. He was like we had never seen him before. He never loved a woman like that, and we go back twenty years. But Kate's marrying that other guy, so what does she want with Rey?"

They stopped walking, and James and Seby stared at each other. Seby, in his usual animated way, quipped, "Marrying? Hell no, she quit her job the day after the opening because she couldn't stand that guy. What made you say that?"

A light drizzle started to fall, bringing a cool breeze with it. Approaching Rafa and Paco's vehicles, they stopped and beeped open the cars to settle jackets and bags inside. As he threw out the cigarette, Rafa said, "Look, we were in Chile, and that guy was there. First, he goaded Rey into a fight and then taunted him with Kate becoming his wife. So we just figured that it was true. We thought Rey was going to kill him. A younger Rey would have beaten the crap out of him, but he's older now, and his body hurts all the time." Rafa shrugged and then patted James on his arm and continued. "It was good seeing you guys, but I have nothing, man. Rey could be anywhere, and he destroyed his phone just like he did Angie. That was one of the saddest days of my life." Rafa looked away and shook his head in disbelief before he rolled up his sleeve and extended his hand for handshakes. Everyone said farewell, and James and Seby lingered and waved as the musicians pulled their cars out of the parking spaces and drove away.

As they drove back to New York City, James and Seby agreed not to mention to Kate anything about her supposed marriage to Trevor. The news of not knowing where Rey could be would be devastating enough as she moved along in her pregnancy, but Kate was one step ahead of them already. After they returned with negative news regarding Rey, Kate went to where he lived to confirm this for herself. She was feeling desolate without news of him and wondered if he was hurt. On the taxi ride down, she recalled their last conversation and cringed at his words to her. *When you love someone, you don't throw that love away like garbage.* Her entire life, she wanted what she had with Rey yet ran away because she feared that the circumstances of their encounter would be wrong in the eyes of others. *What a fool I am,* was one of the many musings in her head. *If he wasn't really there, then maybe the neighbors or the people in the restaurant might know.* She wondered.

Her head ached and her back hurt from the stress. Getting out, she went into the building and spoke with the doorman, who promptly confirmed what she already knew, but he did add, "Mr. Aguilar said good-bye and gave me a nice tip. He also told me to be careful with women." This was the second time she cringed in one day and was grateful for the baggy tunic that hid her bulging baby bump.

Exiting the building, she walked across the street and entered the well-known and quaint restaurant. Chef Rocco Varela knew nothing except that he was very sad to see Rey go because he had been such a good customer. After shaking hands, she went to exit when one of the waiters recognized her. He walked up and said hello in a heavily accented English. "Hello, Kate. It's me, Carlos. Do you remember me? I was always your waiter here." It took Kate a minute to remember him, but when she did, she gave a warm smile and acknowledged the slender and charming man with the bright blue eyes and shiny black hair. He ensued a conversation by the door asking Kate, "Table for one?"

Embarrassed, she looked at the crowded place with late lunch guests and said, "Actually, I thought I would find Rey, but I guess I was wrong."

Looking puzzled, he saw a quiet sadness in her eyes. She started to apologize when he surprised her with, "Rey? He's not in New York. He took Captain and moved to his house in Formentera."

Kate's eyes flew open with the sudden information. "Formentera? Where is this place?"

He smiled and took out his phone to show her photographs of his wife and kids back home on the small island. "Formentera is one of the Balearic Islands of Spain. See here?" He swiped to show her a young woman holding a baby on her hip and the hand of a small boy. "This is my wife, Claudia, and that's Miguelito and my baby Anna Luisa."

Not certain why he was showing her these photographs, she graciously acknowledged the beautiful family. "Your wife and children are so beautiful. What a pretty place with so many flowers," Kate said sincerely.

Pointing to the image on his phone, he said softly, "Well, you see that white house up there far away with lots of pink flowers?" She peered at the photo and saw the side of a house overflowing in pink and purple bougainvillea. "That is Rey's house, and that is where he lives now."

A sudden twinge pulled at her abdomen, causing her to wince. Carlos took her arm, sat her down, and got her water. She asked excitedly, ignoring the pain, "Are you sure of this?" The funny pain was gone, but she also felt wet between her legs and feared something might be wrong.

Carlos said with certainty, "Of course, señora, he is our neighbor."

Standing up carefully, she hugged and gave Carlos a kiss on the cheek. "You have no idea how grateful I am."

The young man looked alarmed. "Señora, how can I help you?"

AURA POLANCO

Kate felt the weird pain again and fought her fears to say, "Please, get me a taxi."

The cab maneuvered its way over to NYU Langone Medical Center in heavy midday traffic. Kate kept her breathing as steady as she could and noticed her jeans were wet with blood. When she entered the large and busy foyer, she went over to the desk and announced, "I'm five months pregnant and bleeding." Rapidly, one nurse made a phone call, and another whisked Kate through the hallway in a wheelchair and up to maternity, where a doctor performed an examination.

Scared and alone, she closed her eyes and prayed, *Please, God, all I want is a healthy baby and that someday Rey forgive me.*

The young doctor returned with an older female doctor, who also performed the same exam. She removed the gloves and was very matter-of-fact. "Ms. Connor, you are in danger of a spontaneous abortion. We can do a minor surgical procedure called a cervical stitch or cerclage. There are no guarantees, but it is your best choice right now."

With her head spinning from the news of Rey and the fear of losing her pregnancy, Kate asked quietly, "Okay, when will this be done?"

The doctor looked at her watch and said, "Right away. We do not have time to lose here. I'll advise my team, and we will be in to get you within the next thirty minutes. You need to remain in bed, and if you need anything, ring for the nurse. I'll see you in a short while."

James was at a deposition, but within minutes, Seby—who had been shopping at a nearby Morton Williams—came rushing to the hospital with his groceries. Kate could hear him saying loudly near her room, "Yes, she's family. She's my sister!" He breezed into the ward and hugged Kate. "What's wrong with the baby?" He put his backpack and groceries down and took Kate's hand. "You look scared. Talk to me, Kate."

"The baby is in danger because my cervix has opened."

"You know I have no clue about female anatomy. But how is the baby in danger?"

"If the cervix opens before the baby is ready, then it's called a miscarriage or, as doctors like to say, a spontaneous abortion. They have to sew me up to keep the cervix from opening."

"What? Sew you up?" Seby asked with eyes wide open.

"Yes, I'll get an epidural, which is an injection in the spine to numb me from the waist down, and the doctor will sew up the cervix."

Seby wiped his brow and dramatically held up his hand to say, "TMI. I have to text James because this is deep." Wringing his hands, he pulled out his phone and sent James a text. *Get over to Langone because Kate is going for surgery. Hurry!* He ended the text with a frightened emoji.

"Seby, I know where Rey is." Kate's statement was interrupted when an orderly came in with a nurse and started unclamping security stops on the bed in preparation to roll her into surgery.

They kissed on the cheek, and Seby squeezed her hand and whispered, "James and I will be right here when you get back. No worries."

"Thank you, Seby. I love you." Kate was taken to another floor, and she remembered nothing else after she met the anesthesiologist and was given an epidural.

Waiting in hospitals is a despairing affair. James and Seby watched people go back and forth as they waited in the family room. The procedure took forty-five minutes, a little longer than expected. Just when James anxiously went to inquire, the doctor came. She looked at both men and asked, "Who is the father?"

James stepped up and said, "I am her brother. Is she okay?" They exchanged handshakes.

"She is resting now, and we have to see how she will cope the remainder of her pregnancy. Does she live with you?"

"No, she has her own apartment."

"This could be a problem unless we get a visiting nurse for checkups or a temporary attendant to be with her daily. She cannot do stairs or walk around. I am ordering her on bed rest for the remainder of the pregnancy. We can figure this out later with the social worker, but for now, she and the baby are stable. The baby has a strong heartbeat, and we managed to lower Kate's blood pressure."

"Thank you, Doctor, much appreciated."

"You are welcome. Do you have any questions?"

"No. I'm just grateful she and the baby are stable. Thanks, again."

"See you tomorrow. Bye now."

The next morning, Kate was in bed in James and Seby's apartment. They set up the living room as a bedroom to help Kate feel more at home. They were also, taking turns staying by her side. She was feeling a little crampy and generally uncomfortable, which added to her also being cranky. Remaining in bed was the last thing she wanted to do when what she desired was to go to Spain. James was done arguing with her when he said, "Listen, I get that you want Rey back and you want to get on a plane for a seven-hour flight to go beg for his forgiveness, but if you lose his baby, that will work against you, so stop it and relax." He left the room to make some sandwiches. James had already decided to go back to the restaurant and inquire with the waiter on Rey's address in Formentera. Finding Rey was crucial for Kate's well-being.

CHAPTER 23

Bougainvillea Heaven

I t rained mercilessly for three days. Frustrated tourists huddled in cafés and tapas bars in an effort to be light and jovial as the rain-washed away their hopes of a sun-drenched holiday. Farmers welcomed the rain to nourish the orange, lemon, and fig trees; olive groves; and all other Mediterranean crops that grow abundantly in this warm climate. While the cafés and tapas were making a handsome profit with all the tourists seeking refuge from the rain, the owners knew it would be short-lived. The rain was only a tease in preparation for the glorious heat and rays from the sun. Worshippers yearning to brown their skin and curl pale toes in the white sandy beaches of Llevant or Ses Illetes eagerly waited for the rain to cease and the sun to warm their faces. The island of Formentera was sun-drenched with three hundred days of sunshine. It was the least populated of the Balearic Islands, and it was not uncommon for the sun to set after nine in the evening, giving tourists and locals alike a longer day for activities.

Overlooking the sapphire waters and bursting with trees and walls of cheerful pink and purple bougainvillea stood a whitewashed house with royal blue shutters. To get to it, one had to walk along the secluded beach and climb up a series of stone steps that led to a natural walk with fig trees providing a shady canopy. Another way to reach the house was by driving or walking up the steep hill off a dusty and rocky road. A writer seeking inspiration and escaping the crowded city of London built the house in the 1960s. Daniel Foster died in the late 1990s, and the house stood abandoned until 2013, when Rey Aguilar—with the same ideas of peace and remoteness as Mr. Foster purchased it from the trust that held it.

After purchasing the downtrodden property, Rey set out to paint the exterior with support from local men who needed work. He also intended to install wide plank, cherry wooden floors throughout the entire house. Neighbors, who took a liking to the affable and charming Rey, warned him against wooden floors, as they would scratch easily from all the sand being trekked throughout and insisted he consider a sturdy stone tile instead. He listened to all their ideas, and once the floors had been installed, he welcomed the nearest neighbors to an alfresco seafood paella dinner. Solid friendships were formed from that day forth.

Several neighboring families moved around the house and marveled at what he had done in the short time he was there. They admired how pretty from the outside the now-white house looked, with its window boxes bursting in colorful flowers and lawn chairs matching the blue of the shutters. He hired local craftsmen to build a large pergola and farm table that could easily sit ten. Rey wasn't certain why he needed such a large table at the time but had it built anyway.

The interiors were spacious with a great room containing a large wood-burning stove to heat the house in the cool winters and a rustic kitchen off to the side. Upstairs, there were two average-sized bedrooms, each with views of the sea and sharing a bathroom between them. The main bedroom was large enough to have a walk-in closet, its own bathroom, and an ample terrace overlooking the sea yet large enough to catch a glimpse of the nearby juniper forest. From this level, a winding staircase led to a magnificent rooftop terrace, complete with outdoor patio furniture and lounge chairs for sunbathing. Burnt-orange-colored terra-cotta tiles were laid down across the entire roof.

For Rey, the pearl in the oyster of the entire space was the expansive views of the sea from three sides and the forests from the other. This was Rey's nirvana and where he sat for hours, contemplating his life while his skin took on a rich bronze color. The accident derailed his life for two years and kept him from returning to the sun and caressing Mediterranean waters. Everything about this small house embraced Rey, but even its comfort and the natural beauty around him could not fill him with joy or peace. Returning to it was his way of reinventing himself and regaining a sense of self after Kate shredded his heart.

His neighbors noticed that, unlike three years before when the boisterous and happy man had everyone over for drinks and food, this returning man was quite different. His nearest neighbors, Amalia and Pablo Azcona, invited him over for dinners, which he repeatedly and graciously turned down. Even the local single women seeking husbands or just a good time with the tall and handsome man kept their distance, as they saw a remoteness in his eyes that pushed away any chance of encounters. The small village kept his secret of being an international musician and respected his solitude, but wondered about his heart.

Rey needed to be alone to heal and find a purpose. His body was no longer hurting as it did back in New York, and he attributed this to the sun and healing waters of the Mediterranean. Long days were spent walking Captain along the beach and watching him chase the abundant lizards and birds throughout his two-acre lot. For Rey, this small part of the world was where he could open up his wounds and embrace his despair. At one point, he had concluded that what Kate did to him was punishment for her son's death. He believed she had planned it as revenge and had fooled him with her gestures and talk of love. He also wondered if this was life's karma for years of partying and endless women. It was this reality that kept him withdrawn and contemplative. Eventually, he knew he would have to embrace the life around him—but not yet, not now.

On a warm Wednesday after the nearby church bells awoke him, Rey walked down to the beach with Captain and into the ocean for a swim. This was his usual morning routine, a calm swim in the beautiful azure waters of the Mediterranean. Captain swam along as well, and when he tired, he sat on the sand panting and waiting for his master.

Back in the house, showered and drinking a cup of coffee, Rey went up to the rooftop terrace and decided that he would obtain an ordinance from the town hall in Sant Francesc tomorrow to have a saltwater pool put in, but today he would need to secure a car, and the only place he knew this could happen would be in Mallorca or Ibiza, the busiest and most popular of the four Balearic islands. The ferry left in one hour to Ibiza, giving him plenty of time to slip on a pair of sandals and grab his wallet.

While securing a hanging, potted plant for his wife, Pablo saw Rey walk by his house. He called out his name and offered him a ride in his tiny sky blue Renault with a black driver's side door, an obvious reminder of an accident occurring some time ago. Rey squeezed into the compact car, with his knees practically touching his chest, but the ride was pleasant as the men chatted about the local fishing and whose palm to press for obtaining ordinances from the town hall.

After arriving in Ibiza from the pleasant ferry ride, he stepped into a taxi that took him to Pepe's Emporio de Autos. This was the most popular dealership that serviced all four islands for vehicles both new and used. After looking around at some vehicles, he chatted with the rosy-cheeked owner, Pepe. Rey chose a pre-owned practically new white, Volvo XC60 with the condition that delivery must be made to the port in Formentera complete with license and papers of registration. After writing a check for the full amount, Pepe offered Rey a sherry, and the two men drank and contemplated the state of the beleaguered Spanish economy.

The next day, Rey went to the local municipality in the village of Sant Francesc in Formentera and was welcomed by a pretty local woman with hazel green eyes and long blond hair. Because her eyes reminded him of Kate's, Rey kept his from looking directly at hers. He filled out an application, paid the small fee required for processing, and left.

Stopping by the local market, he picked up a variety of fruit, freshly caught fish, saffron, seafood, and potatoes. With his goods in a netted bag, he walked over to the pet store Mascotas and bought a large bag of kibble for Captain and several of his beloved bully sticks. Walking across the plaza, he hailed a cab and went back home.

He walked Captain on the beach and exhausted his dog by repeatedly making him chase after a ball. Later they walked up the short cliff to reach Pablo and Amalia's tiny house. Amalia was watering her window boxes, and Pablo was reading the paper when they saw Captain and Rey approach. Amalia filled with water a cut-off plastic container for the grateful dog, which lapped it up thirstily.

Rey shocked his neighbors when he invited them over for dinner. "If you two aren't too busy this evening, I would like your company for dinner. I'm cooking." The surprised and childless older couple was thrilled to be invited by their reclusive neighbor and happily agreed and offered to bring dessert. After sharing farewells, Rey continued up the side of the hill to reach his property as his neighbors went to gather ingredients for a homemade pie and some bottles of wine.

The evening brought a spectacular sunset of orange and pinks competing for attention in the horizon. Azure waters glistened, and the waves sent soft sounds up to the rooftop of the house, where Rey and his small company were enjoying the delicious peach pie that Amalia had baked and the sherry Pablo brought from home. Earlier they ate a delectable meal of grilled lemon-crusted halibut, asparagus, and buttery mashed potatoes all prepared by Rey. Soft jazz in the background and a local Rioja complemented the meal.

For Rey, his neighbors were his family. When he arrived three years ago, they brought him food as he renovated the house and invited him to participate in local community festivals. Doing this helped Rey develop friends and establish respect in the community, which he had grown to feel very much a part of. Amalia reclined on a lounger with more wine as Rey and Pablo looked over and talked about his idea of a pool. Pablo pointed out that putting the pool to the side of the house instead of behind would give him views to the sea. He considered this and acknowledged that, while the pool would then have to be smaller, it would also be more impressive.

The night ended with friends hugging when Amalia asked Rey in Spanish, "Que te paso en Nueva York, querido?" She inquired about what had happened in New York.

He shrugged and responded, "Una mujer hizo pedazos de mi corazón." He thought about what he had said out loud—that a woman had torn his heart to bits—and gave Amalia an embarrassed, sheepish grin. After the temperature cooled and the stars made their appearance, Rey escorted his friends to the front door, where they hugged again and exchanged kisses on both cheeks.

Two months later, Rey had grown frustrated. Anyone expecting speed in Formentera was in for a disappointment, as life here went slowly. People enjoyed their siestas, and dinners were late affairs with music and laughter. Life was to be enjoyed, and people who did not understand or accept these differences struggled when expecting things to move quickly.

Although he was rapidly becoming a master at relaxing, Rey still expected people not to be late and builders to be finished when their contract stipulated they would be. It took one additional week to dig up and create a twenty-five-foot infinity pool. Local craftsmen made the six-sided royal blue tiles that adorned the wall of the pool, and it took another painstaking month of labor to complete the job before they could lay the floor tiles. With an expansive gold tile border, the craftsmen, at Rey's request, designed an image evoking black tile musical notes surrounding a gold saxophone for the floor of the pool.

As this came together, Rey imagined kissing Kate in the pool and pushed the thought out of his mind because any thought of her caused pain and longing. Every fiber of his body and cell in his brain missed and needed her terribly, but he knew she wanted nothing to do with the man who killed her son, accident or not.

To pull Kate out of his mind, he remained focused on the men working and observed how the plain water of the pool was transformed with a saltwater system. He was particular about having a saltwater pool, as it was better for the joints and relaxing. The daily swims in warm ocean water heated by the rays of the sun were a powerful combination that had served him well. Rey noticed how the back problems that had plagued him for the past three years were minimal and no longer interfering with his mobility.

Two weeks later, on a quiet Sunday morning, he took his first plunge into the new salt water, infinity pool. Swimming to the edge, he reached his arms up and looked down onto the ocean and gave way to the rawness of his emotions to explode. Rey cried for the love he lost with Kate and for not being able to share this beauty with the woman he loved.

Swimming back to the ladder, he climbed up and onto the deck. Looking around, he realized that he could use a couple of lounge chairs, some umbrellas, and tables. He even entertained the thought that perhaps another barbecue could be useful down here. Going around to the front of the house, he went to his mailbox to collect the post that was delivered the day before. With the frenzy and workmen completing the deck, the thought of collecting his mail had not even occurred to him.

Several notices of little importance were thrown on the kitchen table when he came upon an overseas letter from James Adderley. Rey stared at the name and address familiar to him and wondered how James found him. He knew Rafa or Paco would never betray him, but he could not imagine how James discovered his exact address. Tearing the envelope along the side, he opened the letter and read it.

Dear Rey,

I hope you are doing well when you receive this letter. I also hope you are not too disappointed to hear from me. Considering the circumstances, I fear I had no choice but to get your address from Carlos, the waiter from the restaurant. Please don't be angry with the poor man, as I practically threatened his life to get your address.

You see, Rey, you must reach out to Kate. Things are very difficult right now for her, and she has no idea I'm writing this letter to you. I cannot tell you why you must contact Kate, but I implore you to do so quickly.

Kate was wrong in what she did, and she realizes this, but she needs you now more than ever.

I never sent you this letter, so please don't betray my trust.

Respectfully,
James Adderley

Rey put the letter down and proceeded with his daily chores of feeding Captain, watering the plants, and sorting the mess of newspapers he left from the night before. His head was racing with questions regarding the sketchy communication in the letter, but to keep calm and not jump to conclusions, he went about his business. After doing all these mundane tasks, he went up to his room to shower and change into a crisp white shirt and a pair of summer weight jeans. Slipping into a pair of sandals, he grabbed his keys and whistled for Captain to follow him into the car.

He drove to the main port, La Savina, and moved the car onto the port space, where he waited for his turn to board the ferry. Once on board, he opened all the windows, turned off the engine, and rubbed Captain's head, which he did every time he was leaving him alone. The dog knew to stay and be quiet until Rey returned. On cue with tourists sporting T-shirts with the names of the islands, he waited patiently to purchase his round-trip tickets to Ibiza and back to Formentera. Back in his car, he played soft music and took in the sea air, while Captain reached his massive head out the window and barked at seagulls flying overhead.

In Ibiza, the vibe was immediately different. Tourists were everywhere as were vendors, music, and noise. Of the four Balearic islands, Ibiza was the one all the partygoers went to for the beaches and popular nightlife. Rey was there to buy a phone. He headed northeast toward Passeig Joan Carles I, where he made a right. Four roundabouts later, he reached the third exit onto Central Santa Portinatx and arrived at INTECAT iStore. A half hour later, he purchased the latest iPhone and had all his contacts and personal information retrieved from his iCloud account.

They walked calmly along the street, where the dog tinkled in several places as Rey placed a call to Paco. Paco's voice mail came on, and he left him a quick message as to his whereabouts and that he was doing well. His next call went to Rafa, who answered immediately when he saw it was Rey on the other end.

"Rafa, it's Rey. How are you, brother?"

"Wow, you live! Anytime you call is a good time, *hermano*. What the hell, six months later! Really!"

"I have been keeping busy fixing the house, and I just bought the phone I'm calling you from minutes ago. So how are things back there? How is the new guy coming along, and more importantly, how are you?"

"Well, let me put it this way. You can't force a square peg into a round hole." He guffawed into the phone before adding, "Johnny is a great musician. The problem is he has gigantic shoes to fill. But that's our problem, not yours. You will be happy to know that I am seriously dating a teacher. Imagine me with a teacher? That's like karma for being such a class clown." He laughed harder at his own words.

Rey laughed into the phone and caught himself, as he had not laughed out loud since the day his relationship with Kate ended. He sat on a bench overlooking the clear blue Mediterranean Sea with palm trees neatly lined up and swaying in a calm and warm breeze. People from different places walked by while he continued his conversation with Rafa. "Wow, a schoolteacher, huh. Well, if anyone needs some schooling, it is you. Go easy with Johnny. He's dedicated to his craft, so just be patient. Rafa, I wanted to ask you something."

"Of course, ask away."

"I received a letter from James. Just wondering if he, at anytime, approached you as to my whereabouts."

"He and Sebastian showed up when we were playing in New Haven last September asking about you."

"Oh yeah?" Rey uttered as he watched Captain attracting the admiration of several young women, but it was Rey who caught their eyes with his swarthy good looks and tall figure. He smiled at them, got up, and walked to his car, where he settled in with Captain. "So what did they want?"

"I honestly don't know, but I can bet it had to do with Kate."

"I don't get it. Isn't she with that jerk Miles?"

"Not true. According to these guys, Kate wants nothing to do with him. But you sound almost like yourself except, I can tell, you are not 100 percent yet."

Knowing Kate had nothing with Trevor filled Rey's mind with all sorts of thoughts. He needed to think and decided to get back home. "I'm doing all right. You know, this stuff takes time, but when you come to visit, you will love my new pool."

"What? You put in a pool! Now I'm definitely coming over."

"Look, I have to get back to catch the next ferry, so we'll continue this talk later. My invitation stands for you and your schoolteacher. You'll love it."

"Rey, you made my day with this call. I have been worried about you. Take good care of yourself."

"I'm really trying, *hermano*. Catch you later." Rey slipped the phone in his jean pocket, pulled the car out of the space, and drove to the ferry with thoughts of Kate invading his mind. Now that he had a phone, he desperately wanted to call and hear her voice, but he knew that was not possible. Every cell in his body ached for Kate, as he needed to touch her, and inhale her scent. With enormous effort, he pushed those thoughts out because it was she who had ended what they had.

Remembering this consumed his thoughts until he reached his front door, entered the kitchen, and saw the letter on his kitchen table. Reading it for a third time, he crumbled it up, threw it angrily into the wastebasket, and went upstairs to change for a swim. The ocean embraced Rey as he swam until his body ached from the effort against the waves. Not even the focus he needed against the power of the ocean could help ease his mind from Kate. He knew she needed him and determined to call her as he staggered onto the sand.

Four times, he pressed her number; and each time, he ended the call before it had a chance to ring. Frustrated, he left the phone and went to shower. It was now early evening, and he figured Kate would be up and about. He took the phone and a cold beer up to the rooftop terrace and looked out over the magnificent little world he had carved out for himself; he understood how none of it meant anything to him without her to share it with. He dialed her number and waited. Beads of sweat rested above his eyebrows, and then he heard her lilting voice fill his heart with bliss. It was so surprising to him that he called out,

"Kate," before realizing it was her recorded message. Annoyed, Rey ended the call, as he would not leave a message.

The exhaustion of the day hit his body and mind with the same force of the waves that pounded him earlier. With no more fight left in him, he surrendered to the exhaustion and slept. Two hours later, the gentle breezes from the ocean woke him to find his now-warm beer still by the lounger on the floor. Captain was asleep, snoring loudly, with his belly facing the sun. Rey rubbed his eyes, looked at the phone, and dialed again.

It rang five times before James answered it. "Rey, thank goodness you called."

"Hello, James. Why isn't Kate answering her phone?"

"She's been through some rough months, Rey, but I cannot talk to you about this. Kate needs to talk to you. Are you still in Spain?"

"Yes. What do you mean she has been through some rough months?"

"How soon can you come?"

"I don't understand your question. Why do I need to be there? She wants nothing with me, James."

"She made a mistake, Rey, a big one, and she knows it. As soon as she wakes up, I will tell her you called."

"Is Kate sick? Why is she sleeping when it's around noon over there?"

AURA POLANCO

"Damn it, Rey. I promised her I wouldn't tell you because she has to talk to you herself."

"You realize this conversation is crazy, and I still have no idea what is going on. You wrote me that letter that I just received and that made me go buy a phone. She can call me when she's ready."

"Good. I will share this with her, and again, Rey, please hear her out when you do talk."

"Sure, good-bye." Not knowing what to think, Rey worriedly picked up the warm beer and headed down to the house.

It was well past eight in the evening, and the sun was still bright in Formentera. Pacing around the house was driving Rey mad. He stuffed a tennis ball into the pocket of his shorts and took Captain for a walk on the beach below. An hour later, tired and hungry, man and dog returned home. After feeding Captain, he could not settle himself enough to eat. His mind was racing with all sorts of worries and questions. Just as he was about to call her again, he decided against it and went to the back porch to stare out to the forest.

Rey waited all night, but Kate never called. Still hungry, he made a sandwich of serrano ham and manchego cheese with lettuce and sliced tomatoes and washed it down with a cold beer. He decided to go to bed and wait there for her call. A restless sleep took over, and a nightmare made him sit up in bed, in which Kate was drowning, and he could do nothing for her because he was too far away.

It was two in the morning when he called Kate, and she answered. "Hello? Kate?" His heart was racing, as he did not know what to expect.

"Rey, I have so much to say. When can you come home?" Kate's breathing was wheezy, and she sounded tired.

"You said plenty to me the last time we spoke. What is so urgent? You do remember you dumped me." Rey knew he sounded hurt and aloof.

"I was so wrong, Rey, to say that to you. I made a mistake and want and hope you can forgive me." She did everything possible to hold back from crying as she stared at her swollen belly, now at the end of her seventh month, but her voice gave away her insecurities and fear.

It was exactly those breaks in her voice that softened his heart and helped him lose his bravado and be himself. He wanted to reach through the phone and kiss her fears away but felt impotent, as he could not. Kate was crying quietly, and he could not bear it any longer. "Kate, what do you want with me? You hurt me so much when we last spoke. I don't know what you want. Are you sick?"

"I want you to come home so we can start over. I really need you, Rey." Hearing those words filled him with a mounting despair he had never felt before.

"I no longer have a home to go to in New York, Kate."

"Yes, you do. It's right here with me and our little family." Kate was so emotional that her words were muffled, and her voice was growing hoarse. "Come home, please."

The word *family* sent a shock wave through him that made him stand and walk around his bedroom. "Our family? What are you saying, Kate?"

"Just come. Hurry please."

"Kate, are you pregnant?"

"Yes." Kate was trying to feel comfortable as she sat up in her bed, but the cramps were growing stronger. She knew she had to stay calm, but the conversation was an emotionally charged one and exactly what she was not supposed to do.

Rey stood frozen in place, not knowing what to do, say, or think. He came out of his trance to say, "I will be there, Kate. I promise."

"I'm sorry, Rey, for putting you through that. I was foolish to let someone's words influence me so much." Kate moved with difficulty to get in a sideways position, which was more comfortable for her.

"Never mind all that. We will talk it out, and we'll see. But for now, stay calm."

"I love you, Rey."

"I love you, my Kate." Rey's heart wanted to burst from the emotion in her words.

She ended the call and waved for James, who was waiting outside her door. Hugging her and handing her tissues, he waited until she fell asleep before he went to rest.

Rey moved like a demon around the house. He pulled an overnight bag and filled it with things he needed. He called Pablo and asked him if Captain could stay for a short while with them, to which they gladly agreed, and he also left the keys to the house and asked Amalia to look after it until his return. Pablo drove him to the ferry that would take him to Ibiza. While on the ferry, he contacted British Airways and secured a flight at 11:00 p.m. to New York.

To remain calm, Rey practiced some breathing exercises and focused on combining musical notes in his head to keep from thinking about Kate being pregnant and in obvious trouble. But even that could not calm thoughts of fatherhood that filled him with enormous joy and a rapidly building anxiety. Suddenly, his tranquil and idyllic existence was overflowing with uncertainties. Keeping calm was impossible, as Rey concluded that as a father, he would want to be there 100 percent of the time to participate in the life of his child.

CHAPTER 24

Hope

The flight took seven long and torturous hours until it finally landed in JFK at three in the morning. Rey's long-sleeved linen shirt was a poor cover in the chilly October air, as he grabbed a cab and gave Kate's address to the driver. He sank back in the seat and remained still to calm his nerves. The thought of seeing Kate was building into a mixture of anxiety and fear, as he did not know exactly how he would react to seeing her and what he would find.

Arriving at the building, he walked up to the doorman, who promptly informed him that Kate was staying in her brother's apartment. He walked back out, hailed another cab, and told the driver to speed over to the Upper East Side where James and Seby lived. Upon arriving, he found Seby leaving the building. Happy to see Rey, he quickly informed him that he was heading to the hospital where an ambulance had taken Kate and James an hour ago.

Racing through the entrance of Langone Medical Center, he asked for Kate. The front desk personnel informed him that she was in surgery but that, if he was family, he could wait on the third floor. James was nervously pacing the floor outside of the waiting room when he saw Rey standing in his linen shirt and jeans holding a small overnighter. The look of relief that James gave him made Rey realize how much his presence was needed. After hugs and handshakes, they sat down to talk.

James gave Rey all the details regarding Kate's problematic pregnancy. He said, "In recent weeks, she developed really high blood pressure and was hospitalized twice because she and the baby ran risks if left unchecked. After talking to you, she fell asleep. But in less than an hour, I heard her scream and walked into a bloody mess. This meant that the stitches weren't going to hold another two months, and the baby was coming. The problem now is saving the baby and making sure Kate doesn't run into complications from the high blood pressure." The entire time James spoke, Seby's eyes were teary, but Rey remained stoic, betraying the tornado of concern spinning in his head.

The three men remained in quiet wait for another hour until the doctor walked in with a cautious look upon her face and directed herself to James. "Actually, Dr. Walsh, this is Rey Aguilar, the baby's father."

"Okay then, let's sit down. Mr. Aguilar. Mother and child are safe. Congratulations, you have a daughter." James and Seby smiled and hugged each other, but Rey remained calm and focused on the doctor. He was holding his emotions as best he could to allow the doctor to finish. "The baby is about six or seven weeks early, which brings with it several complications. We will have to keep the baby in the neonatal intensive care unit until the lungs can work independently and she is out of danger. Kate is stable, but she lost a lot of blood, and her pressure is still high. We had to perform a cesarean section because the baby's heartbeat was too elevated, and to prevent Kate from possibly suffering complications during labor. Now do you have questions?"

Rey quietly asked, "Will Kate or the baby suffer any long-term complications?"

"It is too soon to tell, but I have had worse cases than this that thrived and had no further complications. For Kate, this is really a matter of getting her stable and keeping her calm. She's quite nervous over her baby and understandably so. Also, she keeps calling for you."

Upon hearing the final comment, Rey's eyes exploded in tears, and his voice broke several times as he managed to ask, "When can I see Kate and my daughter?"

"I think that, if you see Kate now, it will do her a world of good, but the baby will have to be from afar for a short while. The baby will be day to day. It was great meeting you, and it has been really nice getting to know James and Sebastian." She gave handshakes all around and directed herself to Rey. "Are you ready to see Kate and your baby?"

His body was aching, and his back hurt, but his mind was afire with the need to see them. He smiled and followed the nurse into the intensive care unit, where Kate rested. Most of the beds were empty except for one other with a young, pregnant woman attached to all sorts of medical equipment. The doctor opened the curtain to reveal Kate, and when he saw her, he let erupt another flood of tears. To Rey, she was as beautiful as ever. Her long brown hair cascaded over her hospital gown. He approached with caution, as she was asleep.

Rey observed carefully the beeping machines and noticed she was receiving fluids and blood. He leaned over her bed rail, gently kissed her lips, and played with a lock of her hair. Her eyes flew open, and a smile broke on her parched lips. They remained looking at each other for minutes when a nurse came in to adjust the machine that started to beep more so once Kate's eyes opened. She whispered to Rey, "She has to remain calm." He nodded and gazed upon Kate.

She was eager to talk and, in a slight hoarse voice, whispered, "You came."

He smiled at her. "Of course I came. Stay calm and go to sleep. I am not moving from this place."

"Rey, have you seen the baby?"

"Not yet."

"She's so beautiful. Her hair is so shiny, but she has not opened her eyes yet."

"I know that, when she does, they will be as stunning as yours. Now, enough with the talking. I am going to sit here and go to sleep myself." He leaned down, kissed her more profoundly on the lips, and rubbed his cheek against hers, causing a whimper to escape from Kate's lips. Rey made a gesture of silence when he placed his index finger on his lips and sat back on a cushioned chair. Kate's eyes remained on his until she succumbed to sleep, but Rey's mind raced with worry over Kate and the baby.

When he was certain that Kate was asleep, he moved over to the nurse's station and asked to see the baby. A nurse from the unit arrived with garments and instructed Rey to wear a scrub gown over his clothes, coverings on his shoes, a hat, and a mask. She waited as he clumsily placed paper-thin coverings over his own clothes before

AURA POLANCO

following her into a warm room where several tiny babies rested in see-through incubators.

The nurse stopped at an incubator with a white card with the name Baby Connor. It contained a tiny baby weighing four pounds and wearing pink diapers and hat. On her feet, there were monitors marking her heart pulse and pressure. Tape covered her eyes, and tubes giving her oxygen were in her nostrils. The nurse said firmly, "Five minutes only." He was oblivious to her command as he gazed upon his daughter. His heart was pounding at the sight of her little body as it made involuntary movements.

At that moment, Rey had found his home in the four pounds of flesh and blood that was his baby. With certainty, he understood what he had to do and became calmer as he maintained his eyes on the little one before him. The nurse returned and, in a gentler voice, said, "Time is up. You can see her again in the next hour." He glanced at the gentle face of the nurse, nodded in agreement, and followed her out.

Kate awoke several hours later and looked around, remembering a dream she had where Rey was by her side. She glanced up and saw the machines she was attached to. Disappointed to find no one there, she searched for the button to press for help. Within seconds a friendly, large nurse came in, saying hello with much exuberance. "Rise and shine, sleeping beauty. It's so good to see you opening your eyes." She fiddled with the numbers on the machines and adjusted the pressure of tubes that administered medication into Kate's veins, all while taking notes on an electronic notepad.

Kate yawned and stretched and felt pain in her abdominal area. She remembered she had a cesarean then, with alarm, thought of her baby. "My baby!"

"That pretty little girl is just fine. She's with her daddy."

"Her daddy?" Kate's eyes flew open at the realization that she was not dreaming at all. "How do I look?"

The nurse looked at her in disbelief and said in a joking tone, "You look like you just had a baby and you are recovering from some issues. You look fine, but I will help you get cuter because you do have a fine-looking man. Girl, I understand."

"Oh my goodness, he really came. I thought I was dreaming. Please I just want to brush my teeth and comb my hair."

"No worries, I will set you up in no time at all." The nurse pulled the curtain and assisted Kate with her needs.

Shortly thereafter, the doctor came in and behind her Rey. Their eyes never left each other as the doctor gave her instructions and Rey held her hand. "Kate, we are moving you to a semiprivate room for another twenty-four hours of observation. I'm happy to report that you are stable and can go home by Thursday."

Rey peeled his eyes away from Kate, looked over at the doctor, and asked, "And the baby?"

The doctor put her hand on Kate's and very gently explained, "The baby is progressing as expected, but she is not ready to go home.

AURA POLANCO

We have to keep her in the NICU until she is a little stronger and a few weeks older."

The realization that her baby would not come home was overwhelming for Kate, who started to cry uncontrollably. "I can't leave my baby. I won't leave her."

The nurse came in to offer support, while the doctor explained further. "As of this Thursday, we are in November, which means that, by Thanksgiving, you should have your baby at home. You can spend your days here, and when she's ready, in about one week, you can hold her." The doctor looked up at Rey, who also looked deflated at knowing his tiny daughter would be at the hospital alone and said to him, "And you, Rey, you are welcome as well. But we limit the visits just to the parents."

Rey cleared his throat to say as he focused his attention on Kate's sobbing, "Thank you, Doctor. We understand, and we will be here all day, every day." The doctor and nurse said farewell and moved on, leaving Rey alone with Kate.

He took her hand in his and kissed each knuckle. Her sobs slowed, and her breathing regulated. They did not talk for a long while as they contemplated their baby being alone. Breakfast was brought in for Kate and a complimentary one for Rey, who ate everything, while Kate hardly touched hers. She needed to be with her child, and nothing else mattered. "Rey, how does she look?"

"I hung out with the little lady two times throughout the night. She's as spectacular as you are, Kate. I am in awe at everything about her. You have to be strong for her because she's not ready to be home. We don't want her to get sick, being she is so fragile."

"I'm so afraid something is wrong with the baby."

"No, stop worrying Kate. The baby is going to be fine. I feel it in my heart. She's so beautiful and all her vitals are strong."

"Rey, what about us?" she asked him nervously.

"We will not have this discussion until you are home and we can both be rational human beings. Right now, the focus is getting you strong and on your feet because we will have to spend the next three to four weeks coming here."

"I never had a chance to even buy her a crib or clothes because I have been bedridden since my fifth month. There is so much to do, Rey."

"Well, first I will settle into a hotel room and return later to see you and the baby." Kate looked horrified at his words and said desperately, "A hotel room? No, you have a home in my place. Please Rey, let's talk this out now."

She looked anguished with concern, but Rey calmed her worries with decisive words. "Okay, I will stay there but I'm sleeping on the sofa. About the stuff we need to do, don't worry. I will buy everything we need. You will make a list, and I will buy the furniture and set it up, and in the next two weeks, we will go shopping for baby clothes. The only thing I want from you is to think of her name. Right now, she is known as Baby Connor." Kate knew exactly what he meant. "Besides registering you as her father, we need to think of a name. I was thinking Hope." Rey smiled and acknowledged saying, "That is a perfect name. Our daughter has given me new hope in life and for you the motherhood I robbed." His eyes watered but he looked away when Kate went to comfort him. All she could utter was, "Please forgive me, my love" He grinned at Kate and kissed her forehead. "We will get through this; we have to for Hope," he said quietly.

In the days that followed, Kate and Rey went to the apartment and sadly settled in without their baby. Days before, James had volunteered to go and fix up the place and make the bed with fresh linens. He aired it out by opening the windows and placed discreet bouquets of fresh flowers in every room. At Rey's instructions, the former office space was to remain closed until he was ready to prepare it as a nursery.

As they looked around the apartment, Kate tearfully walked the space as if lost, prompting Rey to help her sit and listen to him. "Kate, you are in need of physical recovery. Our baby needs you there every day, and between now and when the baby gets home, you aren't lifting a thing. I already secured the same cleaning lady who works with James and Seby. She will come twice a week, and I will cook."

Kate hugged him and rested her head on his shoulder but noticed he did not return the hug. Looking up at his handsome yet tired face, she noticed more gray hairs on his temples and throughout. The gray hairs did not take away from him but rather enhanced his good looks. Kate was aware that he was lacking sleep because he could not rest well on the sofa, and this bothered her. Sitting up and grimacing as the stitches in her abdomen pulled, she said, "I see you have more gray hairs."

He looked sideways at her before saying, "Well, you would too if I had thrown you into hell with some awful words and broken your heart."

She shifted and rested her hand on his arm. "We both deserve to know how things will be for everyone's sake, especially Hope's." As she spoke, Rey stared into those golden green eyes that mesmerized him. He knew she was right; they had to talk. "Rey, our baby deserves parents who are together or, at best, in peace with each other. I am sorry for having done what I did to you. I was stupid and careless and very selfish—"

He took her face in his hands and kissed her passionately. His kisses trailed all over her face, and when he was ready to tell her, he said, "Kate, I forgave you when you called. I never stopped loving you even if you had a thing with that idiot."

Kate pulled away in shock and glared at him, with her eyes blazing a fiery green. "I never had anything with that man, and don't you ever, ever say that again. What he said about you confused me and sent me into a panic. Rey, I love you now more than I ever thought I could. I want what happened buried forever." She shifted uncomfortably on the sofa.

Putting his arms around her and gently squeezing her to him, he uttered, "Don't break my heart ever again, Kate. You have no idea how close I came to losing my mind and jumping off a cliff."

He kissed her softly on the lips when she barely pulled away to ask, "So we are back again?"

Rey laughed and shouted, "Yes!"

AURA POLANCO

They kissed and laughed, and then Rey pulled out of his jean pocket the engagement ring and placed it on her ring finger. Kate was speechless, and became emotional when he said, "As far as we are concerned, our story together continues from this day forward. Are you sure, Kate Connor, you wish to be my wife, warts and all, forever?" Kate flung her arms around him and kissed his face as she said yes repeatedly.

She pulled away enough to ask, "By the way, why didn't you tell me you had a house in Spain?"

"Well, the idea was to surprise you with a trip there for our honeymoon. We will go when the baby is a little older."

"I wish it were today." Their lips met again and all the fears they shared dissipated in the kiss.

The day before Thanksgiving, little Hope Connor Aguilar came home to an apartment filled with warmth and love and an armoire bursting with clothing in varying sizes. Between Seby, James, and Kate, the child was outfitted in designer best. Kate insisted that, for the baby's first months, she wanted her by her bedside in a bassinet. Hope was now seven pounds and rosy cheeked. She cried when hungry or wet, and the remainder of the time, she slept. Her hair was nearly black, and her eyes were the color of clover honey, just like her father's.

Kate was healing and obsessed over losing her baby weight, prompting Rey to always remark, "I prefer my woman with some meat on her bones."

The house smelled like Thanksgiving with Kate's apple pie baking in one oven and a turkey in the other. She prepared mashed potatoes, and Rey roasted a cornucopia of seasonal vegetables in olive oil and seasonings. James and Seby arrived to dinner with more gifts for Hope. After dinner, as Kate put the baby in her bassinet, they sat down to enjoy coffee and dessert. They chatted into the night and shared their plans for the immediate future.

Being an ocean apart was no longer a possibility for Rey and Kate. Their world suddenly came into focus, with Hope transforming their betrothed status into an instant family. The logistics of where to live and when to make these decisions weighed heavily on their minds, but Kate and Rey were certain that their choice would be the one in the best interest of their daughter.

For Kate, Hope was that light she had lost when Oliver died. Her son would never be replaced, but she had a second opportunity to pour all her maternal love into a new child and raise her to adulthood. In Hope, Rey saw all the good this world held. This tiny, little girl gave him the joy of fatherhood and the realization that he had a greater purpose in his life. He was important to his family, and their dependence on him was humbling. Gone were Kate's insecurities and the sensation that she needed to flee for peace. In Hope's bright honey-colored eyes and in Rey's arms, Kate had finally regained the peace she had lost. Together they started to build a little world where love came to live and hope never died.

EPILOGUE

Four years had passed on the island of Formentera. The shimmering sun was just as bright during the day, but by seven in the evening, it settled with a burst of colors in the horizon. Gone were the summer months and the curious traffic of tourists seeking quieter beaches from the larger bustling islands of Mallorca and Ibiza. It was that time between summers and the cooler months when the harvest had been gathered and the holidays were quickly approaching. During this season, there was a calm and melancholic feel in the air. The year-round beaches were deserted, and the locals came out with more frequency for picnics with family and to enjoy festivals commemorating patron saints. Plazas were filled with concerts featuring guitarists from Spain and throughout the world. The vibe was more artsy with local artists displaying their creations in the streets.

One early evening, while the sun made an outlandish display of its magnificence in a psychedelic array of crimson and gold, an elegant and fashionable group of people gathered and mingled on the beach. Musicians from the newest jazz club in town played for the collected crowd. The jazz club was simply known as Rey's and was popular with the locals. Rey kept the venue low-key out of respect to the island ordinances, but despite this, the place was making quite a name for itself in the music world for the celebrities it attracted. Kate's creative juices were nourished in publishing two books on photographic essays of the Balearic Islands and was preparing a third on Greece.

Surrounded by friends from the jazz world and neighbors, Rey welcomed and greeted guests. Neighbors and friends mingled as numerous torches were lit along the beach. People sat on chairs, ottomans, and pillows with the music playing softly in the background. Resting on the sand by Rey was Captain, his faithful friend and companion of fifteen years. Samu and Aiko's three year-old son, Hiro, held hands with four-year-old Hope as they walked down the sandy aisle. Kate and Rey agreed some years before on waiting to be married to allow for the children to be a part of their wedding. Hiro wore a white shirt tucked into neat sky blue shorts and was barefoot. Hope, also barefoot, held a tiny bouquet of pink and white orchids, and small flowers adorned her long dark curls. She wore a white eyelet dress with a robin's-egg blue sash tied in a bow. As he approached the flowered arch, Hiro wore a very important expression. The guests reveled in the beautiful innocence of the children as Hiro waved to his parents and his grandmother, Mrs. Goto.

But the biggest collective sounds of admiration came when Hope ran up to her father and he hoisted her in his arms. Wrapping her arms around his neck, she kissed his cheek and whispered in his ear, "I love you, Papá." It was such spontaneity and pureness of heart that Rey became emotional. He knew he had been blessed with an immeasurable amount of love, and he was grateful for the gifts he had been trusted with in his life. Loyal friends Paco and Rafa sat with their families. The children settled in their seats, Hiro with his parents and Hope with her uncles James and Seby and Rey's parents, to await the entrance of the bride.

Kate walked slowly along the beach from a distance, wearing a long Grecian-inspired, shoulder-baring white dress. Her hair was swept to the side and adorned with tiny orchids she cultivated in her little greenhouse. She carried an elaborate bouquet of white roses, orchids, and freesias. Her eyes were focused on Rey's as she thought about the moments in her life she was most grateful for. Being a mother to Oliver for ten years was the first moment, and being blessed with motherhood a second time followed this. But besides the blessing of motherhood, Kate was keenly aware that it was her capacity for forgiveness and selflessness that had blessed her with these gifts.

On that little beach in Formentera, after much trial and sorrow, Rey and Kate, continued their lives as one.

CPSIA information can be obtained
at www.ICGtesting.com
Printed in the USA
FFHW02n0639140918
48364324-52217FF